D0578250

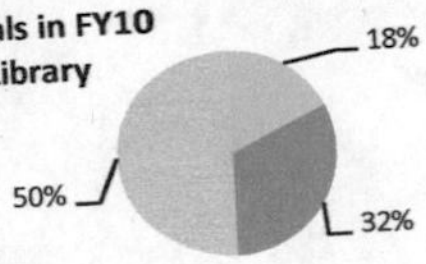

# Shadow Knights

## The Secret War Against Hitler

BY **Gary Kamiya**

WITH ORIGINAL ILLUSTRATIONS
BY **Jeffrey Smith**

DESIGNED BY **Norma Tennis**
PRODUCED BY **Karen Croft**

SIMON & SCHUSTER
New York    London    Toronto    Sydney

Simon & Schuster
1230 Avenue of the Americas
New York, NY 10020

First Simon & Schuster hardcover edition October 2010

SIMON & SCHUSTER and colophon are registered trademarks
of Simon & Schuster, Inc.

For information about special discounts for bulk purchases,
please contact Simon & Schuster Special Sales at
1-866-506-1949 or business@simonandschuster.com.

The Simon & Schuster Speakers Bureau can bring authors
to your live event. For more information or to book
an event contact the Simon & Schuster Speakers Bureau at
1-866-248-3049 or visit our website at www.simonspeakers.com.

Designed by Norma Tennis

Manufactured in China

1   3   5   7   9   10   8   6   4   2

Library of Congress Cataloging-in-Publication Data

Kamiya, Gary.
Shadow knights: the secret war against Hitler / by Gary Kamiya;
with original illustrations by Jeffrey Smith; designed by Norma Tennis;
produced by Karen Croft.—1st Simon & Schuster hardcover ed.
p.    cm.
1. World War, 1939-1945—Secret service. 2. World War,
1939-1945—Secret service—Great Britain. 3. World War,
1939-1945—Military intelligence. 4. World War, 1939-1945—Commando
operations. 5. Great Britain. Special Operations Executive—Biography.
6. Intelligence officers—Biography. 7. Spies—Biography. I. Title.
D810.S7K26 2010
940.54'8641—dc22
2010005898

ISBN 978-1-4391-0904-5

Art and photo credits can be found on page 167.

To my parents, who taught me
to respect courage and hate war.

And to Kate, for everything.

# Shadow Knights

IT IS NOT THE ROCK, which does not know whether a king or a beggar, a holy man, or a wicked person stands upon it. It is not the angels, who have no heart to feel with and for another; they feel the praise of God, they praise God. It is man who has been given a heart.

...We should first try to become human. To become an angel is not very difficult; to be material is very easy; but to live in the world, in all the difficulties and struggles of the world, and to be human at the same time, is very difficult. If we become that then we become the miniature of God on earth.

—Hazrat Inayat Khan,
"Character-Building" (From *Sufi Teachings,* vol. 8,
*The Sufi Message of Hazrat Inayat Khan*)

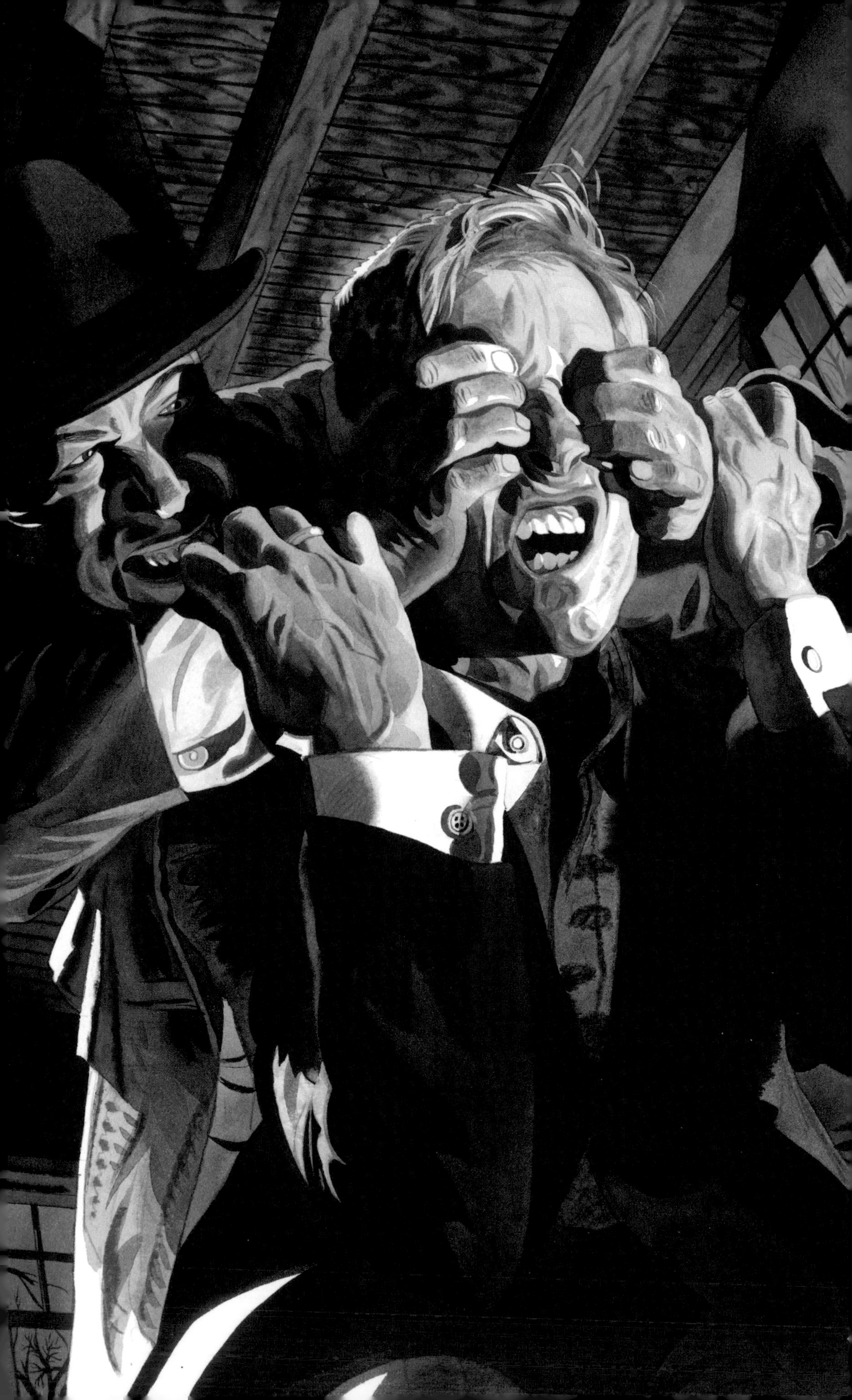

## 4:10 p.m.
## November 27, 1943
## Charmont, near Besançon
## France

They were making small talk now, but the Gestapo man's gun was still pointed at Harry Ree's midsection. The British secret agent would have to make his move soon. More Germans were on their way.

"How about a drink?" Ree said. The Gestapo man nodded, following Ree's movements with his pistol. Ree found a bottle of Armagnac in the cupboard and poured out two drinks. When his captor stretched out his hand for the tumbler, Ree saw his opportunity and smashed the bottle as hard as he could on the man's head.

The German must have had a skull of stone. He jumped up from his chair, hissing, "Ah, so that's your game." Ree gripped him by the throat. The man pushed his pistol into Ree's ribs and pulled the trigger. Ree heard the shot, but he felt no impact. More shots; six in all. "Is he shooting blanks?" he wondered.

**Harry Ree gouged the Gestapo man's eyes. But they wouldn't come out.**

Ree was still strangling the German, but now his enemy hit him over the head with the butt of the gun. Ree saw stars, but found the strength to lunge at him, forcing him to drop the pistol. Ree knocked him to the floor and tried to stomp on his head with his heel, but the man spun away and rose to his feet. They started punching each other, staggering out of the kitchen and down the cellar steps.

Suddenly the Gestapo man rushed at Ree and got a headlock on him. Ree couldn't escape. The man squeezed Ree's neck harder and harder. He began to feel faint.

When Ree had parachuted into France seven months earlier, his wife, Hetty, was about to give birth to their second child. Soon after he landed, hiding in a farmhouse, Ree listened as a BBC announcer ran through a long list of cryptic announcements, coded messages sent by his friends in London. Straining his ears, he heard the faint voice say, *"Clèmentine ressemble à sa grand-mère"*—"Clementine resembles her grandmother." It meant nothing to anyone in the world except Ree. But it told him that his wife had given birth to a baby girl.

Now, as the Gestapo man strangled him, that memory jolted Ree. "Look here, old man," he told himself, "if you're ever

If he didn't keep **fighting**, thought Ree, he'd never see his **baby girl** back home.

going to see your daughter, you've got to get out of this one." He swung his arms back, the way he had been trained in Scotland, and smashed the man below the navel. Grunting in pain, the man released him. But they both immediately returned to the fight, a surreal battle of brief, violent pummeling interrupted by moments in which the exhausted enemies stood panting, staring at each other across the room before they rushed at each other again.

The slow-motion struggle went on and on. Finally Ree fought past the man's fists and bashed his head against the wall. As the German fell to the floor, Ree tried to remember all the dirty tricks he had learned during his training, but all that came to him was the scene in *King Lear* in which Gloucester is blinded. He gouged at one of the man's eyes, but it wouldn't come out. He tried to bite off his nose, but it was too tough. Then Ree shoved his forefinger into the German's mouth, between his teeth and his cheek, and pulled up hard. The man squealed in pain and sent Ree flying over his head.

Both men staggered to their feet. Ree knew he must finish him off. If the other Gestapo men arrived, he would be as good as dead. He rushed at the man again and smashed his head against the wall, harder this time. The German slid down, his face turned to the wall. Ree stepped back to do it again, but the man whispered, "Get out...go to hell..."

Ree stumbled down the front stairs to his bicycle, but he was too unsteady to mount it. He headed for the back garden. He knew that if he ever needed to escape in a hurry, the back way would take him to the next village without crossing the road. He climbed over a muddy ditch and over a bank and pushed into a bramble patch. Stuck in the brambles, Ree slumped to the ground and began to pass out. He was just conscious enough to realize that the jackbooted SS men would catch him if he stayed there. He pulled himself out of the thicket and began to walk across a field.

Darkness was falling, and it had begun to rain hard. Ree was approaching a swollen river. It would be too dangerous to cross on the bridge. He would have to swim. He felt himself getting wet under his coat and put his hand underneath to see how wet. When he pulled it out, his hand was slippery with blood. A lot of blood.

"God," he thought. "They weren't blanks!"

Ree did not know it then, but he had been hit with all six bullets.

He stepped into the dark river.

## October 18, 1942
## 1,000 feet above the
## Hardangervidda
## Norway

Shortly before midnight on October 18, 1942, four young Norwegian men hurled themselves out of the belly of a British Halifax bomber and dropped through the night sky toward a landscape so vast, white and endless it looked like a desert of snow. The commando team—code-named "Grouse"—had been charged with carrying out one of the most crucial missions of World War II. To survive, they would have to overcome not just an army of Germans, but the most desolate place in Europe.

An enormous, barren expanse in the Telemark region of southern Norway, the Hardangervidda is too harsh a place for most plants and animals, let alone

humans. During the six-month-long sub-arctic winter, it is a frozen, forbidding wasteland—2,500 square miles of ice and snow-covered rocks, glaciers, fjords, narrow valleys and jagged mountains, all of it entirely above the tree line. Its sudden, deadly blizzards, the worst in Europe, are legendary. It is a place where nature's knife edge can be unsheathed in an instant.

The four young Norwegians were on a daunting assignment. They had to make their way across this unforgiving terrain

The desolation of the Hardangervidda

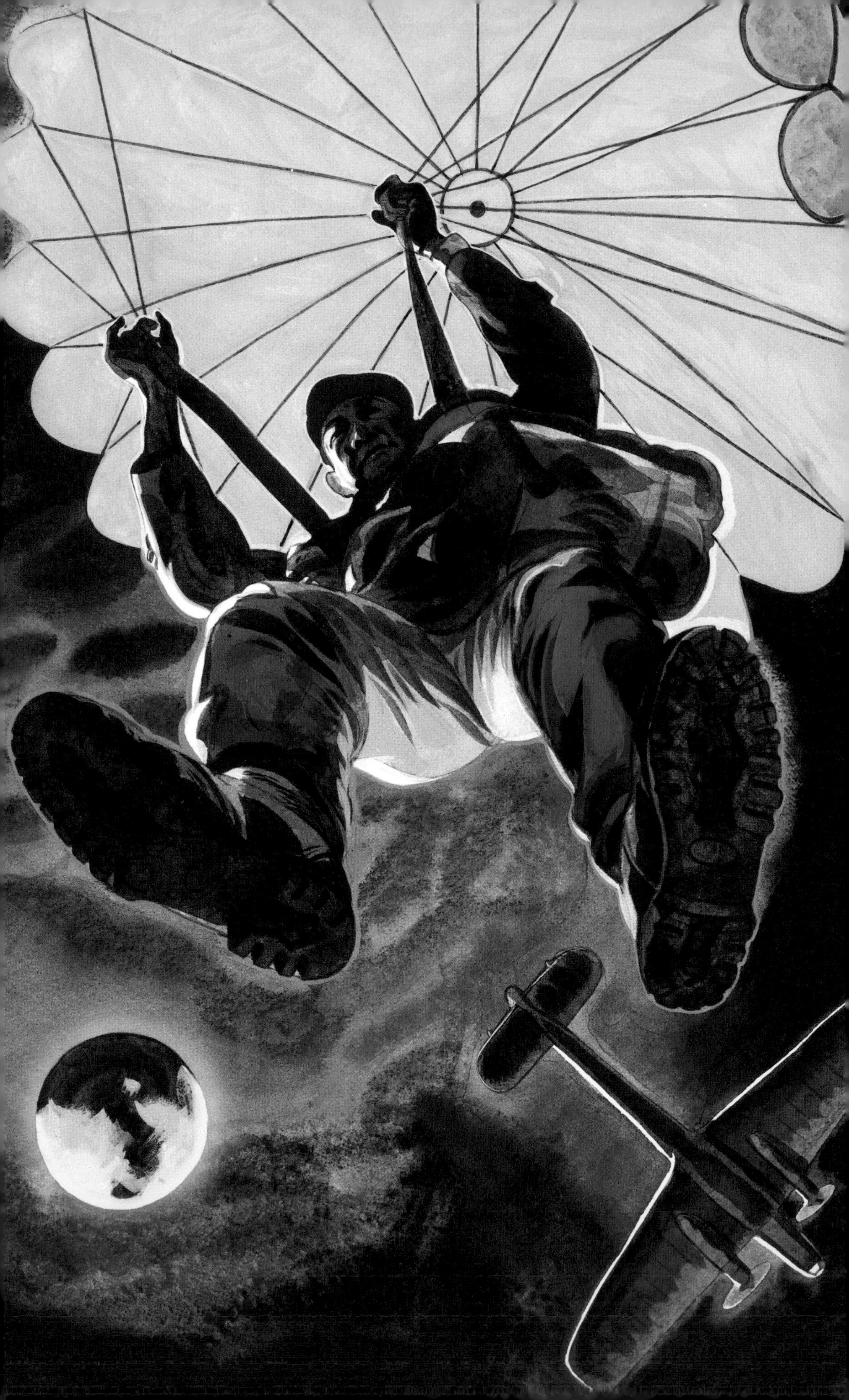

carrying 650 pounds of supplies, find a landing strip, guide in two gliders filled with British commandos, and secretly lead them to a heavily guarded plant built on the edge of a precipitous gorge just outside the wild plateau. Once at the site, they had to kill or neutralize the guards, blow up the plant's machinery and somehow make their escape, avoiding the thousands of German troops who would be searching for them. Through it all, they would have to survive everything the Hardangervidda could throw at them.

It amounted, they knew, to a suicide mission.

**The Norwegians' top-secret mission: Stop Hitler from building an atom bomb.**

But the four Norwegians did not know what only a few Allied commanders did: that their mission was to stop Adolf Hitler from building an atom bomb.

If you were allowed to pick any four people in the world to send into the Hardangervidda on a sabotage mission, you could not have chosen better than these four men drifting down through the frigid air. First, there was the simple fact that they were Norwegians. No other country in the world could have produced men so well suited to surviving the Hardangervidda in winter. There is a reason that tiny Norway, with a population of five million, has won more medals at the Winter Olympics than any other nation. The four men were supremely fit, expert skiers, with a lifetime's experience dealing with the Norwegian wilderness. But perhaps even more important, each of them possessed the intangible qualities that turn a group of individuals into an unbreakable team: resiliency, a sense of humor and an indomitable spirit.

**Most SOE agents parachuted into enemy territory by the light of the full moon.**

The Grouse team's leader, 24-year-old Jens Poulsson, was a tall, powerfully built man whose trademark was his ever-present pipe. Poulsson had spent much of his life camping on the Hardangervidda and was an expert hunter and crack outdoorsman. Like all but one of the quartet, he had grown up in Rjukan, the closest town to the plant, and his family still lived there. Being hometown boys gave Poulsson and his fellow commandos some crucial advantages, but if the Germans discovered their real identities, their loved ones would likely be sent to a concentration camp or executed.

Poulsson's escape to Britain after the German army overran Norway had required an epic odyssey. While most Norwegians who wanted to fight the Germans remained in Norway and joined the Milorg, the national resistance movement, others headed for Britain, where they had heard they could get special training and join an all-Norwegian company. Most made their way via small boats that sailed between the Norwegian coast and the Shetland Islands north of Scotland, a flotilla so reliable it came to be known as the "Shetland bus." But because Poulsson had crossed the border to neutral Sweden, from which no flights to Britain were available at that time, he was forced to circle almost the entire globe to make it to a destination only 400 miles away from where he started. He traveled overland through

# Shadow Knights

Jens **Poulsson**, Knut **Haugland**, Claus **Helberg**, Arne **Kjelstrup**

Finland, the Soviet Union, Turkey, Syria, Lebanon, Palestine and Egypt, took a ship to India, another to South Africa, and finally a transatlantic ship to Trinidad. From there, he flew to Canada. On the last leg he sailed to Britain on a regular convoy. Clearly, he was not a man to be daunted by obstacles.

The second member of the team, Knut Haugland, was an equally strong-willed character. Haugland, who had been a radio operator on a cargo ship, had joined the Norwegian army and fought against the Germans at Narvik in the far north. He was an unflappable man and a superb radio operator—a skill that would prove essential in the days ahead.

The next member of the team, Claus Helberg, was a devil-may-care risk-taker and the best skier in the group. Helberg's desk had been next to Poulsson's at school, which gave the team leader a front-row seat from which to observe Helberg's talent for first getting himself into trouble, and then somehow wriggling out of it. Like a mischievous tomcat, Helberg always seemed to get away.

Finally, there was Arne Kjelstrup. A plumber from Oslo, he was short but brawny, with an irrepressible sense of

humor. And, like his compatriots, he backed down from nothing. Shot in the hip while fighting the Germans (a pair of wirecutters partially deflected the bullet), he and another man escaped from a Nazi-controlled hospital, commandeered a machine gun and took on an entire German column, killing several of the enemy before they were forced to flee. He had accompanied Jens Poulsson on his long, globe-circling escape to Britain.

There was to have been a fifth member of the Grouse team—a muscular outdoorsman with a philosophical bent named Knut Haukelid. Haukelid had to withdraw after he accidentally shot himself in the foot while training for the raid in Scotland. But his role in the saga was far from over.

The four young Norwegians were facing almost impossible odds. But they had two things in their favor. First, they were back on their own soil, fighting to free their country, knowing that most of their countrymen would risk their own lives to help them. That knowledge would be a giant hand that would lift them up when strength and will were failing.

And these extraordinarily brave men had something else on their side: nature itself. The extreme harshness of life on the

Hardangervidda was their trump card. The Germans, unaccustomed to its near-Arctic conditions, were so terrified of the high, frozen wasteland they refused to spend the night in it. Even when pursuing their foes, they turned back after half a day to ensure they would be able to make it out in daylight. But the Norwegians understood the Hardangervidda. They knew they could not outfight the infinite power of nature, what one of them called the "trolls of Norway." They had to yield to it, roll with its punches, burrow into its huge, indifferent heart.

The Hardangervidda could save them, if it did not kill them first.

# July 25, 1943
# 3 Boulevard Richard-Wallace
# Neuilly, Paris

Noor Inayat Khan had been in Paris only ten days when her secret world fell apart.

Noor had flown into a disaster. The British-organized resistance circuit she had been sent to join, code-named Prosper, had been smashed by the Nazis immediately after she landed in the French countryside. Her cover had been blown. The circuit's leaders had just been seized. Many other members of the underground were being hauled in.

The Germans had an accurate description of Noor's appearance. They knew she had been sent into France to work as a wireless radio operator for Prosper. They even knew her code name:

Noor Inayat Khan

Madeleine. They ordered their sophisticated wireless-detection teams, which could pin down the exact location of a covert transmission in 20 minutes, to begin searching for her radio.

Ten days in, and Noor was living on borrowed time—and not a lot of it. In 1943 the average life expectancy of an underground wireless operator in Europe was six weeks.

The secret British organization that had sent her knew that her situation was dire. Her commanding officer, Colonel Maurice Buckmaster, offered to bring her home. Anyone meeting Noor in her former life would have assumed that she would jump at the chance to flee.

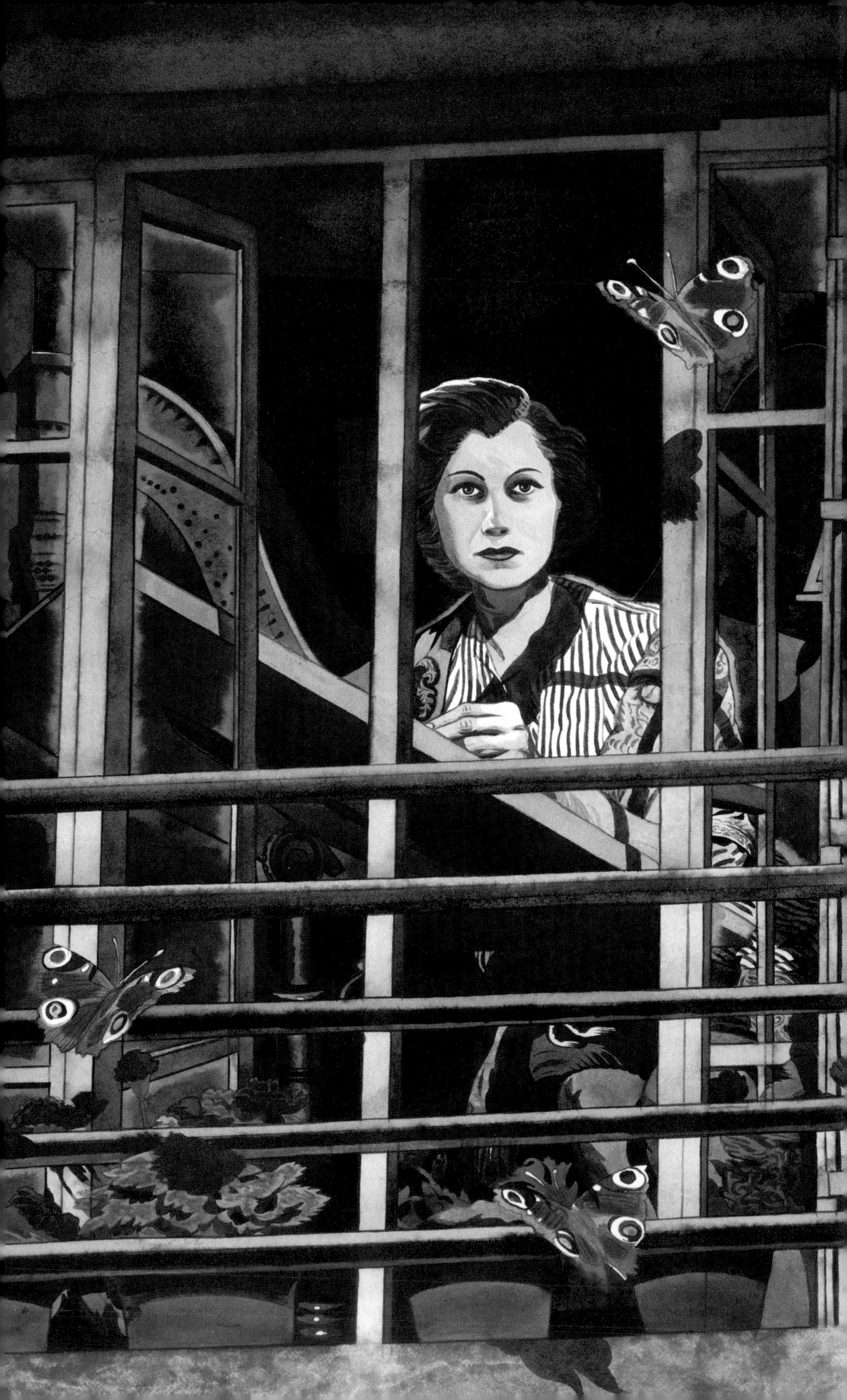

# Shadow Knights

Noor Inayat Khan was perhaps the most unlikely secret agent ever sent into the field. She was an ethereal figure, a butterfly who had somehow fluttered into the iron jaws of the Third Reich. A gentle, otherworldly soul, she played the harp and had written a children's book before the war. Her beloved father, who had died when she was still a young girl, was an eminent Sufi mystic who had raised her to believe in a transcendental philosophy of cosmic harmony and divine truth. The person she was closest to was her mother, a deeply spiritual American woman who had become increasingly frail after the death of her husband.

Short and slight, with a high, soft voice, Noor was a dreamy young woman, still haunted by the terrors of her childhood. An old family friend, who once watched the young Noor freeze with terror while crossing a busy street, believed that "fear was always in her nature." During her training to become a secret agent, Noor flinched at the sound of gunfire. Many of the people charged with her performance believed she was completely unsuitable for the job.

But there was something immovable in Noor, a mysterious force that was not obvious to the casual observer, maybe not even to herself. Whatever it was, it would not allow her to back down.

Noor radioed Buckmaster back. She did not want to fail her comrades. She planned to help rebuild the shattered Prosper circuit. She wanted to stay.

**Noor was a butterfly who had somehow fluttered into the iron jaws of the Third Reich.**

Buckmaster knew that if he allowed Noor to stay in Paris, she would almost certainly be caught, tortured and killed. But Noor was now his only wireless operator in Paris, the sole link between London and the most important resistance network in France. It was a war; she was a soldier. He agreed to let her stay.

Noor began searching for other safe houses. She had grown up in Suresnes, a northern Parisian suburb just a short walk from the Bois de Boulogne. By coincidence, she found an apartment in the building closest to the bridge that crosses the Seine to Suresnes, an elegant modern white apartment block on the Boulevard Richard-Wallace.

The ethereal child-woman had ended up only a few hundred yards from the place where she once played. But in this game, to lose was to die.

The gentle Indian princess, the indomitable Norwegian commandos and the intellectual British schoolteacher all had one thing in common: They were agents of the Special Operations Executive. SOE was a secret British organization, formed in desperation by Winston Churchill in 1940, that grim year when Britain stood alone against Hitler. Its mission was to foment sabotage and subversion behind enemy lines. Churchill called it "the ministry of ungentlemanly warfare." The Nazis called its agents "terrorists" or "gangsters" or "bandits." SOE agents worked with resistance movements in Axis-occupied countries, providing them with the training, communications and arms they needed to strike back at their oppressors.

Scorned by the British military establishment, SOE started out as an amateurish group led by upper-class old boys with no training in clandestine war. But by D-Day, it had grown into a professional paramilitary organization that employed 10,000 men and 3,000 women, about half of them in the field, and operated in almost every country touched by the war. Its agents assassinated Nazi officials in occupied Europe, hijacked ships in Africa, cut telephone lines in Madagascar, sabotaged factories in France, kidnapped a German general in Crete, used canoes to blow up Japanese ships in Singapore and traded black-market money in China. But their primary mission was to help men and women living under occupation fight the Nazis.

Some SOE agents were transported into action by light plane, some by boat. A handful were landed by submarines or simply walked in. But the majority of SOE agents parachuted in by the light of the full moon. The enduring image of SOE is of a lone man or woman drifting down under a canopy of moonlit silk into enemy territory.

SOE agents came from all nationalities and walks of life. They were royalty, soldiers, prostitutes, crooks, journalists, bartenders, racing-car drivers, criminals, shopgirls, playboys and businessmen. No fewer than 50 of the agents SOE sent into France were women—an unprecedented development that was deemed too controversial to reveal until after the war. Some agents were battle-hardened vets who had killed men in combat, others were pacifists. One agent, who later became movie star Douglas Fairbanks Jr.'s butler, was a flamboyant gay man who lived in Paris for a time with a German

Winston Churchill was **fascinated** by guerrilla war.

lover. Another was an American newspaperwoman who roved around France, undeterred by a wooden foot she called Cuthbert. What they all had in common was a determination to fight the Axis in their own way. Instead of making a separate peace, they made, in a sense, a separate war.

Their war was a war of improvisation. It involved diplomacy as much as it did dynamite. It was fought under the constant shadow of torture and death. And it was a war they fought alone.

All soldiers in war possess courage, but SOE agents needed a special sort. Soldiers in regular units are surrounded by their comrades. Most of them do not risk their lives for flag and principle: They stand up to bullets because they don't want to let their buddies down. Neither SOE agents nor the resistance fighters they worked with had such support. They could sometimes open up to a few trusted comrades, but only with extreme care: Many of SOE's most effective agents never slept in the same house for more than a few nights in a row. Even their own families rarely knew what they were doing or where they were.

Except on the very rare occasions when they wore uniforms, SOE agents were not protected by the Geneva Convention. If caught, they were usually executed. Agents sent to France were told that their chances of survival were about 50-50. Those were appalling odds, though better than those faced by crews in the Royal Air Force's Bomber Command, who statistically stood no chance of surviving their assigned 30 missions. In fact, "only" about one in four agents sent to France did not return. But to focus merely on their odds of surviving is to ignore the fact that agents also knew that if caught, they would probably be tortured before they were killed. The thought of being beaten, burned or held underwater to simulate drowning was so terrifying that some agents, once in the field, simply froze up and refused to take any risks at all. One agent is said to have died of fright.

SOE Headquarters, 64 Baker Street, London

Clandestine warfare is as old as the Trojan Horse, and the British had been practicing it in one form or another since the 15th century. But nothing quite like SOE had existed before, and there has never been anything like it since. Because it had to invent itself, there was more than a whiff of classic British upper-class amateurism about SOE. It was initially run by a handful of men who knew each other from elite public schools, such as Oxford and Cambridge and the London gentlemen's clubs where Britain's ruling class congregated. Some of these old boys were clearly in over their head, and their ineptitude sometimes had appalling consequences. Of SOE's leadership, the *Times of London* later commented that "a few could only charitably be described as nutcases."

But SOE's eccentricity was also its strength. From top to bottom, its ranks were filled with ornery, strong-willed men and women, contrarians who disliked taking orders. It was appropriate that SOE's London headquarters at 64 Baker Street—behind a door innocuously labeled "Inter-Services Research Bureau"—was a stone's throw from the fictional home of Sherlock Holmes, another legendary amateur who used guile and unorthodox methods to defeat wrongdoers. The dean of SOE historians, M. R. D. Foot, noted that "SOE was full of people with personalities like sledge-hammers." Military historian Max Hastings wrote, "[I]t is striking to note that there was absolutely no common denominator between the men and women of SOE beyond their courage...Each was entirely an individual, often whimsical and elusive." One agent said, "We were all individualists... We didn't want a stupid colonel ordering us to advance into a screen of bullets when we didn't agree with the order—we weren't the Light Brigade." George Millar, whose bestselling account of his dangerous months with the French underground, *Maquis*, is one of the finest accounts of an agent's life in the field, wrote, "Britain is strong because of her cranks... In times of war, and especially in odd organizations like the one in which I found myself...you see the importance of the great body of Britishers who occupy themselves seriously with crazy things."

These mavericks—the Baker Street Irregulars, as they sometimes called themselves—could irritate more conventional types in Whitehall (the colloquial term for the British government, taken from the street where many ministries were located) and the military, but they had the right—or wrong—stuff to get the job done.

SOE waged war without rules, and its romantic, quixotic, sometimes zany elements are an undeniable part of its fascination. In China, a shady businessman and wit (who immortalized himself in doggerel as "Garrulous, old, impulsive, vague, obese / Only by luck not 'known to the Police'") ran a black-market currency operation that netted 77 million pounds for SOE. One agent put itching powder in German troops' underwear. Another arranged for French prostitutes to give German pilots heroin to damage their eyesight. Yet another wrote that SOE required him to variously play the parts of "journalist, commercial traveler, politician, brigand, gigolo and, finally, smuggler." To which could be added "party animal": One operative was landed in Denmark wearing a tuxedo over which a bottle of brandy had been emptied, so he would look and smell like a harmless late-night reveler.

But for all of its hijinks, SOE was nonetheless an instrument of war, and its agents faced the same deadly risks and had to be prepared to use the same brutal tactics as other soldiers. One agent was shocked to be asked at his preliminary

Pearl Witherington: "There was **nothing civil** about what I did."

interview, "Have you any personal objection to committing murder?" SOE agents had to be prepared to, and did, kill their enemies. They dealt mercilessly not just with traitors but with people who might possibly be traitors. One SOE agent working in France shot a middle-aged woman in the back of the head because her husband had informed on them and her own security was suspect. She probably posed no threat, but the agent and his comrades couldn't take that chance. Pearl Witherington, the only female agent to command a circuit in France, turned down her knighthood when she learned she had been given the civil instead of the military version, saying, "There was nothing civil about what I did."

In a crisis, agents had to be prepared to act with incredible audacity. A wireless operator code-named "Felix" once got off a train in Toulouse carrying his transmitter in its suitcase. As he approached the barrier, he observed two French policemen checking papers. Behind them stood two SS men, who were checking everyone with luggage. Felix knew he was doomed if he tried to pass, so he held his suitcase over his head and called out authoritatively in German, "Get me a car at once, I have a captured set." A German driver took him away in a car. Felix ordered the driver to pull up in a side street, shot him and escaped.

# Shadow Knights

But for all the virtuoso moves, there were also mind-boggling blunders. One agent, completely forgetting all his training and his cover story, checked into a hotel under his own name. (Luckily, he was able to retrieve the fatal reception slip in time.) One of SOE's best agents, Benjamin Cowburn, once left the plans for a train demolition job chalked on a classroom blackboard. The mission, and Cowburn's neck, were saved only by an alert schoolmistress with an eraser.

Being undercover may at times have felt like being in a play, but it was a play that never ended, and one in which to flub a line was fatal. The wrong kind of suit, an inappropriate hairstyle, an English cigarette stub or London Tube ticket in one's pocket, a cover story that was too easy to check out, not knowing where your fake mother was born, unfamiliarity with some petty detail of life under occupation—any of these slip-ups could result in arrest and torture.

When French agent Pierre de Vomécourt ordered a cognac in a station café, the barman told him, "It's our day without." De Vomécourt had no idea what he meant and repeated his order. When the barman irritably repeated, "It's our day without," de Vomécourt realized he had blundered and quickly slipped aboard a train. Tipped off, the Germans stopped the train, but he had wisely gotten off at the stop before. He had almost been killed because he was not familiar with a new French law that allowed cafés to serve alcohol only on alternate days.

But the greatest danger was betrayal. Informers were everywhere, and even well-intentioned people could crack under

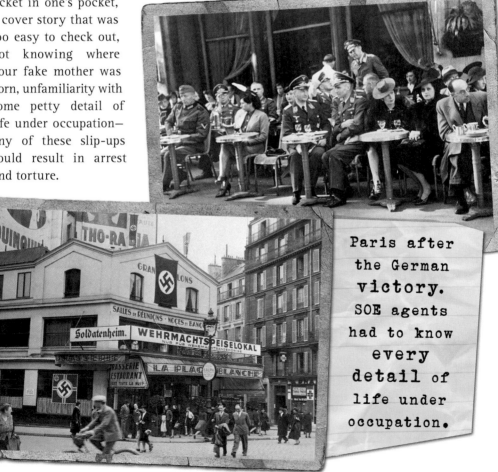

Paris after the German **victory.** SOE agents had to know every detail of life under occupation.

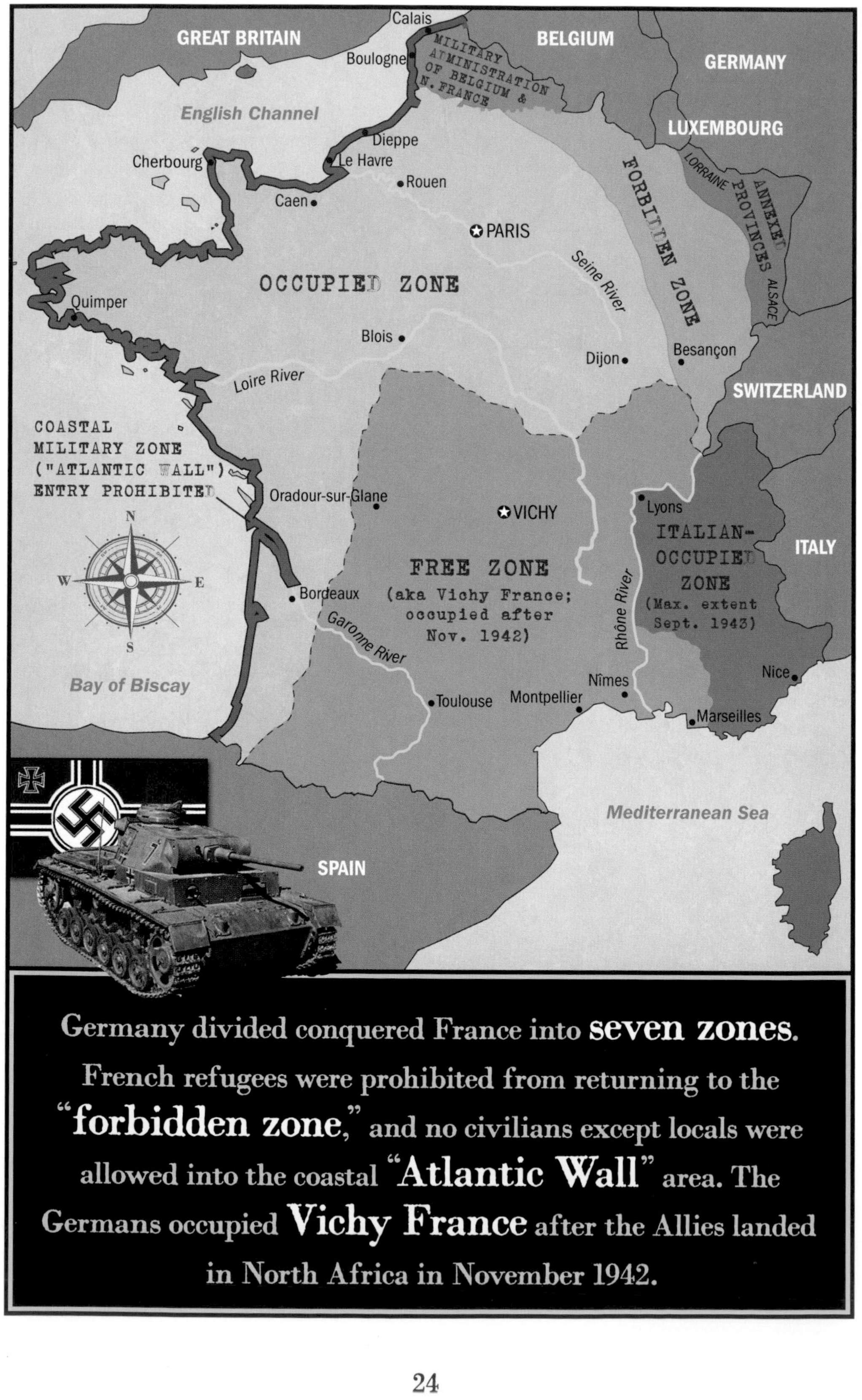
GREAT BRITAIN
Calais
Boulogne
MILITARY ATMINISTRATION OF BELGIUM & N. FRANCE
BELGIUM
GERMANY
English Channel
LUXEMBOURG
Dieppe
Le Havre
Cherbourg
Rouen
Caen
FORBIDDEN ZONE
LORRAINE
ANNEXED PROVINCES
ALSACE
PARIS
Seine River
OCCUPIED ZONE
Quimper
Blois
Dijon
Besançon
Loire River
SWITZERLAND
COASTAL
MILITARY ZONE
("ATLANTIC WALL")
ENTRY PROHIBITED
Oradour-sur-Glane
VICHY
Lyons
ITALIAN-
OCCUPIED
ZONE
(Max. extent
Sept. 1943)
ITALY
N
W
E
S
FREE ZONE
(aka Vichy France;
occupied after
Nov. 1942)
Bordeaux
Garonne River
Rhône River
Bay of Biscay
Nîmes
Nice
Toulouse
Montpellier
Marseilles
Mediterranean Sea
SPAIN

Germany divided conquered France into **seven zones.** French refugees were prohibited from returning to the "**forbidden zone,**" and no civilians except locals were allowed into the coastal "**Atlantic Wall**" area. The Germans occupied **Vichy France** after the Allies landed in North Africa in November 1942.

pressure. George Starr, organizer of the Wheelwright circuit in Gascony, said, "Building a network is like making a ladder. You fix one rung. You stand on it. You jump on it. If it holds, you build the next one. It takes time. The people who wanted to do it in five minutes got caught. I was bloody lucky."

SOE made more than its share of disastrous mistakes. Wily German counterintelligence officers outwitted SOE again and again, resulting in the deaths of dozens of agents. Some have even charged that Baker Street deliberately sacrificed some of its own agents as part of an Allied deception scheme. (See sidebar.)

But for all its faults, SOE played a vital role in the Allied victory. By strengthening resistance movements, it forced Axis leaders to commit precious divisions to rear-guard duties and entire theaters they could otherwise have ignored. Its constant pinprick of attacks demoralized enemy troops and distracted Axis leadership: At one point during the war, Hitler—his fear of British assassination attempts heightened after the successful SOE murder of *Reichsprotektor* Reinhard Heydrich—spent at least half an hour a day poring over German military intelligence reports of SOE activities.

A **triumphant Führer** poses in front of the Eiffel Tower.

SOE operatives also played a little-known role in some of the war's most crucial operations. It was an SOE agent, for example, who radioed London that the pride of the German navy, the *Bismarck*, was trying to break out from its hiding place in Norway into the North Sea. That intelligence led Britain to dispatch a task force that sank the mighty battleship, in one of the epic naval battles of the war.

And when D-Day came and the hour finally tolled for the resistance to rise up, SOE answered the call. SOE's existence would be justified if it had never done anything except train and arm the thousands of French *maquisards* whose guerrilla attacks in south and central France delayed the German Panzer divisions racing toward Normandy, and who two months later cleared the path for American troops driving north after the Dragoon landing in the south of France.

But perhaps SOE's most enduring legacy exists not in the pages of military history but in the secret history of human courage. Like the ring bearer Frodo and his companions in *The Lord of the Rings*—a book that J. R. R. Tolkien began writing as the Third Reich dragged the world into its bloody nightmare—they chose to walk straight into Mordor. This book tells the true story of three of their missions.

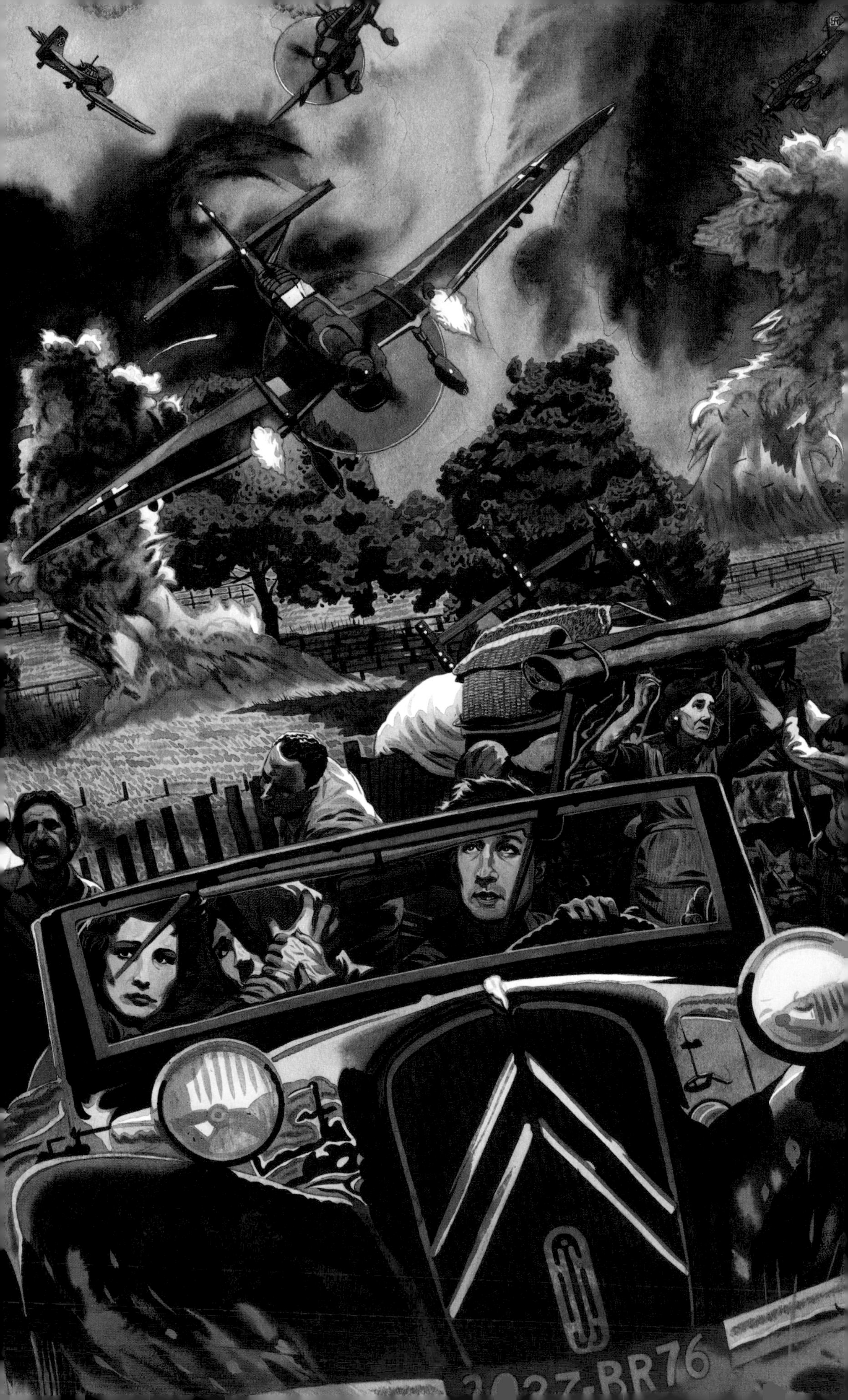
BR76

## June 5, 1940
## Southern outskirts of Paris
## France

An evil scream came straight down from the sky. Noor and her family looked up in terror as the Stukas dropped on them, their nose-mounted sirens shrieking. Then the road exploded. Cars, bicycles, children, old people stumbling along with pushcarts piled with pots and blankets, the whole ragged desperate procession fleeing Paris was suddenly ripped apart. Ahead of her and behind her, Noor saw cars explode.

At the wheel of the car, Noor's brother Vilayat, a thoughtful young man who had never contemplated killing anything, swore he would join the RAF. As the dive-bombers banked and wheeled to come back for another free shot at slaughter, Noor hugged her trembling mother.

> **The Stukas screamed down on the desperate convoy fleeing Paris, leaving a trail of death and destruction.**

Nothing that Noor had experienced in her 26 years had prepared her for this tableau of death. Noor was the great-great-great granddaughter of the legendary Tiger of Mysore, the fiery last Mogul emperor of southern India, who led a rebellion against British rule. Her father, Hazrat Inayat Khan, was a celebrated musician and one of the most eminent living practitioners of Sufism, the ancient mystical sect of Islam. Hazrat Inayat Khan's life's mission, personally entrusted to him by his spiritual master, was to "unite East and West through the harmony of his music." Inayat Khan traveled to America, where he established the first Sufi centers. At a lecture in San Francisco, he met a young American woman named Ora Ray Baker, with whom he fell in love. They were married in London, then traveled to Russia on a musical tour. On January 2, 1914, in a monastery near the Kremlin, Ora Ray gave birth to a baby girl named Noor-un-Nisa Inayat Khan. Her name meant "Light of Womanhood."

From birth, Noor and her three younger siblings were steeped in an atmosphere of deep, idealistic spirituality. As children growing up in London, they would be lulled to sleep by their father with sacred Sufi songs. Inayat Khan felt that Noor was especially close to him, and her family nickname was Babuly, which means "Father's Daughter."

The young Noor believed passionately in fairies, and one day she insisted she had seen them in Gordon Square. When other children told her that fairies did not exist, she was devastated. She and her brother Vilayat went to their father, who told them, "Children, when something exists in the imagination of anybody you can be sure there is a plane on which it has real existence."

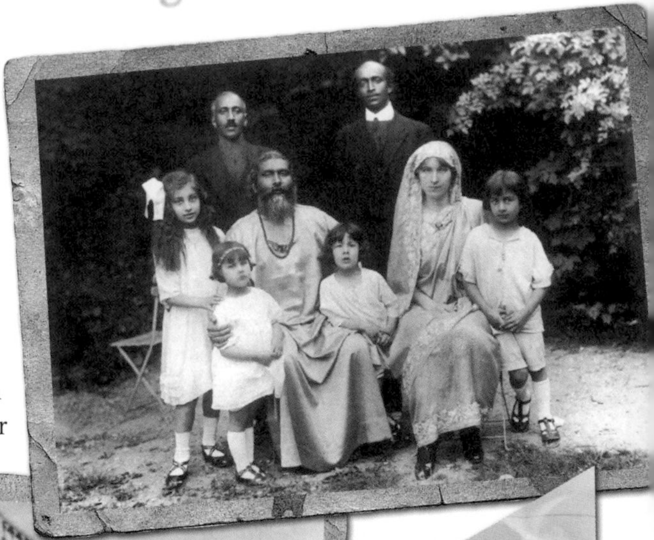

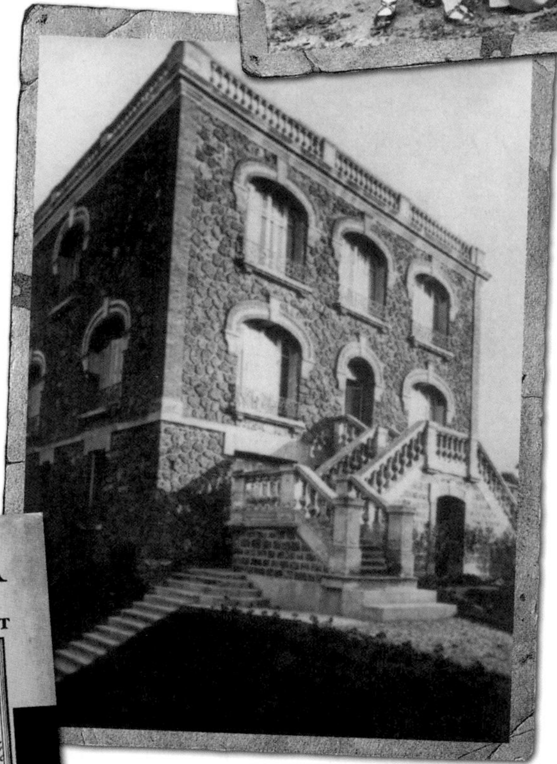

The Inayat Khan family; their Paris home, the Fazal Manzil; Noor's book Twenty Jataka Tales.

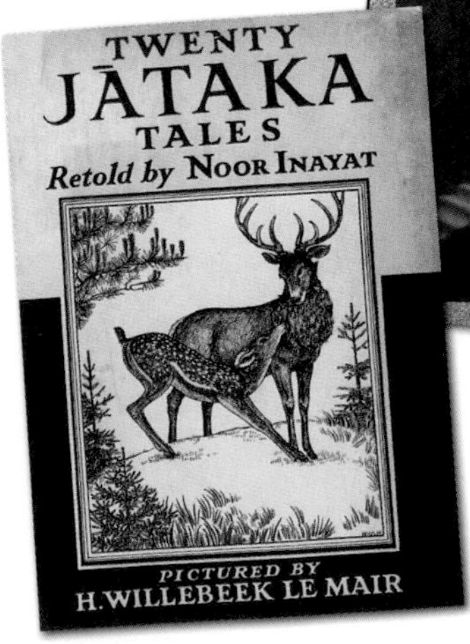
TWENTY
JĀTAKA
TALES
Retold by NOOR INAYAT
PICTURED BY
H. WILLEBEEK LE MAIR

Noor was an affectionate, thoughtful, timid little girl who worshipped her father and solemnly embraced his philosophy of cosmic harmony and the unity of all religions. But her childhood did not prove to be so idyllic. Financial troubles, and British disapproval of mixed marriages, led Inayat Khan to move his family to Paris, where he found a stone house on a hill in the suburb of Suresnes. He named the house the Fazal Manzil—the House of Blessing.

In 1927, her father told his family that his destiny called for him to return to India, and he made it clear to them that he would not come back. Less than five months after his departure, word came that he had died. Devastated, Noor's mother became a recluse. At age 13, Noor had to take care of the entire family. The steel beneath the silk was being forged.

Following in her father's footsteps, Noor entered the École Normale de Musique, where she studied the piano and the harp. Then she took a degree in child psychology from the Sorbonne and began a career as an author. Her children's book, *Twenty Jataka Tales,* retellings of famous stories about the Buddha's selfless deeds on behalf of others, came out in 1939, the year that World War II began.

Her favorite story, "The Fairy and the Hare," was about a hare who offered himself as food for the hungry by jumping into a fire. But the flames, created by a kindly fairy, did not burn the hare. Explaining that the fire had been only a test, the fairy honored the hare by drawing his picture on the moon.

Noor had paid little attention to politics, but Hitler's menace was now undeniable. Nazism was utterly repellent to Noor and her siblings. They were appalled by the Nazis' persecution of the Jews, their cruelty and lust for power. But they had been raised to greet hatred with love.

Noor studied **harp** and **piano** at the École Normale de Musique in Paris.

On June 3, the Luftwaffe bombed Paris for the first time, killing more than 250 people. Two days later, the German guns could be heard in the east. Noor and Vilayat could not put off their decision any longer. The city was about to fall. Should they stay in Paris and try to keep the Sufi movement alive? Or should they fight?

Noor and her brother had a fateful discussion in the living room of the Fazal Manzil. They realized they could not simply be priestly keepers of the holy flame. Their beloved father's teachings demanded spiritual idealism in action, not just in words. Their duty was to fight.

France had fallen, its invincible Maginot Line breached and its mighty army routed in six weeks. Noor and Vilayat's only hope was to take their family to Britain, the one hostile country in Europe that Hitler had not defeated.

But Britain was on the ropes. The day before Noor and her family fled Paris, the last British troops had been evacuated off the burning, corpse-littered beach at Dunkirk.

The mighty Luftwaffe was preparing to launch the greatest aerial assault in history against London. Would there be a Britain for Noor to escape to?

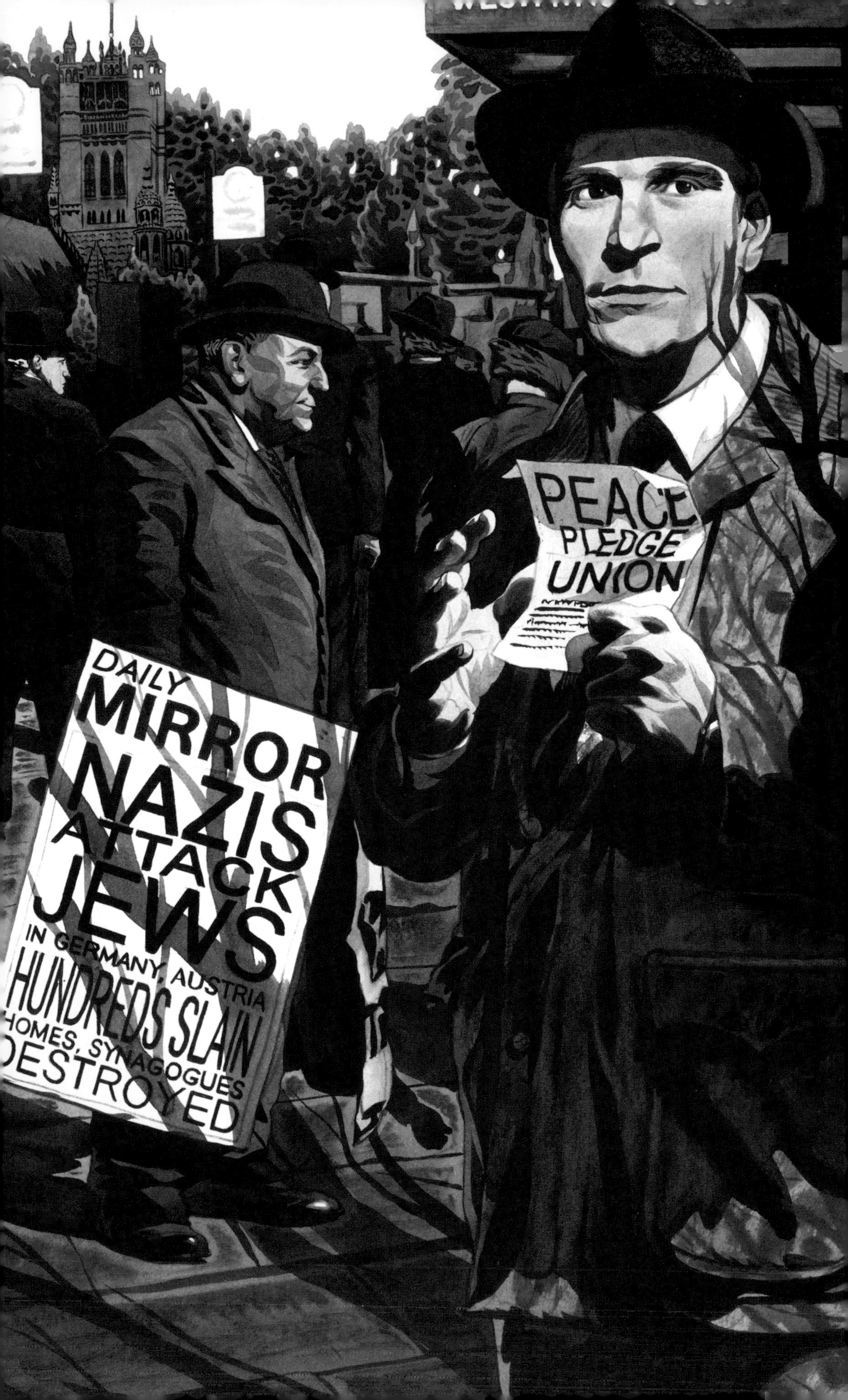
PEACE
PLEDGE
UNION
DAILY
MIRROR
NAZIS
ATTACK
JEWS
IN GERMANY, AUSTRIA
HUNDREDS SLAIN
HOMES, SYNAGOGUES
DESTROYED

# June 1940
# Beckenham County School
# Bromley, London

Harry Ree started out as a conscientious objector. Wry, witty, self-deprecating, highly intelligent, the 25-year-old teacher at Beckenham School was a left-winger who had no desire to fight in a war that he believed would only benefit capitalism. The pointless carnage of the Great War, and the societal inequalities it left in place, had convinced many of Britain's leading intellectuals that all wars were futile. While studying Modern Languages at Cambridge, Ree—like many other Brits, including Vera Brittain, Aldous Huxley and Bertrand Russell—signed the Peace Pledge, a public vow to renounce war and never fight another.

But shortly before the fall of France, Ree decided he could no longer be a "conchie"—a conscientious objector. It was Hitler's racial policies that did it. Ree's father was part Jewish, and young Harry had grown up with a lot of Jewish friends in Manchester. After Hitler's hate-filled rise to power, Ree's political objections to the war didn't make sense. This wasn't a war for capitalist spoils. This was a war to defeat a murderous tyrant who had whipped his nation into a psychotic fever with his ugly, anti-Semitic ideology. Ree had initially volunteered to be a minesweeper, which seemed acceptable for a pacifist. But now he told himself, "OK, I don't mind where I go."

He did not know that the road he'd take would lead him to a cottage in the French countryside, lying in wait to kill in cold blood a Frenchman he knew well.

WARS WILL CEASE WHEN MEN REFUSE TO FIGHT
nansen
PEACE PLEDGE UNION
6 ENDSLEIGH STREET, LONDON, W.C.1.
01-387 5501

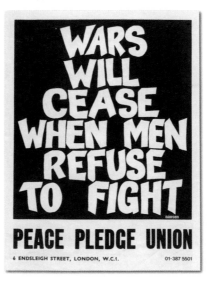

A Peace Pledge Union poster. Like many of Britain's leading intellectuals, Ree believed that war benefited only capitalism.

# July 1940
# Ferry on Lake Mjosa, near Hamar Norway

Standing on the deck of a ferry, 29-year-old Knut Haukelid looked out across the largest lake in Norway. He had just seen his country overrun by Nazis, and he was heading underground.

Two months earlier, on April 9, Germany had invaded Norway and Denmark. It was the end of the "Phony War," the surreal period of false peace that had begun eight months earlier after Hitler invaded Poland. By the end of April the Germans had seized southern Norway and were consolidating their control over the rest of the country. In mid-April, British troops tried to check the Germans in central and northern Norway, but they were ignominiously defeated, and all British troops were withdrawn—a disaster that led Conservative British Prime Minister Neville Chamberlain to resign in May.

On April 9, Haukelid had spent the night with a friend in the northern city of Trondheim. He awoke to discover that German troops already occupied the city. He and his friend collected all the ski equipment they had and sneaked out of Trondheim, intending to join a Norwegian detachment.

Haukelid and a group of students commandeered a railcar and headed to Oslo, then to the front lines. Armed and sent into action, they fought hard, but rifles could not defeat tanks, nor companies defeat divisions. As Haukelid watched the Germans burning farms and livestock, he and his comrades swore they would never give up, even if the Germans won the war.

> **Haukelid and his friends vowed never to surrender, even if the Germans won the war.**

Norway's overmatched army could not hold out long. After his unit was ordered to lay down its arms, Haukelid and three of his men skied across the mountains to join the British, only to find they had fled. Haukelid and three comrades decided to return to Oslo and continue fighting the Germans in any way they could.

On the ferry, Haukelid noticed that one of his fellow passengers was a uniformed member of the Hird, the paramilitary wing of Vidkun Quisling's Norwegian

# Shadow Knights

Nazi puppet Vidkun Quisling (second from right) was despised by most Norwegians.

fascist party. As a "Jossing," a good Norwegian, Haukelid despised Quisling and his followers.

Haukelid looked at his men. They came to a quick decision. When the boat was about 300 yards from shore, they approached the storm trooper. "Heil Hitler," said Haukelid, extending his hand. As the man took it, his comrades seized the man, lifted him over the railing and threw him into the lake. Only his cap floated.

Some women screamed and the captain came aft to investigate. "He jumped into the lake by himself," Haukelid's men told the captain.

"That is excellent," said the captain. "Full speed ahead!"

When the ferry landed, Haukelid and his men stole quickly into the woods, carrying four rucksacks filled with captured German pistols and submachine guns. The powerfully built young outdoorsman set up operations in Oslo, where, in one of the more peculiar resistance plots of the war, his group hatched a plan to kidnap Nazi puppet Quisling, ship him to London and exhibit him in Piccadilly Circus for a shilling a look. But the Germans got wind of the plot and smashed the group.

Haukelid narrowly escaped to Sweden, then flew to England, where he and other escaped Norwegian patriots formed the Linge Company, named after a young Norwegian officer who died leading a commando raid on the Germans. The Norwegian government in exile seconded Haukelid and his countrymen to SOE's Norwegian section, commanded by Colonel Jack Wilson. SOE sent them to a remote camp in the Scottish Highlands where they began arduous physical training. They had no idea what they would be asked to do. They only knew that they were being given a chance to fight back.

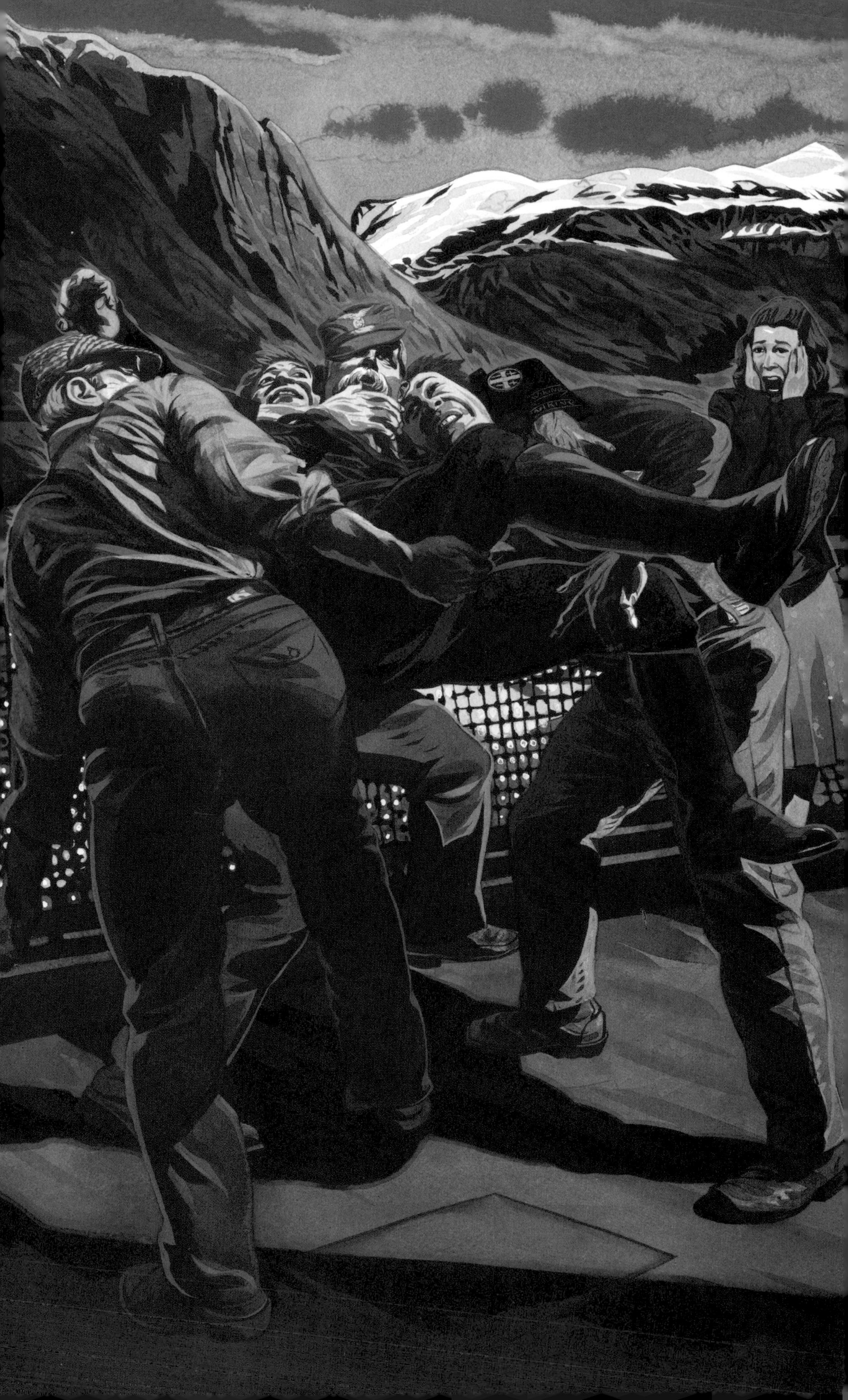

## July 16, 1940
## Late at night
## 10 Downing Street
## London

Winston Churchill had been prime minister for just two months. He had had another long, grueling day, and it wasn't over. Churchill was meeting with his new minister of economic warfare, a loudmouthed Fabian socialist named Hugh Dalton.

Churchill told Dalton he was placing him in charge of a just-created, top-secret organization. Dalton's mission would be to stir up trouble for Hitler by any means available, fair or foul. As the two men parted, Churchill turned to Dalton and said, "And now, set Europe ablaze."

Thus was born the Special Operations Executive.

When Churchill met with Dalton, he knew that Britain had almost no cards in its hand against Hitler. A month earlier, Britain's undersized, underequipped army had almost been destroyed at Dunkirk, rescued only by the famous "miracle of the little ships"—a motley flotilla of 700 small craft, including one open fishing boat only 15 feet long, whose civilian crews braved the Channel to save their boys. The map of Europe was a sea of swastikas. Poland, attacked by both Germany and the U.S.S.R., was a Nazi slave labor camp. Germany had overrun Norway, Holland, Belgium and Denmark. France had collapsed and signed an armistice ceding three-fifths of its territory to the Germans. Italy had come into the war on Germany's side, threatening North Africa, the Mediterranean and the oil supplies of the Mideast. Nor was there hope from the two most powerful Allied nations. Stalin had signed a nonaggression pact with the Nazis, and the United States, whose army was smaller than Poland's, was firmly committed to neutrality.

**Haukelid and his men tossed the Quisling overboard.**

So Britain was forced to grasp at straws. Whitehall seized upon the chimeras of "economic warfare" and "popular revolt." A bombing campaign and a sea blockade would starve Germany, leading to "widespread revolt in her conquered territories," or so the British military command fantasized in May. SOE, under the control of Dalton's new Ministry of Economic Warfare and headed by executive director Frank Nelson, was to provide the spark that would set off the revolt of the oppressed.

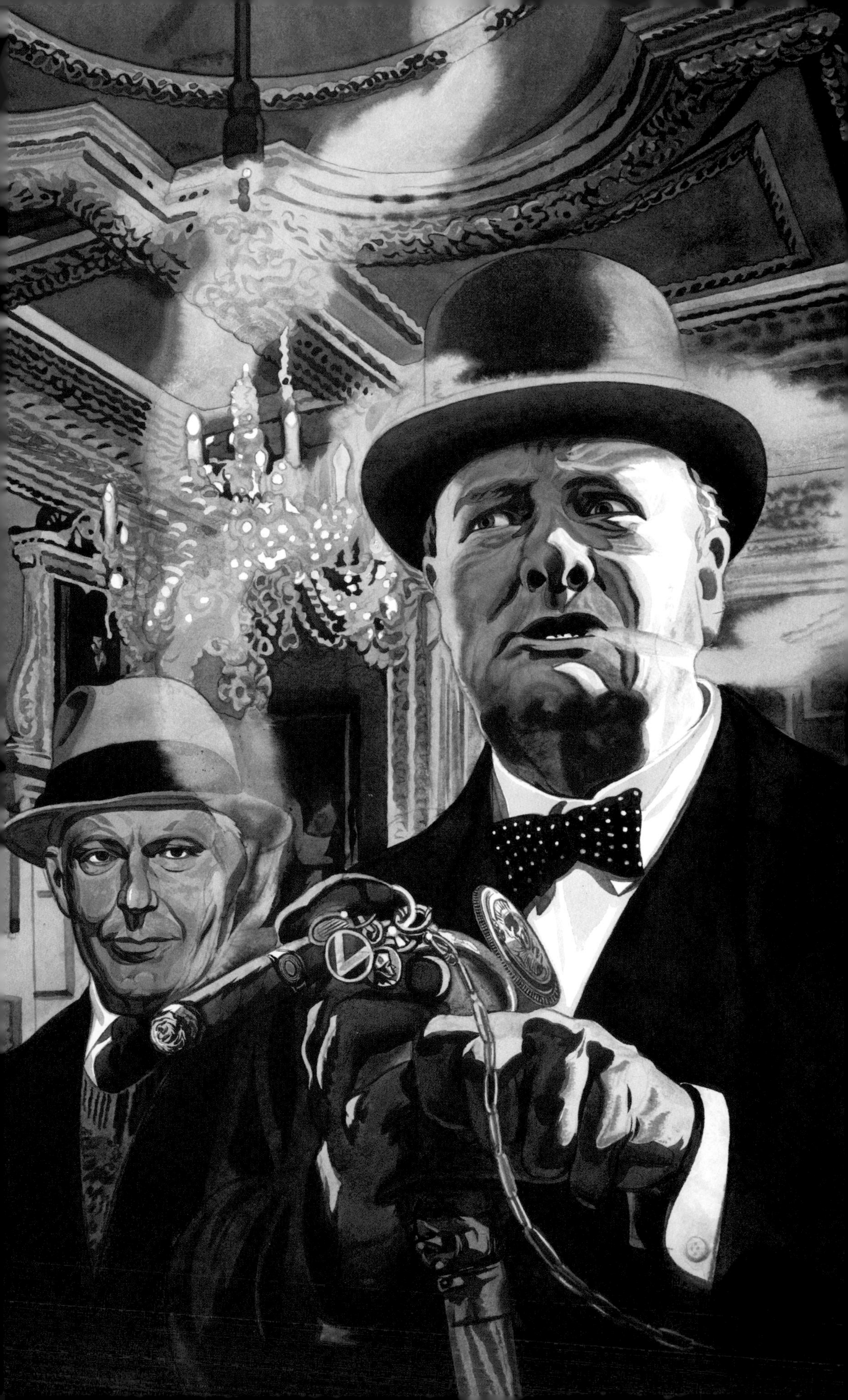

Ironically, the man who, on Churchill's instructions, signed the founding charter for this fierce organization was none other than Neville Chamberlain, who had resigned in disgrace as prime minister. Chamberlain's creation of SOE was his last political act: he died less than four months later. The man who appeased Hitler at Munich made some amends for his folly at the end of his life.

The overblown hopes Whitehall vested in SOE quickly came crashing down. For the first year of its existence, SOE accomplished almost nothing. Its one major coup took place in January 1941, when a businessman named George Binney, assisted by SOE agents, hijacked six unarmed British merchant ships from their berths in Sweden and brought them through a German blockade to Britain. Their cargo, a million pounds' worth of ball bearings, was vital to the British armaments industry. But aside from the ball-bearings run, and a hand in helping topple the pro-Nazi Yugoslav Prince Paul, SOE had precious little to show for itself. It did not even manage to parachute an agent into France until May 1941.

**"And now, set Europe ablaze": Churchill's famous words gave birth to the SOE.**

Its slow start was hardly surprising, for SOE was basically starting from scratch. The Firm, as it was sometimes called, had been cobbled together from two small military research organizations dedicated to subversion, neither of which had many resources or achievements. But even if SOE had sprung into the world like Athena, fully armed, it would not have been able to do much in its first year or two. Its raison d'être was to support resistance movements, but in most of Europe the occupied population had been stunned or intimidated into passivity, and resistance movements barely existed. There were large underground movements in Poland and Czechoslovakia, but distance and the Nazi iron fist made assisting them impractical. Only in Yugoslavia, where thousands of partisan guerrillas were led by a tough, resourceful Communist named Josef Broz, aka Tito, did SOE have any immediate prospects.

Throughout the war, SOE also had to deal with the enmity of powerful forces at home. Setting Europe ablaze was an admirable goal, but as a top British official drily observed, SOE "sometimes came nearer to setting Whitehall ablaze." Dalton's abrasive personality did not help: One of his political rivals described him as "the biggest bloodiest shit I've ever met," and Churchill had no love for Dalton either. "Keep that man away from me," he once said. "I can't stand his booming voice and shifty eyes."

But the real problem went beyond personalities. By its very nature, SOE was doomed to clash with three of the most powerful forces in the British wartime establishment: the intelligence service (SIS, also known as MI6), the Royal Air Force (RAF) and the Foreign Office (FO). All three of these established entities regarded SOE as essentially a private army, a loose cannon. As a top Baker Street official noted, "At the best, SOE was looked upon as an organization of harmless backroom lunatics which, it was hoped, would not develop into an active nuisance."

The most poisonous rivalry was with the SIS. Baker Street had invaded the spy agency's turf, which angered its formidable head, Stuart Menzies. More substantively,

SIS feared that SOE's operations would endanger its intelligence agents. The mutual antipathy was extreme. Members of SOE called SIS the Bastards of Broadway, after the street where the intelligence service had its headquarters. For their part, Menzies and his aides regarded SOE as a disreputable gaggle of untrained and incompetent amateurs.

SOE's conflicts with the RAF were less nasty but more consequential. The problem was planes: SOE always wanted more than the RAF wanted to give. It soon became clear that the only viable way to get agents into the field was by air—either by landing them in light planes or parachuting them out of bombers. And supplies could only be dropped from bombers. But the RAF was loath to give any of its precious bombers to the upstart organization. The head of Bomber Command, Arthur "Bomber" Harris, was convinced that he could bomb Germany into submission, and saw no reason to waste planes on SOE. Charles Portal, chief of the Air Staff, expressed the dominant view not just of the RAF but of the orthodox military establishment when he said to a top SOE official, "Your work is a gamble which may give us a valuable dividend or may produce nothing. It is anybody's guess. My bombing offensive is not a gamble. Its dividend is certain; it is a gilt-edged investment. I cannot divert aircraft from a certainty to a gamble which may be a gold-mine or may be completely worthless."

At least at the beginning of the war, the RAF, like much of the military establishment, also had moral qualms about SOE. At the end of 1940, SOE devised a plan to ambush German pathfinder pilots, who guided the Luftwaffe's nightly attacks on Britain. The elite pilots were reportedly taken to the airfield every night in buses, which SOE planned to ambush. When Portal learned of the plan, he insisted that the party be dropped in uniform, saying, "I think that the dropping of men dressed in civilian clothes for the purpose of attempting to kill members of the opposing forces is not an operation with which the Royal Air Force should be associated." Such gentlemanly strictures faded as the war progressed, but SOE was always regarded as somewhat disreputable by the regular forces.

Tensions with the Foreign Office were the most complex. There was an inherent conflict between SOE's short-term military goals and the Foreign Office's long-term political ones. SOE's mandate was to defeat Germany and Italy (and later Japan), and toward that end it would work with any groups that would kill the enemy. But many of the most active resistance movements, especially after Hitler

Charles Portal and Winston Churchill

invaded Russia, were Communist. The establishmentarians in the Foreign Office, along with the Prime Minister, wanted to preserve the status quo and were vehemently opposed to empowering Communists. SOE was thus put in the impossible position of being asked to perform simultaneously as a fighting force and as an instrument of grand policy. And it was blamed by Whitehall when those imperatives inevitably collided.

JOHN
STEINBECK
The Moon
Is Down

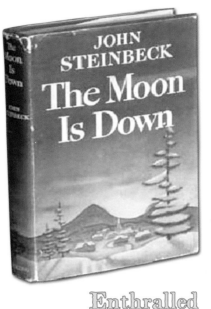

**Enthralled by a Steinbeck novel, Churchill urged SOE to give civilians little bombs to use against their occupiers.**

But SOE had two aces up its sleeve. One was the support of Winston Churchill. Despite his conservative politics, the prime minister had been infatuated with popular resistance and guerrilla war ever since 1895, when as a young newspaper correspondent he watched Cuban guerrillas confound a far larger Spanish force in Cuba's successful revolt against its colonial rulers. A stint in Afghanistan during an uprising in the Northwest Frontier furthered his respect for irregular warfare, and his experience in the Boer War in South Africa cemented it. Captured by the Boers, whose effective partisan tactics he observed firsthand, Churchill staged a daring escape, stealing 300 miles through enemy territory. The experience brought him worldwide fame and left him with a lifelong admiration for subversive movements.

Churchill's romantic enthusiasm for heroic underground fighters was not always rational. He became so excited after reading John Steinbeck's 1942 novel *The Moon Is Down,* a stirring fable about resistance to tyranny, that he urged SOE to emulate the book and drop explosives to civilians all across Europe, so they could strike back at their Nazi occupiers. Nor was it consistent. He raged against SOE on numerous occasions and came close to disbanding it more than once. But in the end the fiery leader stood by Baker Street, and it was only his support that saved the maverick outfit from being shut down by its bitter rivals in Whitehall.

The most important asset SOE had was a piercing-eyed 44-year-old Scot named Colin McVeigh Gubbins. Brigadier Gubbins had led one of the only units to acquit itself well during the disastrous Norway campaign—a newly created unit called the Independent Companies, forerunners of special forces like the British Commandos and the American Green Berets. Gubbins lost the battle in Norway, but as SOE's driving force, he was to bedevil the Germans and their allies a thousand times over.

Gubbins was exactly what the fledgling, civilian-dominated organization needed: a professional soldier who was tough enough to translate Dalton's vague plans into action, imaginative enough to think outside the military box and charismatic enough to inspire the men and women who would be asked to risk their lives for him.

Gubbins was a born leader. A short, dark, intense, no-nonsense man who nonetheless radiated energy and enthusiasm,

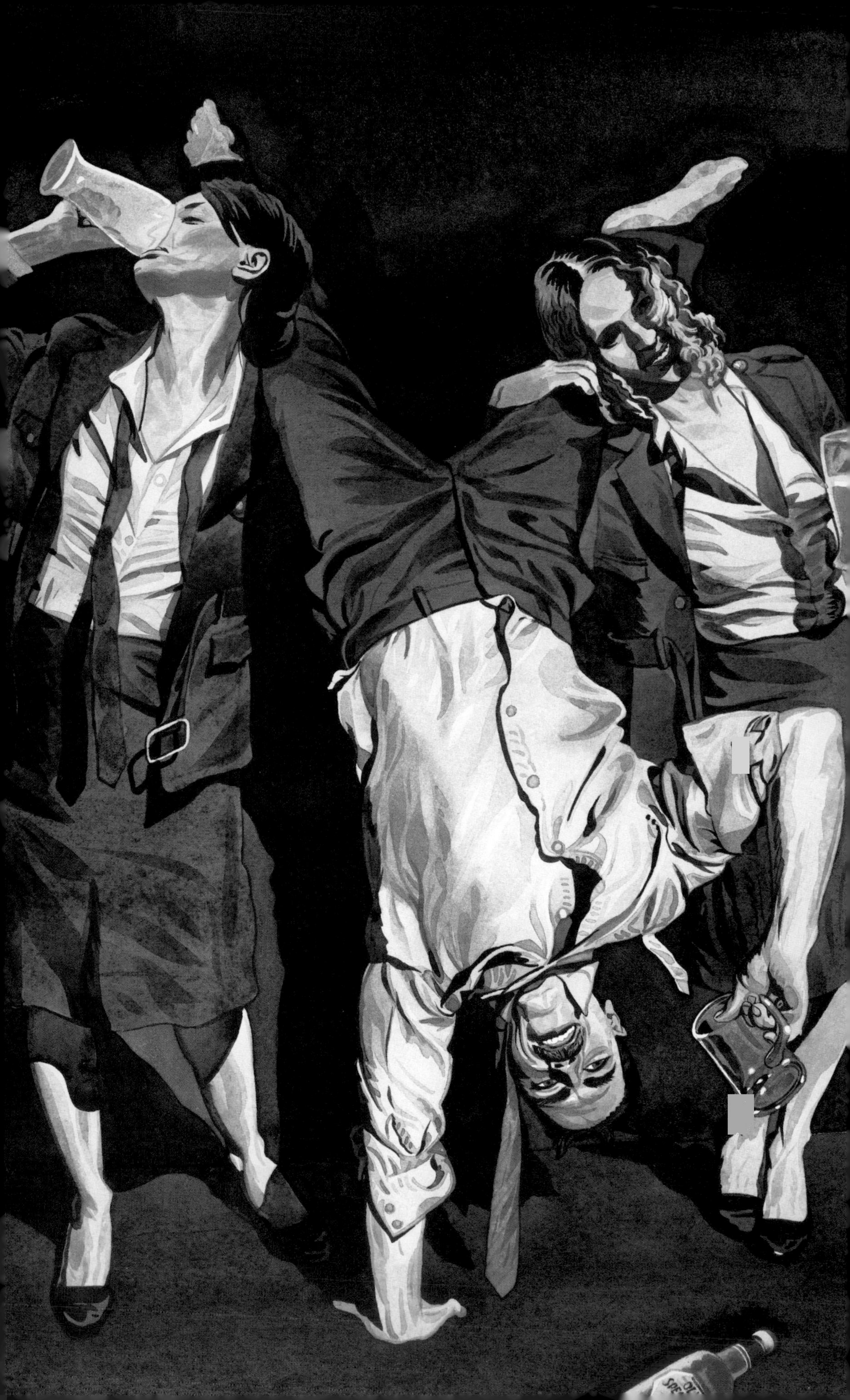

he was described by one agent as "a real Highland toughie, bloody brilliant." Hired as SOE's director of operations and training in November 1940, he quickly became its linchpin.

Gubbins seems to have been as much a swashbuckler in his private life as in his professional one. He was married, but his all-consuming and secret work life placed the marriage under severe stress. According to Kim Philby, the Soviet mole in British intelligence who helped create the SOE training course, "It was rumored that [Gubbins] could only find time for his girlfriends at breakfast. But he was man enough to keep them." An SOE secretary recalled that there were a lot of "bedtime stories" at Baker Street and that "Gubbins was a lech." In a diary entry written during their official mission to Poland and subsequent escape to Romania after the war started, Gubbins's biographer and SOE colleague Peter Wilkinson wrote, "Went to Nippon where Gubbins and I got a bit bottled and had two very amusing girls and two bottles of fizz for one pound sterling though this entailed fighting a rearguard action through the swing doors—and so to bed, scarcely able to remember when I had last had a full night's sleep."

**Gubbins's favorite party trick was drinking a half pint of beer while standing on his head.**

Gubbins was known to party all night, sometimes wearing a kilt, with members of FANY—the First Aid Nursing Yeomanry, which provided cover for female agents sent into the field and whose gently bred female members played an indispensable role in SOE. On special occasions, he would show off a party trick in which he would stand on his hands, call for a half pint of beer, slowly lower himself down and then drink it, still standing on his head.

When it came to his work, however, "the mighty atom"—as the short-in-stature Scot was called—was deadly serious. He knew how effective guerrilla war could be from personal experience in Ireland, where he had run guns to the British-backed rebel faction. He had studied South Africa's Boer guerrillas, the Arabian desert campaign against the Turks led by the legendary T. E. Lawrence, the Spanish Civil War and the 1930s Arab revolt in Palestine. After the war broke out he briefly headed the Auxiliary Units, a kind of homemade guerrilla force intended to wage partisan war against the Nazis if they successfully invaded Britain.

Gubbins summed up what he had learned in two little pamphlets on guerrilla tactics. Translated into 16 different languages and distributed all over Europe and Southeast Asia during the war—sometimes printed on rice paper so they could be swallowed—they predated Mao and Ho Chi Minh's more famous pamphlets by several years.

But to wage clandestine war, Gubbins needed to turn SOE recruits into professional secret agents. He established an unprecedented network of schools and training centers from Scotland to Surrey, a far-flung Dirty Tricks Academy where prospective agents would learn about everything from safecracking to silent killing to industrial sabotage to wilderness survival to spy tradecraft. Many of these schools were located in august country houses, leading wags to nickname SOE "Stately 'Omes of England."

Gubbins had the right ideas. He had a core of trained agents to carry them out. Now it was time to find out what the Baker Street Irregulars could do.

# PORTABLE TRANSMITTING AND RECEIVING EQUIPMENT, TYPE B. MARK II.

## GENERAL DESCRIPTION

This is a completely portable transmitting and receiving station, capable of working from A.C. Mains or from a 6-volt accumulator. The whole (apart from accumulator) together with a box of spares has been sent out in a suitcase, but is now despatched in two watertight containers.

In the larger container is the transmitter and receiver and in the smaller is the power pack and spares box. When A.C. Mains are not available a large-capacity 6-volt battery of the automobile type should be used and provision made for keeping it fully charged.

## THE TRANSMITTER

Two valves are employed, and oscillator-doubler driving a Class C amplifier, crystal controlled. Provision is made for frequency doubling. Plug-in tank coils cover 3.0 to 16 Mc/s. A multirange meter on the panel measures voltages and currents and facilitates tuning.

## THE RECEIVER

This is a four-valve seven-stage superheterodyne receiver essentially designed for C.W. reception. A three wave band selector gives a coverage of from 3.1 to 15.5 Mc/s.

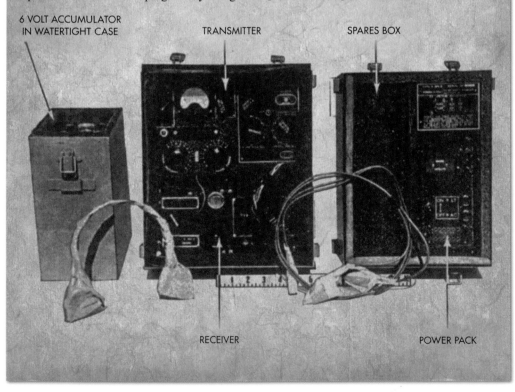

6 VOLT ACCUMULATOR IN WATERTIGHT CASE      TRANSMITTER      SPARES BOX

RECEIVER      POWER PACK

# November 6, 1942
# Sandvatn hut
# Hardangervidda
# Norway

On November 6, the four members of Grouse staggered into a hut near a frozen lake and collapsed. It had taken two weeks to reach this sanctuary in the Hardangervidda, and the trek had nearly killed them.

The four Norwegians had been dropped 10 miles from where they were supposed to land. After they parachuted into the icy wilderness, they had spent two days just collecting the scattered containers, air-dropped with them, that held their heavy equipment and supplies. Bad luck put their skis in the last container they found and made their task exponentially harder. The third day, the first winter storm of the season broke over them. The snow was deep and wet and their skis were not properly waxed. They broke through thin ice while crossing streams with their bulky packs, sometimes getting soaked to the waist and risking fatal hypothermia. They had lost the fuel for their stove, which forced them to change their route and slog through valleys to find birch brush they could burn for cooking and warmth. On one of their last marches, they covered only three-quarters of a mile in a full day. Their rations were grossly inadequate for such exertions, and they began to suffer from malnutrition.

Realizing they were in danger of starvation, leader Jens Poulsson dispatched Claus Helberg, the strongest skier on the team, to return to an empty farm they had stopped at earlier and bring back as much food as he could carry. But after Helberg left, another ferocious storm broke and gale-force winds drove in from the northeast. Although the farm was only three and a half miles away, an inconsequential distance for a first-class Nordic skier like Helberg, he barely made it back to his companions. As he looked at his comrade's gaunt, exhausted face, a Norwegian proverb came into Poulsson's mind: "A man who is a man goes on till he can do no more, and then he goes twice as far." It could have been the motto for their entire mission.

> One of the **rugged** wireless radios SOE's agents used to **communicate** from the field.

When the party finally made it barely alive to their operational base, the Sandvatn hut, their first order of business was to contact London. No one at SOE knew if they were alive or dead. The Grouse team had to send Baker Street information about landing places for the impending British glider mission, code-named Freshman. The Norwegians also desperately needed fresh supplies. Radio operator Knut Haugland rigged up aerials to the hut, but his radio had gotten so wet it would not turn on. He had to wait three days for it to dry out.

Finally, on November 9, the radio crackled into action. Haugland lay in his sleeping bag, only his sending hand exposed. It was too cold to transmit any other way. Painstaking, patient and a perfectionist, Haugland was by far the best wireless operator in SOE, and he needed every bit of his skill. "Sorry to keep you waiting for message," Haugland signaled. "Snow storm fog forced us to go down valleys. Four feet snow impossible with heavy equipment."

The message was received by a coder at SOE's coding station at Grendon Underwood, in Buckinghamshire, northwest of London. But she was suspicious. Wireless messages were transmitted in encrypted Morse code, using a sending key depressed by the operator. Every operator had a unique sending style, as distinct as a fingerprint, which was recorded on a special machine before they left. It was one of a coder's jobs to learn an agent's sending style, or "fist," and raise the alarm if their fist changed—it could mean the agent had been captured. Because Haugland could use only the frozen tips of his fingers, the coder did not recognize his fist. Worried, Baker Street asked him a series of security questions, finishing with a whimsical one to which only he knew the answer: "What did you see walking down the Strand in the early hours of Jan. 1, 1941?" When Haugland replied, "Three pink elephants," jubilation broke out in the coding room. Grouse had survived.

Ten days later, Haugland sent a message to London that the weather in the region had finally cleared up. A few minutes later, an SOE operator sent back the code word *Girl.* The glider raid was on. Freshman would fly that night.

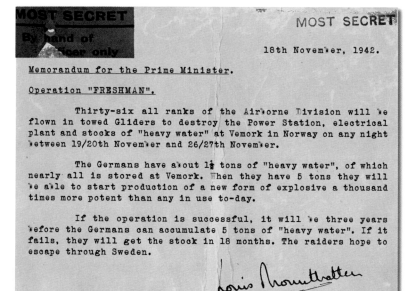

MOST SECRET
By hand of officer only

MOST SECRET

18th November, 1942.

Memorandum for the Prime Minister.

Operation "FRESHMAN".

Thirty-six all ranks of the Airborne Division will be flown in towed Gliders to destroy the Power Station, electrical plant and stocks of "heavy water" at Vemork in Norway on any night between 19/20th November and 26/27th November.

The Germans have about 1½ tons of "heavy water", of which nearly all is stored at Vemork. When they have 5 tons they will be able to start production of a new form of explosive a thousand times more potent than any in use to-day.

If the operation is successful, it will be three years before the Germans can accumulate 5 tons of "heavy water". If it fails, they will get the stock in 18 months. The raiders hope to escape through Sweden.

Louis Mountbatten

Chief of Combined Operations

**The memo from Mountbatten to Churchill sent the day before Operation Freshman was launched.**

## 4 p.m.
## November 10, 1942
## Room 238, Hotel Victoria
## London

The man in the dingy, almost empty room looked across the table at Noor. His clean-shaven face was bland, unreadable, a polished mask. But Noor could tell that behind it a keen and probing intelligence was evaluating everything about her.

The man did not tell her his name. He said a few words in English, then switched to French, which he spoke flawlessly. He asked Noor how she had come to speak French so well. They chatted for a few minutes about her family and her life story. She told him that she had published a children's book and described her family's flight from Paris. He already knew that she had joined the Women's Auxiliary Air Force and had been chosen at random for training as a wireless radio operator.

Noor had joined the WAAF because her beloved brother Vilayat had volunteered for the RAF. "If he becomes a pilot," she said, "he will be risking his life every day." She did not want to do less than her brother.

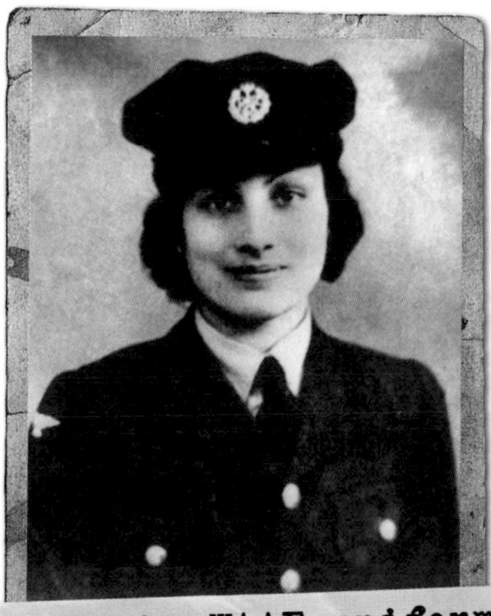

Noor in WAAF uniform

It was her skill as a wireless operator and her fluency in French that had drawn the attention of the organization for which the man worked. The organization was SOE.

The preliminaries over, the man came to the point. He told Noor that if she agreed to join his organization, she might eventually be sent into occupied France as an underground wireless operator, working with other secret British agents who were engaged in sabotage.

The man told her that the work would be extremely dangerous. If she was caught, he said, she would be interrogated by the Gestapo. Since she would not be in uniform, she would not be protected by the international laws of warfare. In short, she might not return. He told her that her odds of returning were about even.

Noor had listened carefully. Then, raising her head, she said simply, "Yes, I would like to do it."

The interviewer—an SOE officer named

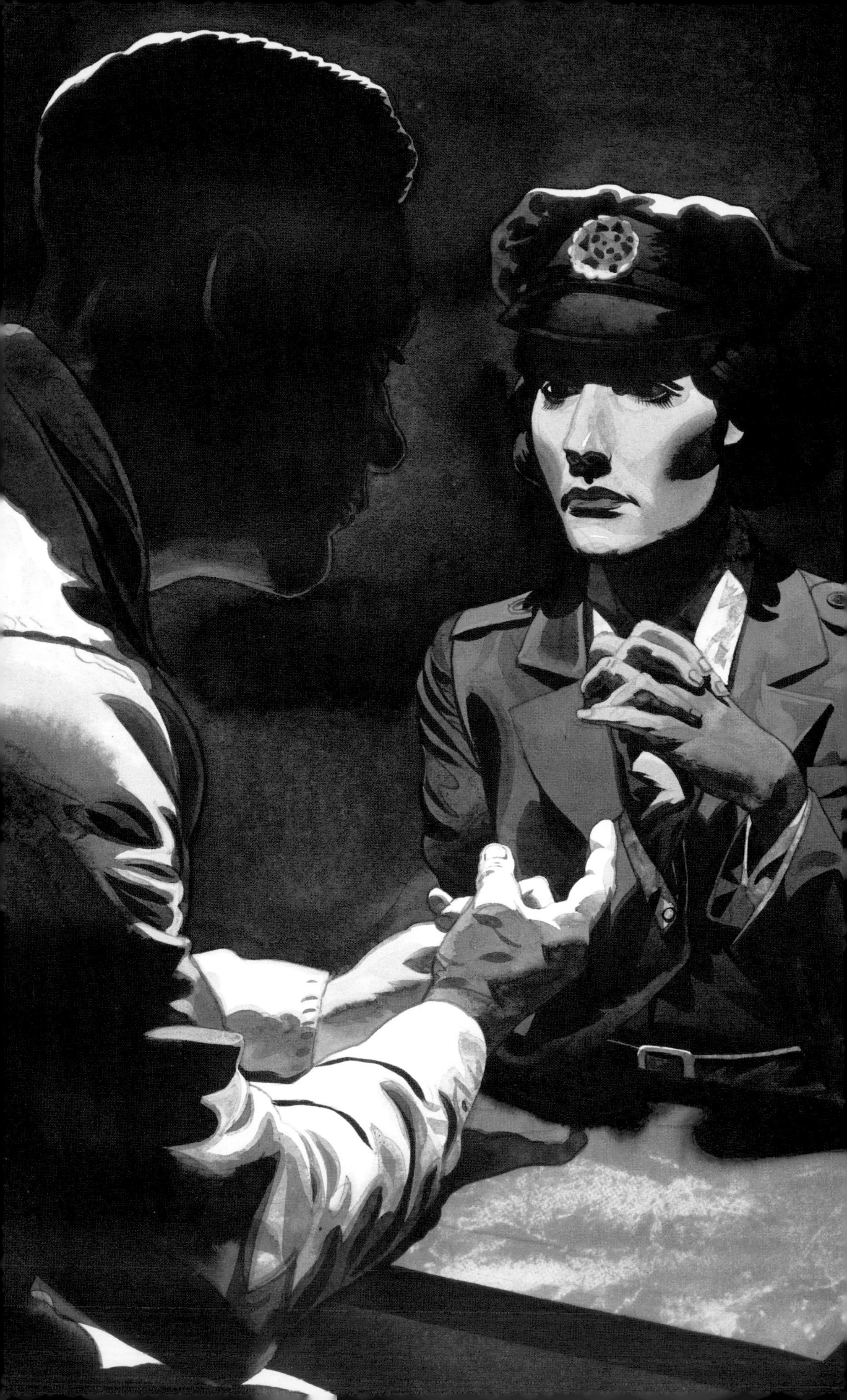

Selwyn Jepson, who had been a novelist in civilian life—was ordinarily suspicious when a potential recruit immediately agreed to sign up. It usually meant that the person had not thought through what he or she was being asked to do, or was driven by some personal motive that might make them unreliable in the field. Impulsiveness was dangerous. But Jepson had an uncanny ability to immediately size up the people who walked into his grim office. And Jepson's instinct told him that Noor was the real thing.

But as he looked at the diminutive, earnest young woman across from him, Jepson suddenly found himself impelled, against his professional duty, to try to persuade her not to take the job. Speaking to Noor as a fellow author, he suggested that it would be understandable if she decided she could help humanity more by writing books for the children who would have to rebuild the world after the war was over.

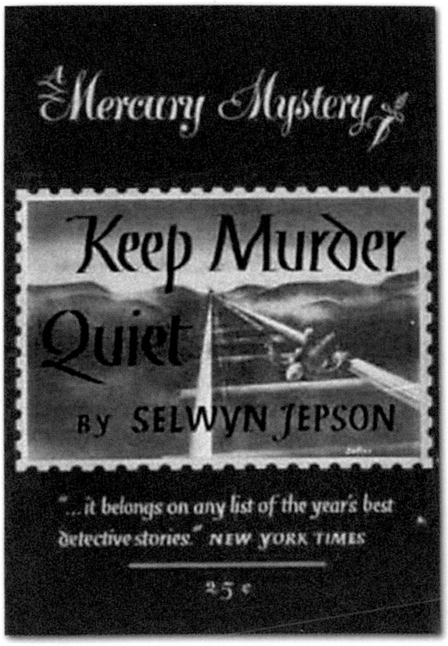
Mercury Mystery
Keep Murder Quiet
BY SELWYN JEPSON
"...it belongs on any list of the year's best detective stories." NEW YORK TIMES
25¢

**The ironically appropriate title of one of Jepson's novels.**

**Jepson found himself trying to convince Noor not to take the job.**

Noor shook her head. If Jepson thought she could make it, she would like to try to become an agent.

Jepson always felt a sense of bleak distress at this fateful moment in the recruitment process, and as he looked at Noor, he felt it more acutely than ever. But he had a job to do. Jepson told her he was sure she would make it. He agreed to take her on.

Ten years later, Jepson was still haunted by the memory of that afternoon in the Hotel Victoria. "I see her very clearly as she was that first afternoon, sitting in front of me in that dingy little room, in a hard kitchen chair on the other side of a bare wooden table," he told Noor's biographer, Jean Overton Fuller, who had become friends with Noor in London and, like everyone who met her, could never forget her. "Indeed, of them all—and they were many—who did not return, I find myself constantly remembering her with a curious and very personal vividness which outshines the rest...the small, still features, the dark, quiet eyes, the soft voice, and the fine spirit glowing in her."

The next day, Noor wrote Jepson a letter formally accepting the offer. Her one qualm had been about her frail mother, who had never recovered from the death of her husband. But, she wrote, she had realized that her mother would eventually get used to her going overseas, and the extra money Noor would be paid as an SOE agent would make her mother's life easier.

"Besides," she wrote, "I realize how petty our family ties are when something like winning this war is at stake."

# The Shanghai Buster

The distinguished faculty at SOE's training schools was rumored to include an agent named Fifi whose job was to use her sexual wiles to loosen the tongues of male agents. But the most memorable of SOE's instructors was a mild-mannered, middle-aged man named William Fairbairn—aka The Shanghai Buster.

Fairbairn earned his moniker working as a cop in the 1920s and 1930s on the Shanghai waterfront. With 100,000 hoodlums, 70,000 prostitutes, a booming opium trade and astonishing rates of murder, kidnapping and armed robbery, it was the world's nastiest piece of real estate. Fairbairn learned every deadly trick in the book there. After nine of his fellow policemen were shot, Fairbairn and colleague Bill Sykes devised a new method of "instinctive firing," in which trainees under attack were taught to fire two shots instantly and accurately without bringing their guns up to eye level—a method he introduced to SOE and which is still taught by the U.S. Army and other military and police forces today. The two men also invented a highly lethal double-edged fighting knife, which was used by the British commandos in WWII and by U.S. forces in Korea and Vietnam.

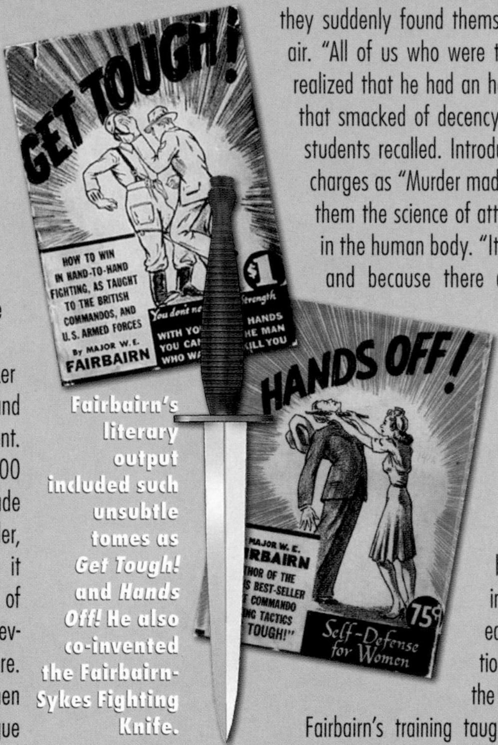
GET TOUGH!
HOW TO WIN IN HAND-TO-HAND FIGHTING, AS TAUGHT TO THE BRITISH COMMANDOS, AND U.S. ARMED FORCES
By MAJOR W. E. FAIRBAIRN
$1
HANDS OFF!
75¢
Self-Defense for Women

Fairbairn's literary output included such unsubtle tomes as *Get Tough!* and *Hands Off!* He also co-invented the Fairbairn-Sykes Fighting Knife.

Fifty-five years old in 1940 and of medium height and build, Fairbairn hardly resembled a killing machine. But any doubts his students may have had about him vanished when, invited to attack him, they suddenly found themselves flying through the air. "All of us who were taught by Fairbairn soon realized that he had an honest dislike of anything that smacked of decency in fighting," one of his students recalled. Introducing himself to his SOE charges as "Murder made easy," Fairbairn taught them the science of attacking every weak point in the human body. "It's fighting without rules, and because there aren't any rules, there aren't any fouls, and it's all fair play," he would tell them. "See, fighting to kill is the only honest fighting there is, see!" His lessons sometimes seemed complicated to his students, but they invariably ended with the easy-to-remember instruction "and then kick him in the testicles."

Fairbairn's training taught SOE agents how to disable or kill an enemy silently and quickly. But more important, it gave them enormous confidence. Agent George Langelaan wrote, "He taught us to face the possibility of a fight without the slightest tremor of apprehension, a state of mind which very few professional boxers ever enjoy and which so often means more than half the battle." Langelaan's only fear was that after the war he might get into a fight and kill someone before he realized what he was doing.

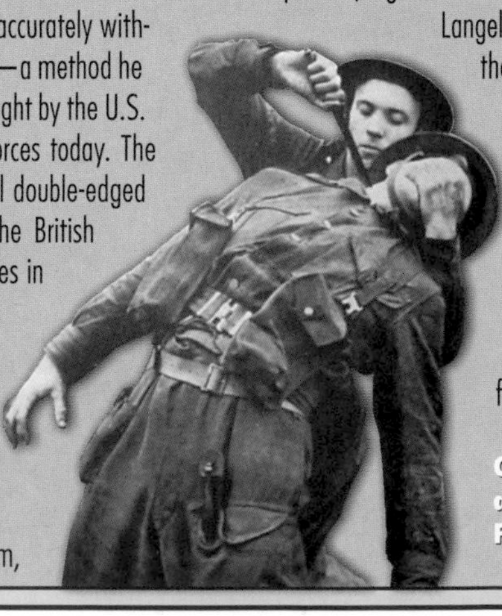

Commandos demonstrate a lethal attack with the Fighting Knife.

## November 14, 1942
## Special Training School #23
## Meoble Lodge
## Inverness-shire
## Scotland

Harry Ree was not happy. He had just endured a grueling four-week paramilitary course at Meoble Lodge in the Scottish Highlands, getting up at the crack of dawn to go on long runs, struggling through grueling obstacle courses, having his internal organs rearranged in hand-to-hand combat training. But when he was finished, his instructors made him repeat the course. All he could do was grit his teeth and do it all over again.

One of SOE's approximately 60 training schools, Meoble Lodge, like the other SOE schools around Arisaig in the Scottish Highlands, specialized in advanced paramilitary training. The 3,000 SOE agents who trained in Scotland during the war went through a rigorous three- or four-week course that included physical workouts, basic infantry skills, rudimentary courses in demolitions, sabotage and Morse Code, small arms practice and, most memorably, a course in unarmed combat and silent killing taught by SOE's most famous instructor, William Fairbairn, aka The Shanghai Buster (see sidebar.)

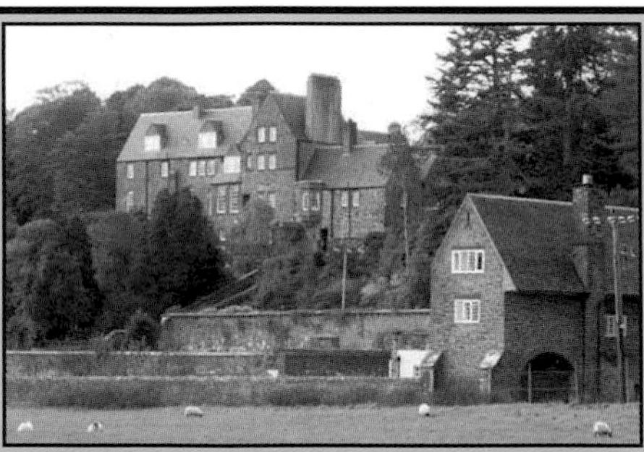

Arisaig House, SOE's **commando** training HQ in the Scottish Highlands

On Ree's second try, he passed with flying colors. In a "Para-Military Report" filed on November 14, 1942, his instructor gave him excellent marks almost across the board. Under Physical Training, his instructor noted, "Very good. Easily the fittest on the course. Groundwork outstanding." He was scored "very good" in Close Combat and "outstandingly good" in Rope Work. The camp commandant commented, "A very nice fellow who has worked very hard and done very well."

Having made it through boot camp, Ree went on to SOE's so-called finishing school at Beaulieu Manor in the New Forest in Hampshire. Beaulieu was SOE's Ph.D.

program. On its stately grounds, students learned the fine points of how to be an undercover agent. They studied conditions of life in the country they were to work in. They had to know every type of security force they might encounter—in France, for example, in addition to the German Gestapo, SD and Abwehr, there were no less than 15 different French police forces. They learned about identity cards, ration cards, curfews and other ever-changing facts of life in their assigned country. They were subjected to mock interrogations. They learned about safe-cracking from a famous Scottish burglar (who mysteriously vanished one day, presumably sent back to jail for using his considerable skills in a way not approved by His Majesty's government). They studied disguises, how to pass messages, and other secret-agent tradecraft. In their final exercise, they were sent off on two- or three-day missions to various British cities, where, working alone, they had to make contact with comrades, avoid the authorities, devise suitable cover stories, send messages secretly and generally do everything a real agent in an occupied country would have to do.

Ree's "Finishing Report"—dated March 1, 1943, only six weeks before he went into the field—painted a less flattering portrait than the one from Meoble Lodge. It read, "Very intelligent and intellectual: very quick but not very practical. In spite of the fact that he is hard working and enthusiastic his excellent mental qualities are seriously marred by a natural erraticism which leads him to gross carelessness. He has a strong character and deep sense of honor and duty, but, at the same

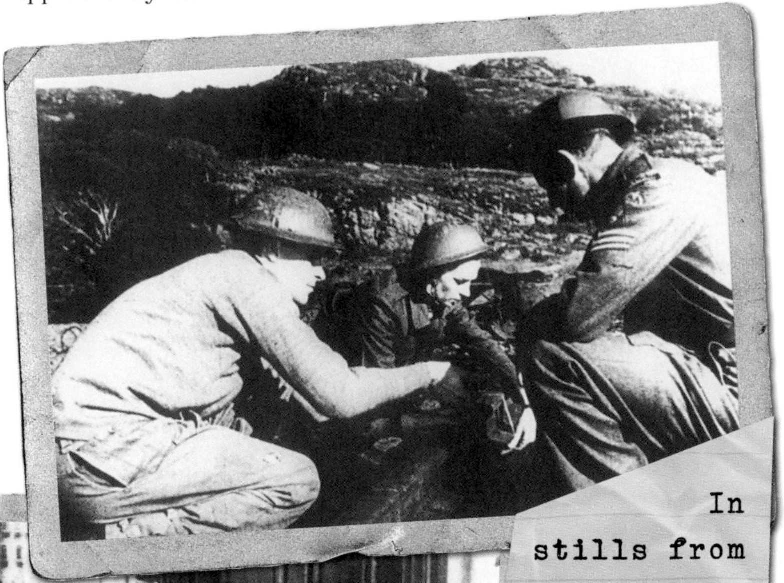

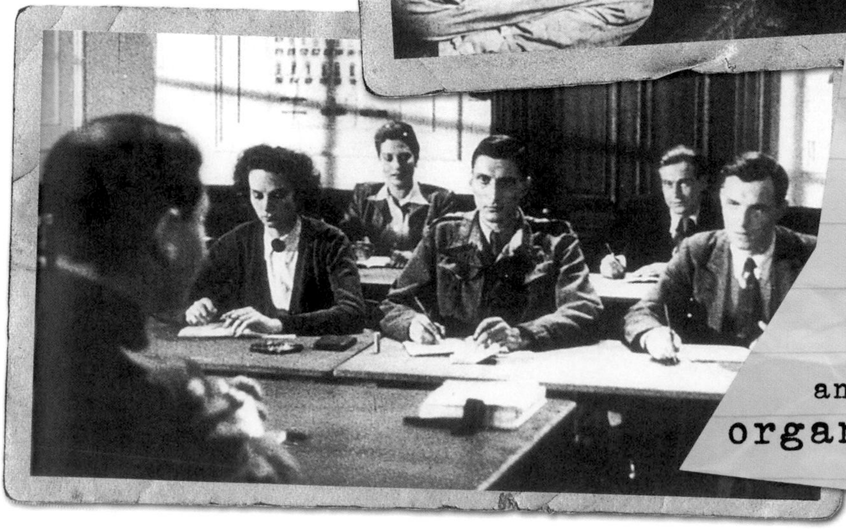

In stills from a postwar documentary about SOE, Ree is shown learning sabotage and circuit organization.

time, he is highly strung and nervy. He is an uncompromising idealist and would be quite ruthless with anyone who roused his moral disapproval. He is very tactless and hates authority as such. Nevertheless, he would always be a loyal subordinate for idealistic rather than disciplinary reasons.

"He has an exasperating personality which many people might find intolerable, but, nevertheless, those who understand him like him very much. In spite of these failings he has certain powers of leadership and would win the respect of those who understand him."

Ree in full parachute gear

Finally—and most alarming—the report raised questions about Ree's ability to withstand the rigors and terrors of the field: "Although he would probably be the last to admit it, he is very apprehensive about the work he has volunteered to undertake. He has serious doubts about whether he is mentally capable of carrying it out. He is worried about his French. As a result of this he has of late been sleeping badly and those who have known him previously were shocked by his change of appearance. All instructors here agree that he is not suited, either mentally or temperamentally for the work for which he is intended, and feel very strongly that he should not be so employed."

Harry Ree was a complex man. A leftist whose great-grandfather was a German freedom fighter who had sat in the famous liberal Frankfurt Parliament in 1848, he was an individualist who disliked authority, a deeply moral person who followed his own ethical code but had no time for dogma, an intellectual who probably was capable of imagining the terrors of the job more acutely than most trainees. In short, he was the sort of person the more hidebound types of military men would dislike.

Not surprisingly, Ree had ended up in SOE because he couldn't stand the regular army. After giving up his conscientious objector status, he was called into the field artillery and trained as an artilleryman for six months, an absurd experience where he drilled with guns on wooden wheels and had a terrifying sergeant who called him "Gonorrhea," a sophomoric play on Gunner Ree. Fortunately, around this time he received a letter from his brother, who told him about a secret organization called The Racket which sent secret agents into France. Ree transferred out of the artillery and enlisted to be trained in field security. He was assigned to SOE's wireless section at Grendon Underwood, where he helped train prospective agents. But after he realized that some of the people he was training spoke worse French than he did, he applied to go into the field himself.

Ree's commanding officer recommended against sending him into the

field, on the grounds that he knew too much about SOE. He also spoke French with an obvious foreign accent. But The Firm needed bodies, and Ree was accepted. After training at Beaulieu, he was sent to SOE's special demolitions school, STS 17, at Brickendonbury Hall, a former school on extensive grounds near Hertford. The head instructor of this school—who also taught the Norwegian commandos how to sabotage the key machines in the heavy-water plant—was a man named George Rheam, who rejoiced in the title "the father of industrial sabotage." Rheam taught Ree how to set fire to massive amounts of rubber. SOE's plan was to send him to sabotage the huge Michelin tire plant at Clermont-Ferrand, which had been taken over by the Nazis.

Ree now held an advanced degree in dirty tricks from the strangest university in the world. Sleepless nights, fearful imaginings, insubordinate tendencies, bad French and all, the contrarian young schoolteacher would soon be dropped into enemy territory.

## November 19, 1942
## Sandvatn hut
## Hardangervidda
## Norway

Soon after Knut Haugland received word from London that Freshman, the British commando team, was on its way, the capricious weather on the Hardangervidda suddenly worsened. Haugland urgently tried to signal London to abort the raid, but he could not get through. There was nothing for him and the other members of Grouse to do but hope they could guide the gliders in safely.

At the landing site, the Grouse men placed torches and set up a homing device called a Eureka to guide the planes in. Around 9:40 p.m., they heard the sound of an airplane and the Eureka beeped. But then the plane turned away. They kept waiting, hearing a faint drone now and then, but the plane never returned. Not knowing what had happened, they returned disappointedly to their hut.

The next day, London informed Grouse that both gliders and one of the bombers had crashed. The four Norwegians, clinging to life on the Hardangervidda, were devastated.

The Norwegians did not know exactly what happened to the six airmen on the bomber and 34 commandos on the two gliders. That was just as well, for their fates were hideous. All the airmen and about a third of the commandos were killed in the crashes—and they were the lucky ones. The Germans brutally executed the survivors. Doctors tortured several badly injured men by injecting air bubbles into their veins as Gestapo thugs strangled them with leather straps. Some who were shot may have been buried while still alive.

The survivors had not tried to escape because they were in uniform, which they believed would entitle them to protection under the laws of war. But just a month before, Hitler had issued his top-secret "Commando Order," which mandated that all enemy troops on commando raids, whether in uniform or not, were to be "annihilated to the last man." It was this illegal order that sealed their dreadful fate.

Knowing the Germans would search the area, London ordered Grouse to hide immediately. The four Norwegians moved to a new hut, Svensbu, in a more remote part of the Hardangervidda. They called it Cousin's Cabin because Poulsson and his cousin had built it before the war.

The Freshman glider disaster revealed just how long the odds were against the mission. But Allied commanders could not write it off. They were convinced that nothing less than the fate of the world hung on its success.

Germany was racing the Allies to build the first atomic bomb, and Roosevelt and Churchill feared the Germans were winning. German physicists had been the first to split uranium in 1938. Heavy water, or deuterium oxide, was a crucial component in making a nuclear bomb. There was only one facility in the world that produced heavy water: a plant called Norsk Hydro, at Vemork in the Telemark region of Norway. In late 1941, the Allies learned that Germany had ordered the Vemork plant to triple its production, to 10,000 pounds a year.

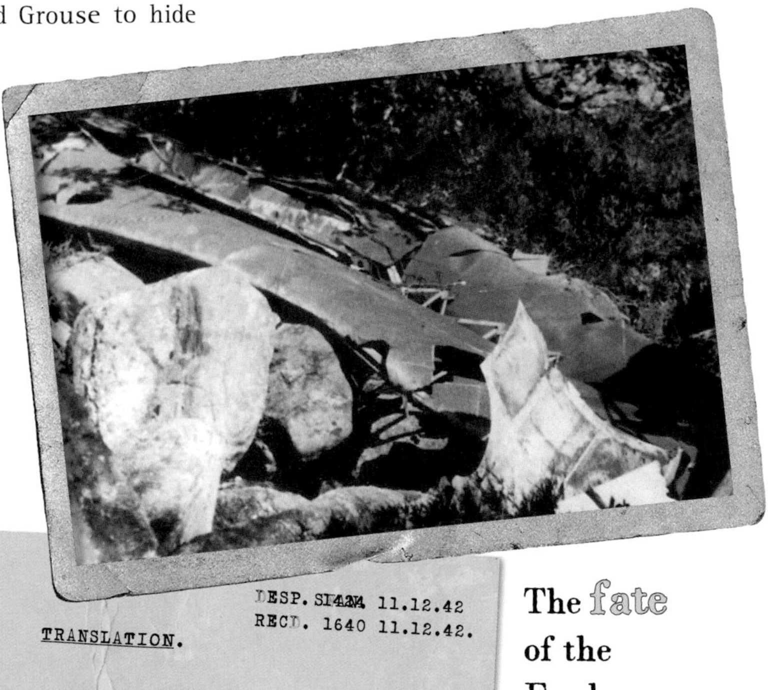

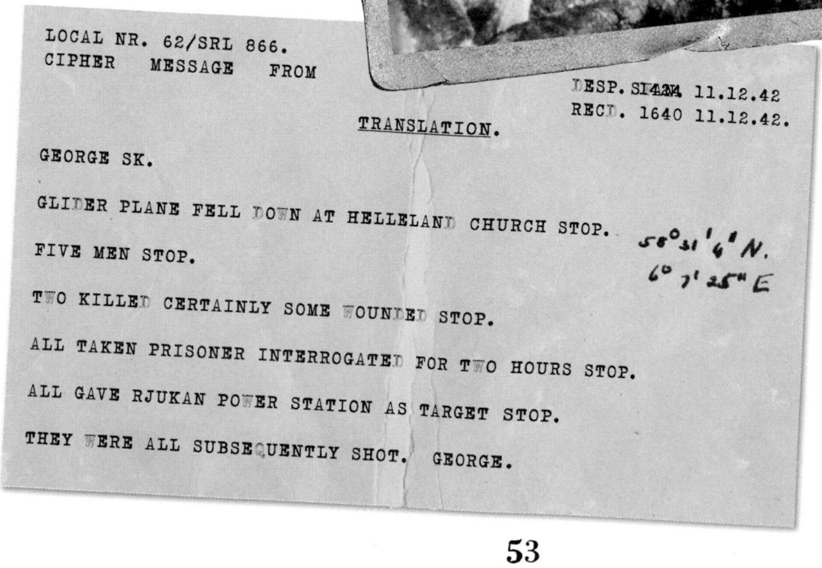
LOCAL NR. 62/SRL 866.
CIPHER MESSAGE FROM

DESP. S1424 11.12.42
RECD. 1640 11.12.42.

TRANSLATION.

GEORGE SK.

GLIDER PLANE FELL DOWN AT HELLELAND CHURCH STOP. 58°31'6'N.
FIVE MEN STOP. 6°7'25"E
TWO KILLED CERTAINLY SOME WOUNDED STOP.
ALL TAKEN PRISONER INTERROGATED FOR TWO HOURS STOP.
ALL GAVE RJUKAN POWER STATION AS TARGET STOP.
THEY WERE ALL SUBSEQUENTLY SHOT. GEORGE.

**The fate of the Freshman glider commandos was hideous.**

# Shadow Knights

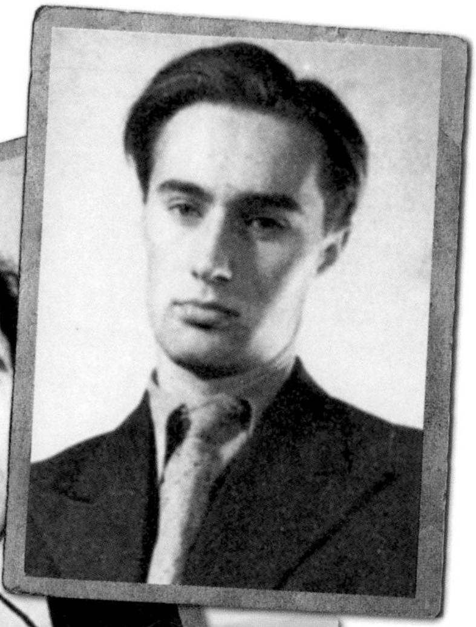

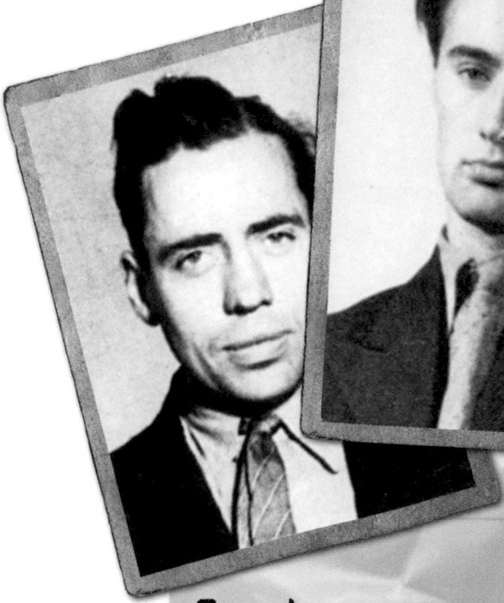

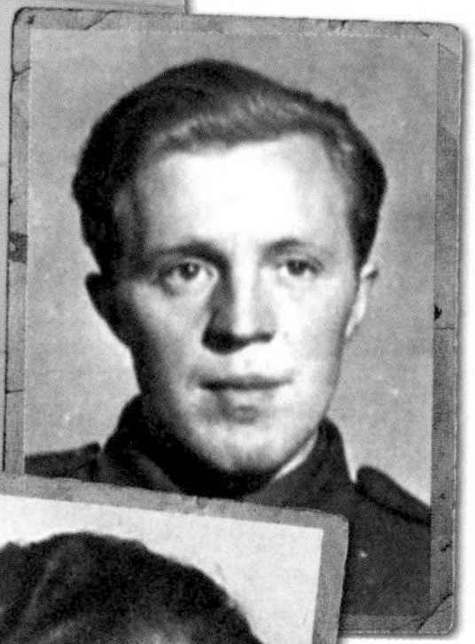

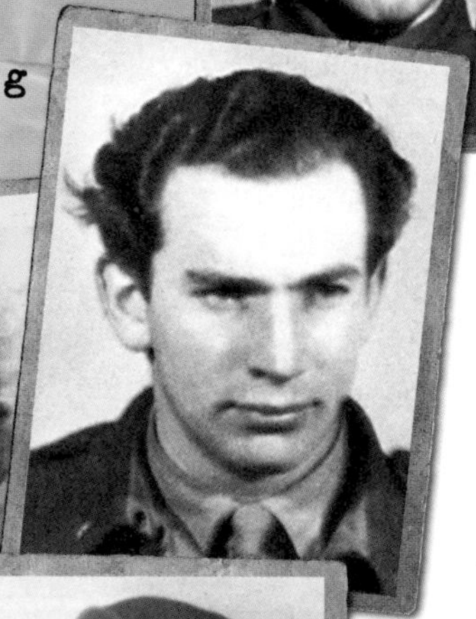

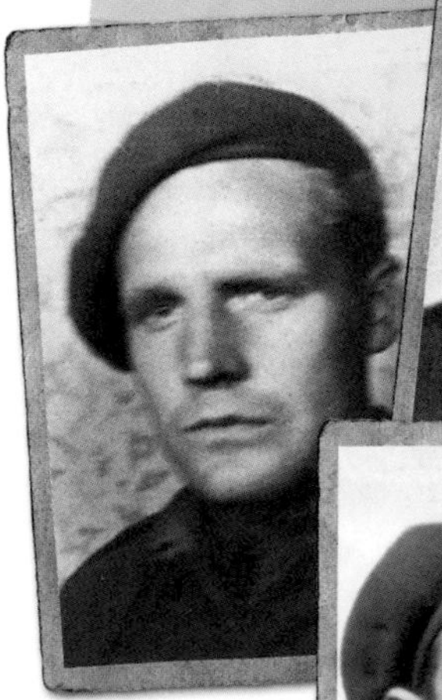

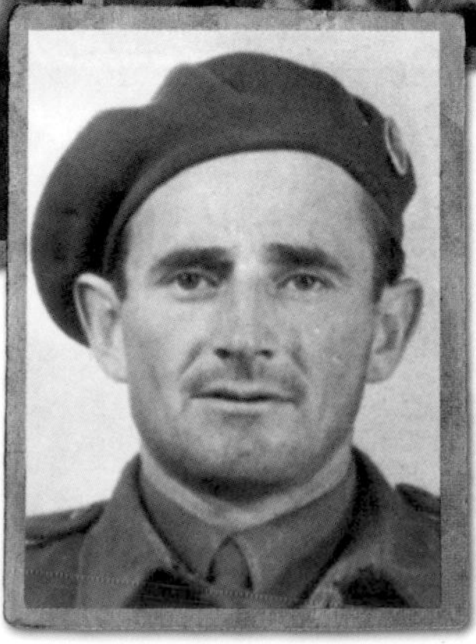

Top to bottom: **Ronneberg, Haukelid,** Stromsheim, Kayser, Idland, Storhaug

If Hitler got the atomic bomb first, he would be unstoppable. Churchill and Roosevelt made disabling the Norsk Hydro plant their top priority.

Freshman had been run by a British military unit called Combined Operations, better known as the Commandos. The catastrophe convinced the military brass to let SOE take complete charge of the operation. Colonel Wilson, the head of SOE's Norway section, proposed that a small, all-Norwegian party of expert skiers do the job. This new group of commandos would jump in, join up with Grouse and destroy the heavy water.

When Gubbins, now a major-general and in charge of SOE's military operations, learned of Wilson's plan, the intense Scot was aghast. "You can't do that!" he said. "It's too difficult." Wilson told him that he had already appointed the leader, who was selecting five other men to go with him. "I'm positive the job can be done, and it *will* be done," Wilson said.

The man SOE selected to lead the raid was named Joachim Ronneberg. Just 22 years old and barely out of college, the strikingly handsome Ronneberg was nonetheless the perfect choice: intelligent, resourceful, good-humored, physically indomitable and mentally tough. Ronneberg selected his teammates as much for their personalities as for their fitness. In particular, he was looking for men who could get along with others and had a sense of humor. He knew camaraderie and the ability to laugh off difficulties would be as essential to the mission's success as fitness and fieldcraft.

Ronneberg's second in command would be Knut Haukelid, the barrel-chested philosopher-fighter who had thrown the

# Shadow Knights

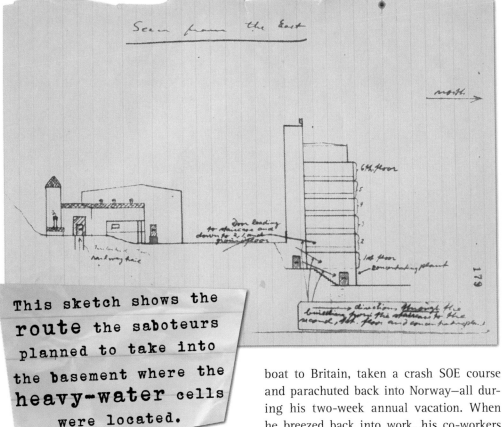

Seen from the East

This sketch shows the **route** the saboteurs planned to take into the basement where the **heavy-water** cells were located.

Quisling off a Norwegian ferry boat and then fled to England. Haukelid, who was nicknamed the General, had dropped out of the Grouse party after shooting himself in the foot. The other four were Birger Stromsheim, Fredrik Kayser, Kasper Idland, and Hans Storhaug. This team's code name was Gunnerside.

The team had gone through SOE's commando-style training course in Scotland. Now they received a crash course in demolitions under George Rheam at STS 17. They were armed with accurate maps of the plants smuggled out by the scientist who designed it, Leif Tronstad, and the plant's manager, Jomar Brun, both of whom had escaped to Britain. They also received up-to-the-minute intelligence provided by a remarkable figure named Einar Skinnarland. Skinnarland, the construction superintendent at the hydro-electric dam near the plant, had hijacked a

boat to Britain, taken a crash SOE course and parachuted back into Norway—all during his two-week annual vacation. When he breezed back into work, his co-workers simply assumed he had been on a skiing trip. Skinnarland—fearless, inexhaustible, a champion skier and a gourmet cook to boot—was to prove invaluable to the mission.

It was crucial that the Gunnerside party get into the Hardangervidda as soon as possible. The Grouse party—whose code name had been switched to Swallow, in case any of the captured British commandos had talked under torture—had been dropped more than six weeks ago. Baker Street did not know just how desperate Swallow's predicament was, but it knew the four men had been pushed to the limit. On December 11, SOE sent a message to Swallow telling them that the fresh team would be arriving within the week.

But bad weather meant that Gunnerside was not to arrive for more than two months—the heart of the brutal Norwegian winter. In their freezing hut on the Hardangervidda, the four men of Swallow would just have to hang on.

# Pirates against Hitler
## The *Maid Honour* raid

In August 1941, a flamboyant SOE agent named Gus March-Phillips and a hand-picked crew of five die-hards sailed a converted trawler named *Maid Honour* to the Spanish island of Fernando Po, off West Africa, where two Axis ships, the Italian merchantman *Duchess d'Aosta* and the German tug *Likomba,* were anchored. March-Phillips's mission: Steal the two enemy vessels.

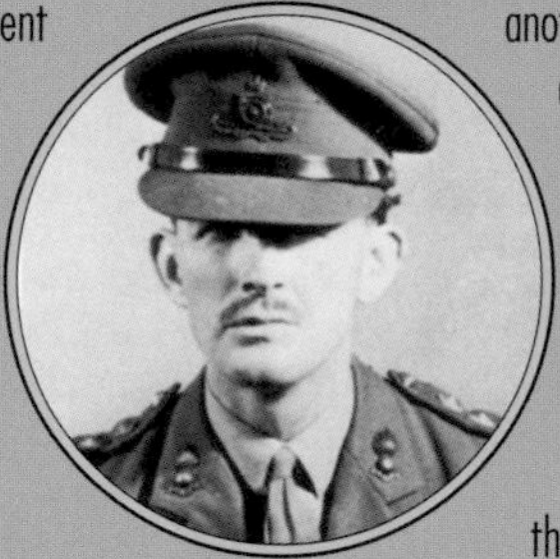

Gus March-Phillips

Because Spain was neutral, the raid had to be approved by Britain's Foreign Office, but there could be no traces of official involvement. Permission was quickly granted, and on a moonless night in January 1942, March-Phillips and his band of brigands, now swollen to 40 men with the addition of "as choice a collection of thugs as Nigeria can ever have seen," sailed into Santa Isabel harbor and stealthily boarded the Axis ships. The pirates met no resistance, because almost the entire crews of both ships had been lured ashore and were drinking heavily at a party at the local casino.

When March-Phillips's men blew up the anchor cables on the target ships with plastic explosives, the confused Spanish shore guards thought it was an air raid and failed to notice that the ships were being towed out to sea. After the German skipper of the *Likomba,* a man named Specht, realized that his ship had been hijacked, he stormed drunkenly into the British Consulate, demanded to know where his ship was and angrily punched a British official. It was a mistake. As an undercover SOE agent who was present reported, another agent identified only as "W.51" jumped up and "put some heavy north of Scotland stuff on him, and literally knocked the shit out of him. When he saw W.51's revolver he collapsed in a heap, split his pants and emptied his bowell's [*sic*] on the floor."

Aside from Herr Specht's pants, there were no casualties. March-Phillips passed the hijacked vessels over to a British warship on the high seas. When the prizes were towed into Lagos harbor, the British governor greeted them from the end of a pier with a whiskey and soda in his hand, cheering loudly.

After March-Phillips made it back to Baker Street—flamboyantly dressed in bush hat, breeches and riding boots—the exuberant Gubbins threw him another party. As he rode the elevator to the celebration, the latter-day privateer began chatting up the female operator. They were married two months later. The next year March-Phillips was killed leading a commando raid in the Channel Islands.

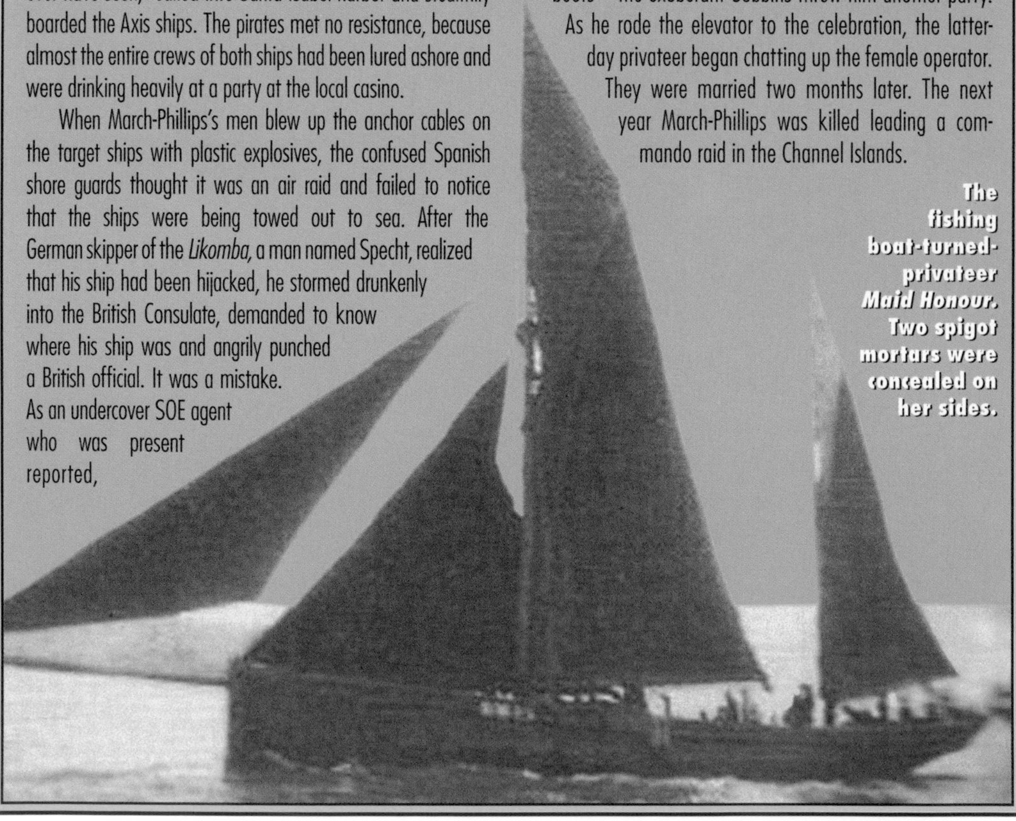

The fishing boat-turned-privateer *Maid Honour.* Two spigot mortars were concealed on her sides.

# December 1942
# 64 Baker Street
# London

**G**ubbins and SOE desperately needed a major success. The year 1942 had begun auspiciously, when one of The Firm's most flamboyant agents, Gus March-Phillips, used a converted trawler, the *Maid Honour,* to pull off an act of piracy worthy of his idol, Sir Francis Drake. After a farewell party presided over by an ebullient Gubbins, who popped champagne and pinned a lucky sprig of white heather to the ship's mast, March-Phillips and a small crew sailed to West Africa, where they stole two Axis ships out from under the noses of the harbor guards and sailed them onto the high seas as prizes of war. (See sidebar.)

For its first two years, SOE's **standing** in Whitehall was **abysmal.**

The *Maid Honour* raid boosted SOE's standing, but like George Binney's 1941 Swedish ball-bearings mission and other flashy SOE coups de main, it was only a temporary shot in the arm. For the first two years of its existence, SOE's standing in Whitehall varied from shaky to abysmal.

SOE's first ministerial head, Hugh Dalton, was disliked by Churchill and despised by Foreign Minister Anthony Eden. Dalton had grandiosely claimed that SOE was about to ignite a vast worker's uprising. When that idea fizzled, Dalton was pushed by Gubbins to embrace a different approach: SOE would arm a host of "secret armies" across Europe. These armies, modeled on the underground forces in Poland and Czechoslovakia, would rise up at London's command and throw the Germans out.

This strategy, which SOE historian David Stafford dubbed the "detonator concept," made more military sense than Dalton's delusional dream of a proletarian uprising, but it proved equally unrealistic. To supply such armies, SOE would need every bomber in the RAF, and the RAF made it clear it was never going to get them.

With SOE floundering, Dalton was replaced in early 1942 as minister of economic warfare by Lord Selborne, a close friend of Churchill's. Gubbins was relieved. Now Baker Street would have a ministerial head who knew how to navigate Whitehall's treacherous currents.

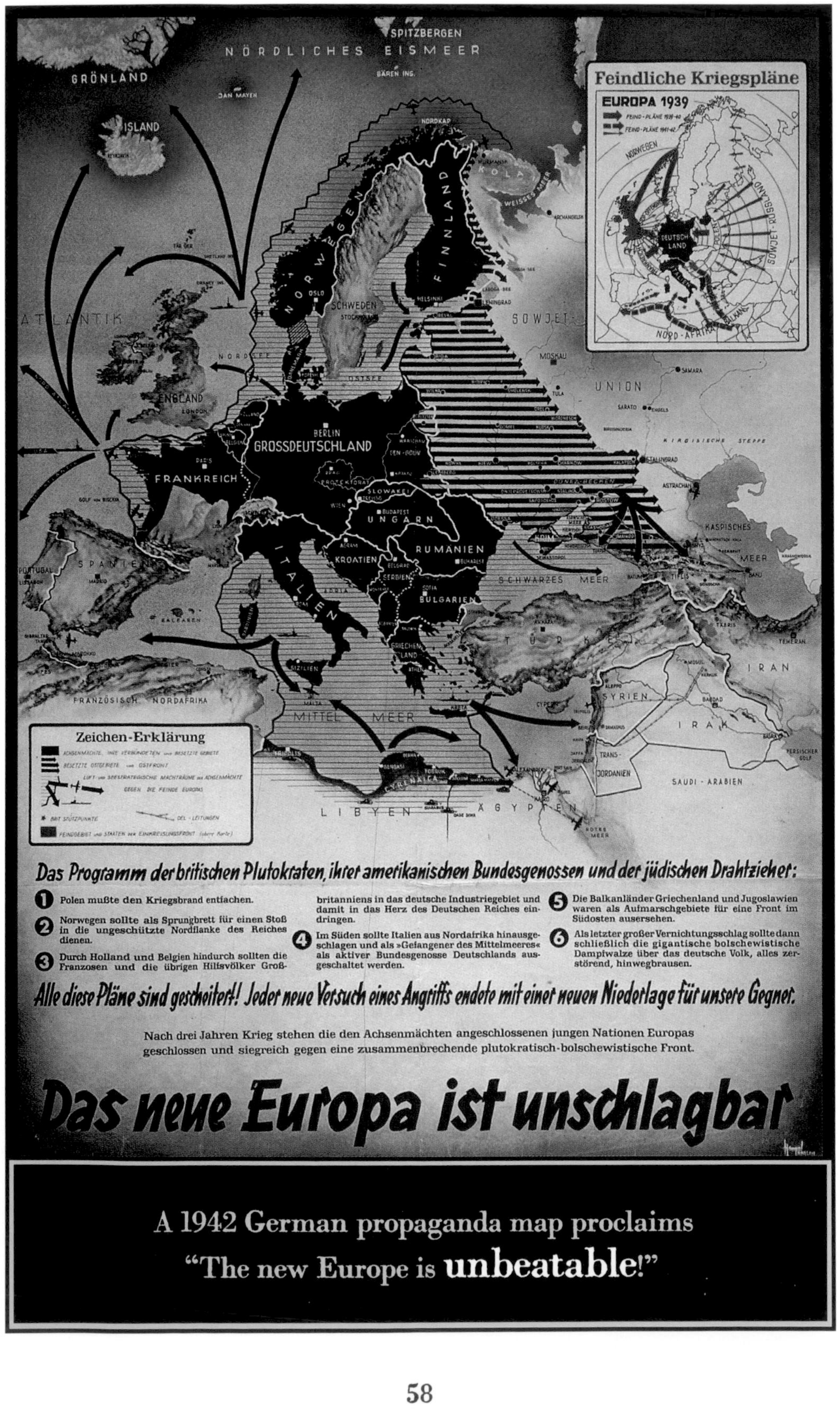
NÖRDLICHES EISMEER
SPITZBERGEN
GRÖNLAND
ISLAND
Feindliche Kriegspläne
EUROPA 1939
NORWEGEN
FINNLAND
SCHWEDEN
ATLANTIK
SOWJET-UNION
MOSKAU
ENGLAND
BERLIN
GROSSDEUTSCHLAND
FRANKREICH
SLOWAKEI
UNGARN
RUMÄNIEN
KROATIEN
ITALIEN
BULGARIEN
SPANIEN
PORTUGAL
SCHWARZES MEER
KASPISCHES MEER
IRAN
SYRIEN
IRAK
TRANS-JORDANIEN
SAUDI-ARABIEN
FRANZÖSISCH NORDAFRIKA
MITTEL MEER
LIBYEN
ÄGYPTEN
Zeichen-Erklärung
Das Programm der britischen Plutokraten, ihrer amerikanischen Bundesgenossen und der jüdischen Drahtzieher:
1 Polen mußte den Kriegsbrand entfachen.
2 Norwegen sollte als Sprungbrett für einen Stoß in die ungeschützte Nordflanke des Reiches dienen.
3 Durch Holland und Belgien hindurch sollten die Franzosen und die übrigen Hilfsvölker Großbritanniens in das deutsche Industriegebiet und damit in das Herz des Deutschen Reiches eindringen.
4 Im Süden sollte Italien aus Nordafrika hinausgeschlagen und als »Gefangener des Mittelmeeres« als aktiver Bundesgenosse Deutschlands ausgeschaltet werden.
5 Die Balkanländer Griechenland und Jugoslawien waren als Aufmarschgebiete für eine Front im Südosten ausersehen.
6 Als letzter großer Vernichtungsschlag sollte dann schließlich die gigantische bolschewistische Dampfwalze über das deutsche Volk, alles zerstörend, hinwegbrausen.
Alle diese Pläne sind gescheitert! Jeder neue Versuch eines Angriffs endete mit einer neuen Niederlage für unsere Gegner.
Nach drei Jahren Krieg stehen die den Achsenmächten angeschlossenen jungen Nationen Europas geschlossen und siegreich gegen eine zusammenbrechende plutokratisch-bolschewistische Front.
Das neue Europa ist unschlagbar

A 1942 German propaganda map proclaims
"The new Europe is **unbeatable**!"

# Shadow Knights

But Gubbins and the rest of SOE's top brass knew that SOE needed more than bureaucratic victories to sustain itself. It needed tangible achievements in the field. And at the end of 1942, it had precious few of them to boast about—and several unfolding disasters.

The country where SOE most urgently needed to establish resistance forces was France, because, as Gubbins's chief of staff said, "the Allies were obviously going to have to land somewhere there in the end." SOE had two main French sections—RF and F. The RF Section was created to work exclusively with General Charles de Gaulle's Free French resistance forces. The larger F Section, headed by Colonel Maurice Buckmaster, worked independently of de Gaulle. SOE could not afford to put all its French eggs in de Gaulle's basket: The Allies were not sure how much support he really had (the Americans particularly disliked him), and their strategic goals were not always the same as his. For his part, de Gaulle denied that Britain had any right to run agents into France. At their best, relations between SOE and the proud and prickly general were strained.

Throughout 1942, SOE's fortunes in France had been a case of one step forward, two steps back. Hampered by poor intelligence—not until April 1941 did SOE possess even the most rudimentary information about matters like French taxis and trains—SOE had managed to establish only a few reliable *reseaux,* or underground circuits.

But SOE was laying the groundwork for more resistance networks. In August 1941 an indomitable red-haired American

newspaperwoman, Virginia Hall, became the first woman agent SOE put into France, and quickly became one of Baker Street's most effective agents. Unhampered by the wooden foot she nicknamed Cuthbert, Hall played a vital role as contact person, fixer and wireless set distributor. Seemingly every SOE agent in France in 1941 and 1942 passed through her kitchen at one point or another. Meanwhile an energetic Frenchman named Pierre de Vomécourt was busily recruiting resisters and organizing supply drops: two containers packed with Tommy guns, limpet mines, knives and plastic explosive were dropped in June 1941 near Limoges, the first of what were to be nearly 60,000 such drops to fall through the night sky over France before the end of the war.

> The Dutch "**radio game**" resulted in 53 agents being parachuted into **Nazi hands.**

But SOE wasted much of 1942 pursuing contacts with a much-touted French Riviera circuit called Carte, which turned out to be little more than a mirage conjured by a boastful artist. As the year ground to a close, SOE had not come close to establishing a resistance force in France capable of playing a significant role during an invasion.

If France was shaky, Holland was a nightmare. Unbeknownst to SOE, German counterintelligence officers had captured a number of agents, impersonated them and were "playing back" their radio sets, sending fake wireless messages to London. The *Funkspiel,* or "radio game," was to result in 53 agents being parachuted straight into German hands. Almost all were killed. Operation North Pole, as the Germans called it, was the single greatest disaster to befall SOE in its existence. A similar debacle was unfolding in Belgium.

Elsewhere in Europe, particularly Greece and Yugoslavia, SOE found itself increasingly caught up in political cross-currents that limited its effectiveness and led to ugly confrontations with Eden's Foreign Office—and with Churchill himself.

Meanwhile, the Allies were barely hanging on in the field. The Germans and Japanese rolled up victory after victory during the first half of 1942. In the Battle of the North Atlantic, German U-boats were taking a terrible toll on Allied shipping, threatening the survival of Fortress Britain. The Japanese had conquered Singapore and the Philippines. The mighty Wehrmacht was inflicting staggering losses on the Russians. And the Desert Fox, Gen. Erwin Rommel, was relentlessly driving the British forces back across North Africa. Against this grim backdrop, the upstart SOE's contributions looked puny indeed.

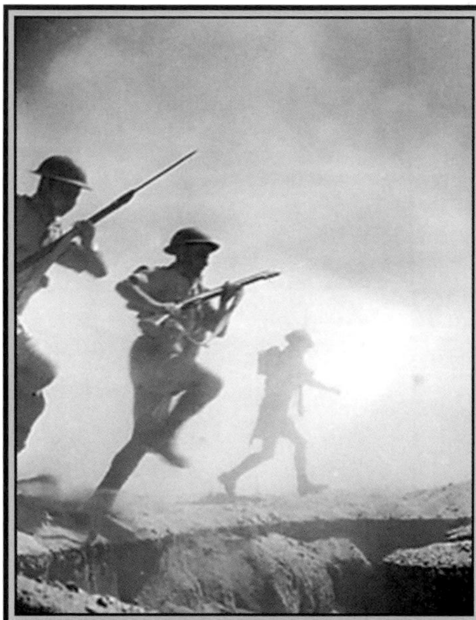

**El Alamein was the Allies' first major victory over Hitler.**

But by the end of the year, momentous events across the globe were ensuring that SOE would play a far more important role in the remaining years of the war.

On November 4, Lt. Gen. Bernard Montgomery defeated Rommel at El Alamein. It was the Allies' first major victory over Germany. In a famous speech to the House of Commons, Churchill marked the occasion with stirring words: "Now this is not the end. It is not even the beginning of the end. But it is, perhaps, the end of the beginning." On November 15, the church bells rang out in celebration all across Britain for the first time in three years. That same month, the Allied landings in North Africa forced the Germans to occupy the rest of France, galvanizing a resistance movement that was to grow more and more potent.

Halfway around the globe, the epic American air and naval victory at Midway in June marked the end of Japanese expansion in the Pacific. And most important of all, on November 19, the same day that the Freshman gliders crashed in Norway, the Red Army launched a great counterattack near a Russian city named Stalingrad that doomed 600,000 German troops, marked the turning point of Hitler's Eastern campaign and decisively tilted the war toward the Allies.

For the people of occupied Europe, these events on faraway battlefields had incalculable psychological effects. When everyone believed that the Germans were going to win, only the bravest dared to resist. But once it became clear that the Third Reich might lose, the floodgates of resistance opened. As 1943 dawned upon suffering Europe, a million tiny flames, fed by the oxygen of hope, began to flicker into life. More than two years after Churchill had issued his famous order, SOE was finally ready to set Europe ablaze.

## Late afternoon
## December 23, 1942
## Hardangervidda
## Norway

Jens Poulsson stared out across the white void, looking for reindeer.

Poulsson was exhausted and nearly delirious. He had been skiing out onto the Hardangervidda for weeks, searching for the great herds of reindeer that migrated seasonally across the high plateau. Back in their hut, his companions were slowly starving. They had never expected they would have to stay this long, and almost all their food was gone. Their daily ration, pathetically scanty to begin with, was down to one and three-quarter ounces of pemmican a day, a handful of oatmeal and flour, four biscuits and a few scraps of sugar, butter, cheese and chocolate. Making matters worse, it was one of the coldest winters on record in Telemark, and the severe cold was rapidly sapping their dwindling strength. Gunnerside, the commando team they were eagerly awaiting, had not been able to drop during the full moon period in December, and there was no guarantee they would make it at all. If Poulsson did not manage to bring home food, some or all of his Swallow team would likely perish.

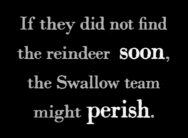

> **If they did not find the reindeer soon, the Swallow team might perish.**

Poulsson raised his binoculars to his eyes again. Nothing. Then he saw a speck. The speck moved. It was reindeer. The herds had come.

Poulsson began carefully stalking the reindeer. After a long pursuit, he finally managed to get almost close enough to shoot—and the skittish animals suddenly bolted. He felt like crying.

The sun dropped and his extremities began to freeze. His strength had almost ebbed away when he managed to get within range. He shouldered his Krag rifle, took careful aim and fired. At first he thought he had missed, but then he saw a trail of blood in the snow. He climbed a hill and saw a wounded young female just over the crest. He fired again and the reindeer collapsed.

Poulsson began to laugh wildly. He pulled out his tin cup, thrust it under the blood spurting out from the reindeer's wounds and drank it before it froze. The

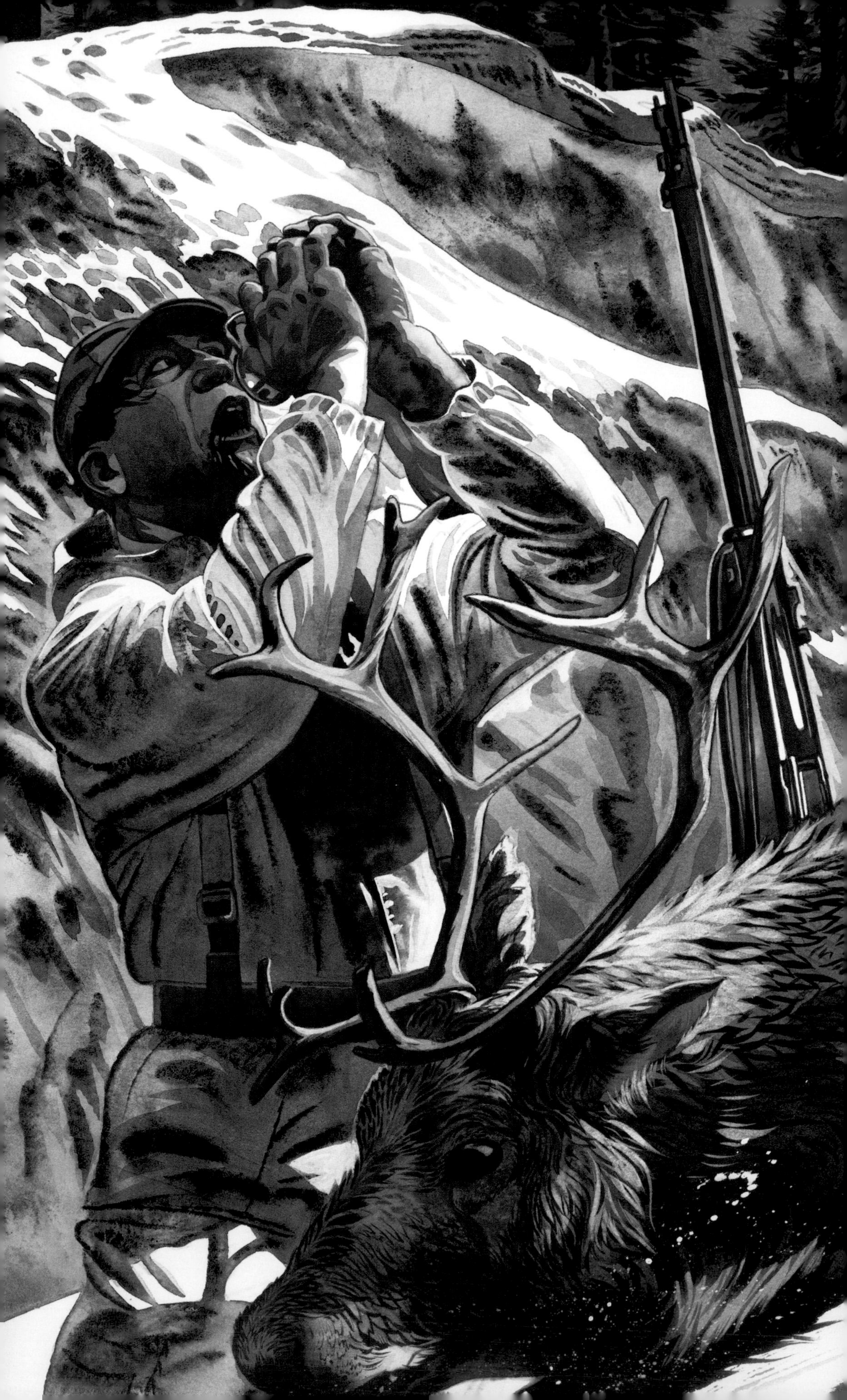

warm blood instantly sent strength coursing through his body. Then he skinned and cut up the reindeer, chewing raw fat and drinking marrow from the legs to keep himself going as he worked. Carrying a pack of meat and a bucket of frozen blood, he staggered back to the hut. When he arrived, exhausted and covered in blood, his three comrades shouted with joy.

That reindeer saved the Swallow party. It gave them enough strength to hold on, and soon they were able to kill more. Over the coming weeks, the four men consumed every part of the animals. They discovered that the lean steaks were the least useful: Their bodies needed fat. They became connoisseurs of the fat behind the eyelids, the marrow, the internal organs and the brains, lips and eyes. They smashed and boiled the bones, turning them into a kind of jelly which they added to their porridge. They ate everything but the testicles and hooves, even unborn fetuses, and hung the skins on the wall of the hut to make it warmer.

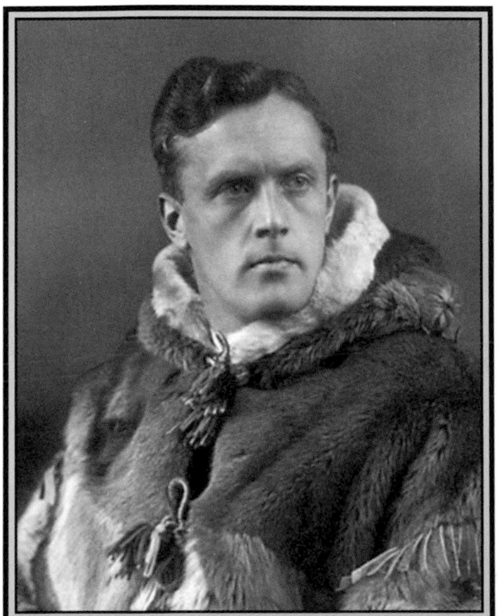

**Explorer Helge Ingstad's books taught the commandos how to survive.**

**The reindeer's hot blood instantly sent strength coursing through Poulsson's body.**

But the real wonder-food was the moss in the reindeer's stomach. Filled with vitamin C and carbohydrates, when cooked with blood it provided nutrition their bodies desperately needed and which they could not have gotten any other way.

In the early 20th century, the most famous Norwegian writer and explorer was a man named Helge Ingstad. Ingstad had abandoned a successful law practice to become a trapper in Canada, where he lived with an Indian tribe called the Caribou Eaters. He later visited the Apaches and lived with the Nunamiut Eskimo tribe of northern Alaska. Ingstad's accounts of his life with the Indians were wildly popular in Norway, especially with young boys. It was from his description of how the Indians survived by eating the half-digested moss from reindeer stomachs that the Norwegians had learned about it.

There are certain uncanny moments when the alpha and omega of human achievement meet, like a circle closing on itself. In Berlin, nuclear physicists were using the most advanced science known to humanity to tap the primordial powers of the universe. A few hundred miles north, the four ragged men who were trying to stop them were staying alive thanks to knowledge handed down from one of the most ancient cultures on earth.

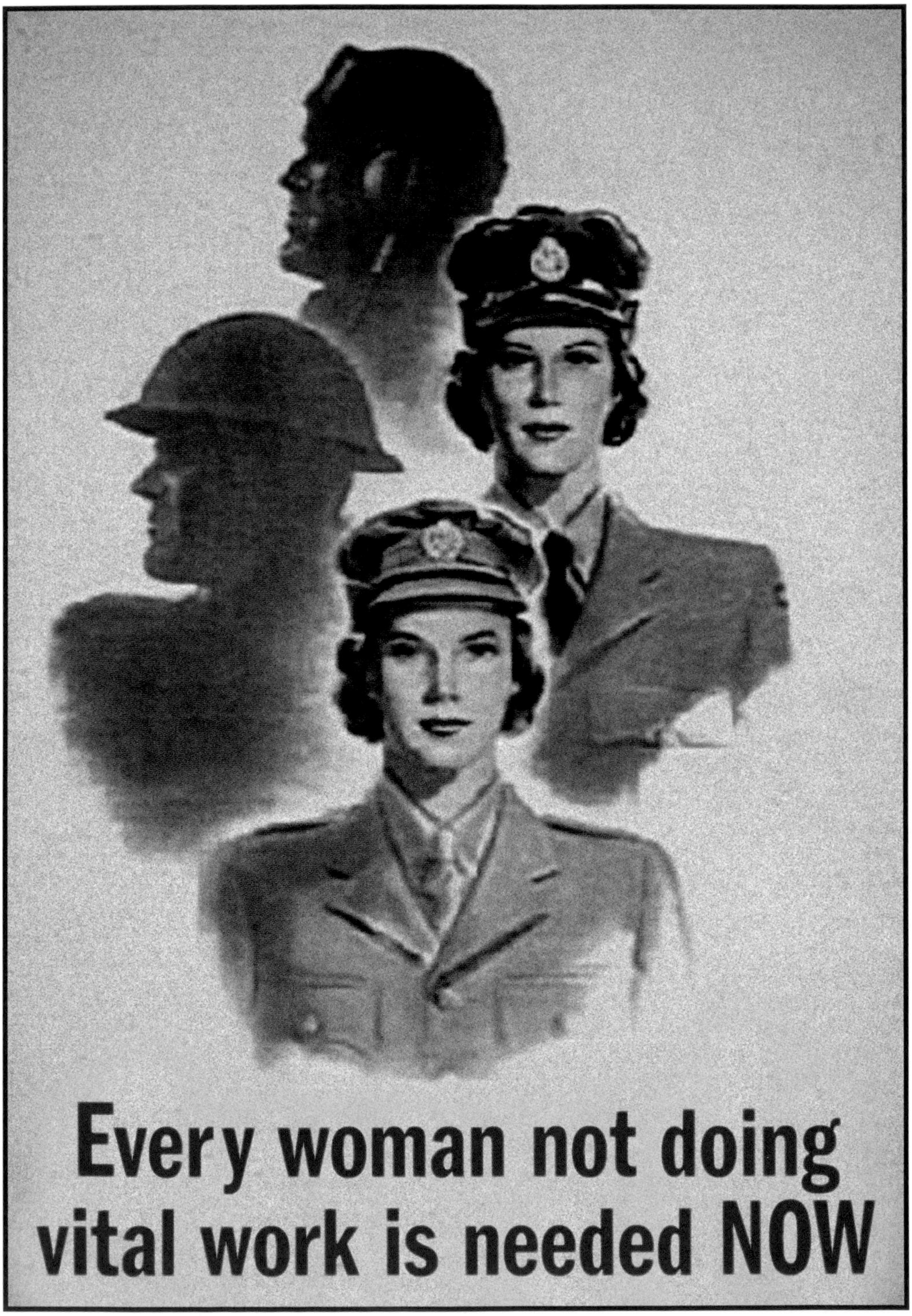
Every woman not doing
vital work is needed NOW

# February 1943
# Wanborough Manor
# Surrey, England

Sometime in February 1943, Noor simply vanished. Her London housemate found her blankets stacked neatly on the bed. She had left no indication of where she had gone.

Noor's disappearance signaled the start of her SOE training. She reported first to Wanborough Manor in Surrey, the handsome country house where F Section agents started. There she was given SOE's introductory course, including physical fitness, unarmed combat, weapons and demolition training Morse coding and wireless training and fieldcraft. Her instructors noted that she was an excellent runner and a skilled wireless operator. She was clumsy at working with explosives and, not surprisingly, "pretty scared of weapons," although her instructors noted that she was game and showed improvement.

"She is a person for whom I have the greatest admiration," wrote her training officer. "Completely self-effacing and unselfish. The last person whose absence was noticed, extremely modest, even humble and shy, always thought everyone better than herself, very polite."

Having passed the first course, Noor now graduated to a more advanced school, at Thame Park in Oxfordshire, where as a W/T (wireless telegraphy) operator she was given specialized signals training. Here she was taught how to encode her messages so that the Germans could not decipher them. The man in charge of SOE's codes was a 22-year-old cryptographic genius named Leo Marks, the Jewish son of the owner of a famed London bookstore at 22 Charing Cross Road. He inherited a system in which agents used memorized poems to send coded messages. Although Marks wrote some memorable code verse himself, he soon replaced this unreliable system with far more sophisticated techniques.

> Heeding the call:
> In 1943, over 2,000
> British women
> **enlisted**
> in the WAAF
> **every week.**

In addition to learning how to code, Noor and her fellow agents had to learn security checks—intentional errors or other

SOE agents learn *instinctive firing*; technicians work on devices in a *secret* workshop.

signals which they would introduce into their messages to alert London that they had been captured by the Germans. The Germans quickly caught on to the security checks, so London came up with a second, "true" check. If an agent failed to use his or her security check, especially the true check, SOE's deciphering staff were supposed to assume the operator had fallen into enemy hands. London's repeated failure to follow this rule had tragic consequences.

Noor's instructor at Thame Park was impressed with her deep commitment to her mission. "This student…has thrown herself heart and soul into the life of the school," he wrote. "The motive for her accepting the present task is, apparently, idealism. She felt she had come to a dead end as a WAAF and was longing to do something more active in the prosecution of the war, something which would make more call on her capabilities and perhaps demand more sacrifice."

Noor's training concluded at Beaulieu, where she was reprimanded for pouring her milk into her cup before pouring her tea, an English custom that would raise suspicions in France.

Finally, Noor was sent off to do a practice mission on the streets of Bristol. Noor performed fairly well in the field, but not during a mock interrogation after she was "captured." Her SOE file noted that she made foolish mistakes during her questioning and nervously gave away too much information.

Noor's performance during her arrest only added to the warning bells that had begun going off about her as her training program grew more intense. Like all prospective agents, Noor had earlier been subjected to a mock interrogation in which she was awakened in the middle of the night and dragged into a brightly lit room by shouting men wearing Gestapo uniforms. That, too, had been disastrous. An observer said that watching Noor was "almost unbearable. She seemed absolutely terrified...As it went on she became practically inaudible."

Noor's instructors and F Section brass were already divided over her fitness to be an agent, and her performance under the second interrogation brought the controversy to a head. Some of her instructors thought she was too dreamy and emotional to be effective, and were particularly worried about security.

Leo Marks wrote that one instructor called her "the potty [i.e., crazy] princess" and said she had "caused more dissension than any pupil in the history of Beaulieu." His fellow instructors unanimously believed that her "crackpot father," the eminent Sufi, was responsible for her "eccentric behavior." "Do you believe what the bastard taught her?" the instructor asked Marks incredulously. "That the worst sin she could commit was to lie about anything."

Noor, he said, had made a series of almost unbelievable security mistakes when she was in field training. During an exercise in which she was carrying her wireless toward a safehouse on her bicycle, Noor was stopped and asked by a policeman what she was doing. "I'm training to be an agent," she told the startled bobby. "Here's my radio—want me to show it to you?" Another time Noor had been so rattled by an unexpected pistol shot that she'd gone into a Sufi-like trance for several hours, emerging from it to consult a Bible. After her disastrous mock interrogation at Bristol, the superintendent in charge told Frank Spooner, Beaulieu's CO, not to waste his time with Noor "because if this girl's an agent, I'm Winston Churchill."

Spooner felt so strongly about Noor's unsuitability for action that he took the unusual step of sending his negative reports straight to Gubbins.

In his final report, Spooner wrote, "Not overburdened with brains...She has an unstable and temperamental personality and it is very doubtful whether she is really suited to work in the field."

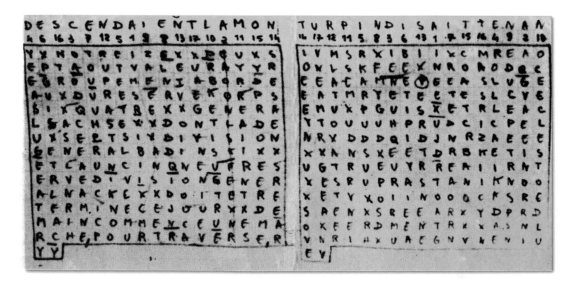

An example of the "double transposition" code used by SOE wireless operators.

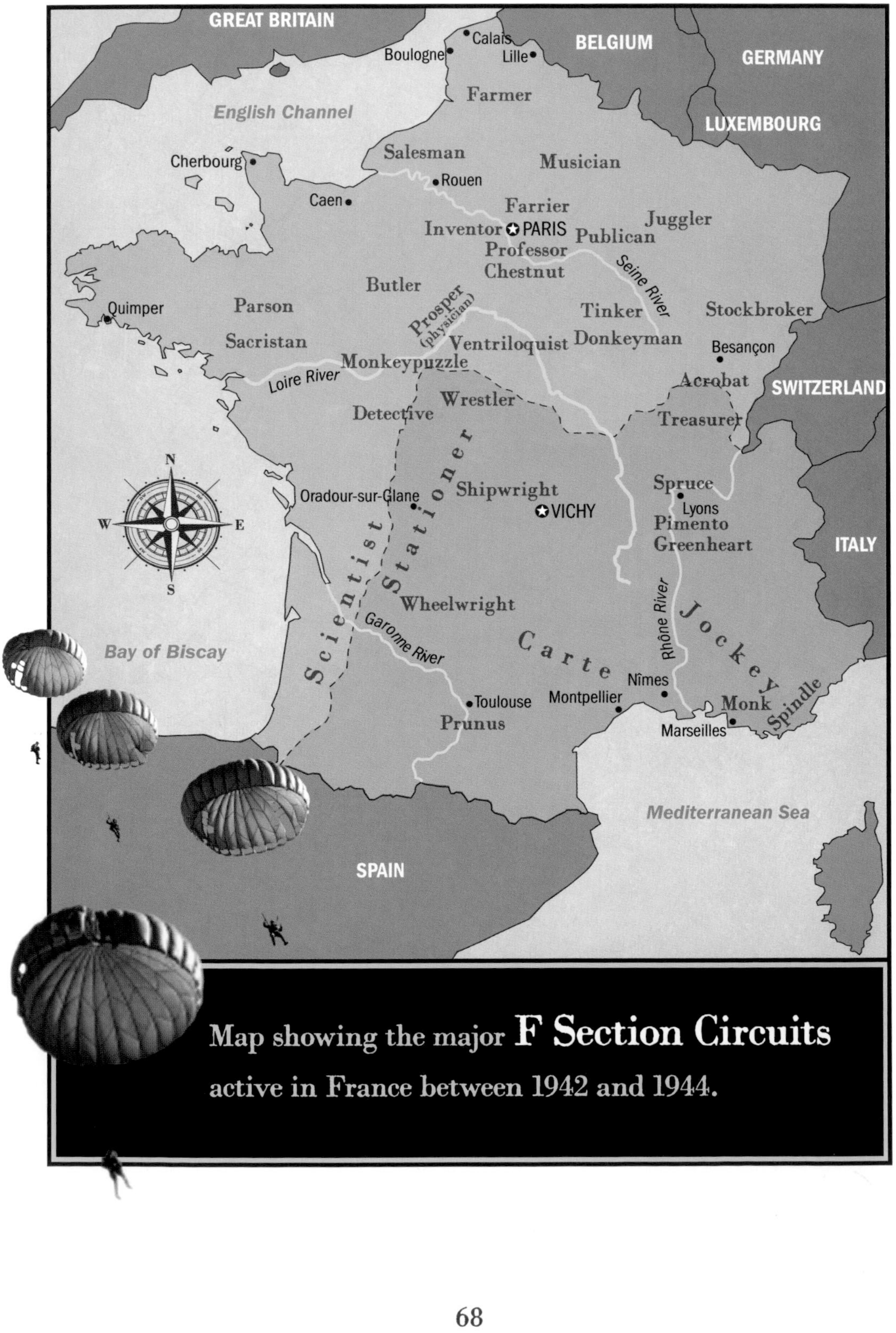
GREAT BRITAIN
BELGIUM
GERMANY
LUXEMBOURG
SWITZERLAND
ITALY
SPAIN
English Channel
Bay of Biscay
Mediterranean Sea
Calais
Boulogne
Lille
Farmer
Cherbourg
Salesman
Rouen
Musician
Caen
Farrier
Inventor
PARIS
Publican
Juggler
Professor
Chestnut
Seine River
Butler
Quimper
Parson
Prosper (physician)
Tinker
Stockbroker
Sacristan
Ventriloquist
Donkeyman
Besançon
Monkeypuzzle
Loire River
Acrobat
Wrestler
Detective
Treasurer
Stationer
Oradour-sur-Glane
Shipwright
VICHY
Spruce
Lyons
Pimento
Greenheart
Scientist
Wheelwright
Rhône River
Jockey
Garonne River
Carte
Nîmes
Montpellier
Toulouse
Monk
Spindle
Prunus
Marseilles
N
S
E
W

Map showing the major **F Section Circuits** active in France between 1942 and 1944.

Noor's commanding officer, Col. Buckmaster, was infuriated by "that bastard Spooner" and "that mob of second-raters" who agreed with him. He vented his spleen on Spooner's evaluation, scribbling "nonsense" next to the phrase "temperamental personality" and irritably writing "We don't want them overburdened with brains."

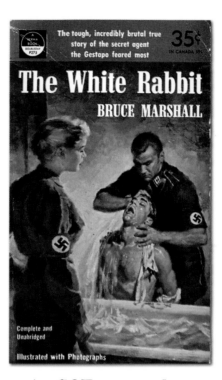

The tough, incredibly brutal true story of the secret agent the Gestapo feared most
35¢
The White Rabbit
BRUCE MARSHALL
Complete and Unabridged
Illustrated with Photographs

**An SOE agent endures a favorite Gestapo torture, waterboarding.**

Buckmaster no doubt believed Noor was up to the job. But he was also under considerable pressure to approve her. Losses in the field had depleted his W/T operators, and Noor was the only one available. Buckmaster was so anxious to get Noor into France that he asked Marks to do him a favor and give her a special coding session, and then write up a report.

Marks prepared for what he called his "appointment with royalty" by ordering Noor's book, *Twenty Jataka Tales,* and reading it twice. One story, the first one in the little volume, he learned by heart.

The story, titled "The Monkey-Bridge," was about a monkey who, after his fellow simians were attacked by a king, saved them by letting them use his body as a bridge. But one monkey jumped on him too heavily and broke his back. As the monkey lay dying, the king, realizing what had happened, asked him, "Who are you, blessed one?" The monkey replied, "I am their chief and their guide...I do not suffer in leaving this world because I have gained my subjects' freedom. And if my death may be a lesson to you, then I am more than happy. It is not your sword which makes you a king; it is love alone."

"Oh, Noor," Marks thought when he finished the story. "What the hell are you doing in SOE?"

Marks duly gave Noor her coding lesson. She made a number of serious mistakes. Knowing her unwillingness to lie, he racked his brains trying to think of a way to get her to take her coding seriously. He told her to think of the letters in her coding as "monkeys trying to cross a bridge between Paris and London...When there's a truth to pass on, don't let your code tell lies." Noor was flabbergasted that the young codemaker had read her book.

Near the end of the session, Marks reminded her that she would have to lie to the Germans about her "true" security check, to prevent them from impersonating her and sending false messages back to London.

Noor rebelled. "There's a better way," she said. "Suppose that I refused to tell them anything at all—no matter how often they ask?"

"It was a statement of intent," Marks recalled. "She'd let her back be broken rather than tell a lie."

Marks fervently hoped that Noor would fail her last coding test, so that he could give her a poor grade and stop her from going into the field. But she performed flawlessly.

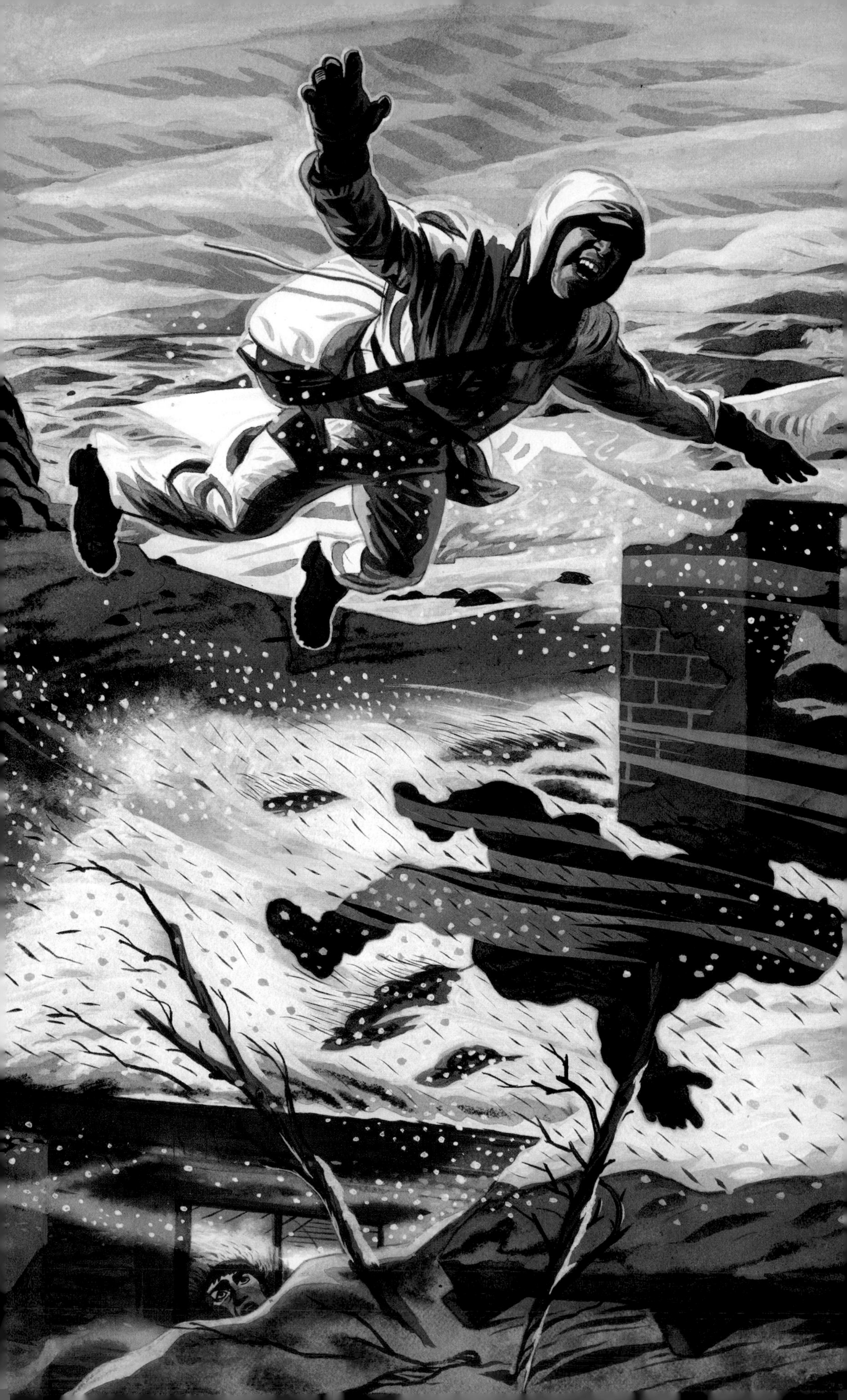

# Midnight
# February 16, 1943
# Near Lake Skrykken
# Hardangervidda
# Norway

Knut Haukelid was climbing the walls. He and his fellow Gunnerside team members had been marooned in a country house near Cambridge for three endless months, waiting to parachute into the Hardangervidda and hook up with his old Swallow compatriots. It was a comfortable place, and the attractive but unapproachable FANY girls kept the men's spirits up, but Haukelid burned to get back into the fight. It was a surreal time, drinking champagne in Cambridge's swankiest restaurants at the War Office's expense while knowing that the next day he might be staggering through a frozen wasteland. In January, his team had flown over the Hardangervidda, but had to turn back because it could not locate Swallow. Haukelid could not stop thinking about his friends down there.

**Ronneberg's body was held aloft by a gust of wind, then tossed ten yards into the snow.**

Finally, on February 16, the weather cleared. They took off in a Halifax from an airbase in Scotland. Shortly before midnight, Haukelid and the other five men jumped out of the hole in the plane's belly and landed safely near frozen Lake Skrykken in the Hardangervidda. With a feeling of reverent joy, Haukelid reached down and touched the snow of his native land. He was home—a free Norwegian soldier on Norwegian soil.

The fiery words of Leif Tronstad lingered in Haukelid's mind. Before he and his comrades left Britain, the Norwegian scientist had roused them with an impassioned speech. "You must know that the Germans will not take you as prisoners," Tronstad told them. "For the sake of those who have gone before you and are now dead, I urge you to make this operation a success. You have no idea how important this mission is, but what you are doing will live in Norway's memory for hundreds of years to come."

But success was a long way away. First the men had to survive.

The next night, the Hardangervidda was hit by one of the worst storms Haukelid had ever seen. Desperately making their way through the whirling snow, by pure luck they literally stumbled upon a mountaineer's wooden hut, called Jansbu. It saved their lives.

The violence of the storm, as they hunkered down inside, was inconceivable.

# Shadow Knights

Visibility was zero. Hurricane-force winds hurled torrents of snow through the air. The sound was high-pitched, constant, deafening. When team leader Joachim Ronneberg climbed onto the hut's roof to fix a broken chimney, he was torn away by a gust that lifted his body, held it aloft for a moment, then tossed it ten yards through the air to crash into the snow.

The severe conditions took a harsh toll on the men trapped in the tiny hut. Two of them became seriously ill, and all were suffering from exhaustion and hunger.

The storm raged on for six days. Finally it broke. The men shakily emerged from their hut and stood looking out at the strange new landscape left by the storm, filled with snow-covered forms thrusting out in impossible shapes. But they had no time to admire the scenery. They had to find Swallow.

They were about to leave when they saw a man on skis approaching the hut, armed with a rifle and dragging a toboggan. They quickly hid. Would he walk past them or see them?

They had no choice: the hunter came right toward them. They jumped up, hauled him into the hut and began questioning him. They had strict orders to kill anyone who might compromise their mission.

They asked the man if he was a member of the N.S., the Quisling party. The terrified man hesitated. "Well, I'm not exactly a member, but that's the party I support," he said. Was he sure? "Yes," he said. He added that he was known to be a supporter of the N.S., but had never actually joined the party. The commandos searched the man and found a large sum of money and a list of black-market customers for his reindeer meat in Oslo.

Most of the party was now in favor of shooting the man. He had admitted he was a Quisling and he was obviously a war profiteer. But Haukelid suspected that the man thought they were Germans and was only pretending to be a Quisling. The Germans had been known to impersonate members of the resistance. So Haukelid asked him if his neighbors could confirm that he was a Nazi sympathizer.

After a pause, the man said, "I have so many enemies down there that they're sure to say I'm not a Nazi, just to make things difficult for me."

Some of the commandos began to have doubts, but Kasper Idland still argued for killing the hunter. Idland was far from bloodthirsty, but he quietly told Ronneberg, "I'll shoot him for you."

Ronneberg held off for the moment. He did not want to jeopardize the mission, but killing a terrified fellow human simply to play the odds went against his gut. He ordered the hunter to guide them to their destination and help pull their toboggan.

They left late at night. Their prisoner was an unbelievably skillful guide, instinctively finding the best route across the contours of the hills. As they skied along, Ronneberg struggled to decide whether they should kill him.

**These re-creations of the Vemork raid reveal how much the men had to carry.**

After four hours, they rested until dawn, then set off again. Suddenly they spotted two skiers coming up a valley. They took cover. Haukelid studied the two men with a telescope. He thought he would recognize any of the men from Swallow, but the figures they saw were so thin, bundled up and heavily bearded he couldn't be sure. So he put on civilian clothes and approached them from behind, prepared to tell them he was a reindeer hunter if necessary. The others hid and covered him with Tommy guns.

Not until Haukelid got to within 15 yards of the men did he finally recognize Claus Helberg and Arne Kjelstrup. They were emaciated, sickly and in ragged clothing, but they were still the same old Claus and Arne: They were arguing over who got to look through the telescope for their comrades first.

Haukelid coughed. The two men whirled around, recognized him and let out wild yells of joy. Hearty back-slapping and much cursing took place as the rest of the Gunnerside team joined them. The Gunnerside men were shocked at the state their friends were in.

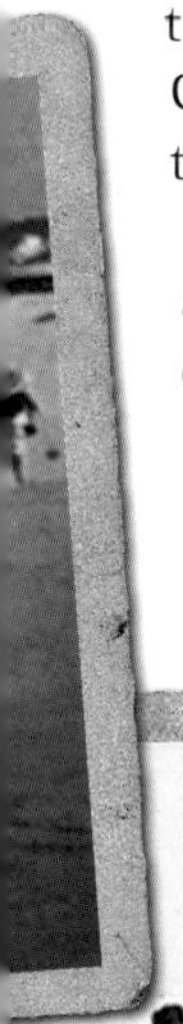

The two full parties were united later that afternoon. Now they had to decide what to do with the hunter. Ronneberg made the final call not to shoot the man. They gave him money and ten days' rations and told him not to return home for three days. They also made him sign a statement that he was illegally hunting reindeer and in possession of an illegal rifle, and warned him that if they were betrayed to the Germans, they would say he was guiding them.

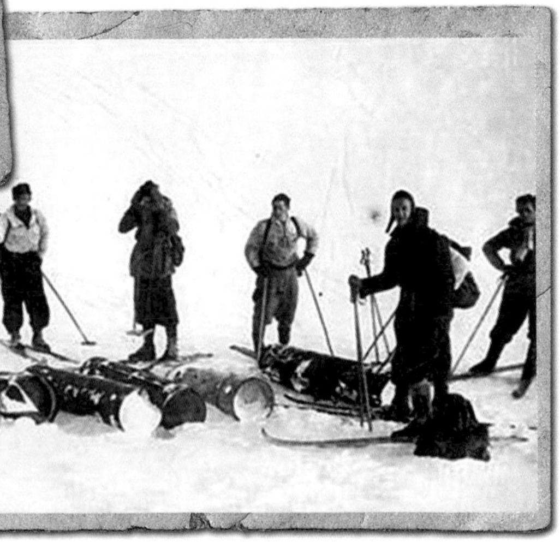

Ronneberg's gamble paid off. The hunter did not betray them.

That night at Swallow's headquarters, Cousin's Cabin, the two parties feasted on reindeer meat and chocolate. The Swallow party entertained Gunnerside with tales about how they had made a delicious soup out of dried-fish dogfood they found in a hut, and how another time Jens Poulsson had dropped the cooking pot, forcing them all to crawl about on the floor lapping up gravy and gnawing on sheep bones. To pass the endless nights, they had given lectures to each other while lying in their sleeping bags, on subjects ranging from "tact and good manners" to how mountain peaks had gotten their names. Arne Kjelstrup even gave a lecture on plumbing. Somehow, they had kept their spirits up, never losing their tempers despite the claustrophobic desperation of their situation. The team had been well chosen.

That night Knut Haukelid read the Swallow team a special message sent by the Norwegian military authorities, laying out their future resistance tasks in the Telemark region. The message had been printed on rice paper so that it could be eaten if necessary. He crumpled it up and was about to toss it into the fire when Knut Haugland stopped him. "Is that food?" the radio operator asked. "Quite digestible," Haukelid replied. "Well, we don't throw away food here at Svensbu," Haugland said, taking the paper and putting it in his mouth.

The men of Swallow had survived four months on the Hardangervidda, facing down every one of nature's assaults. Now they and their Gunnerside comrades would be tested against man. The raid on the heavy-water plant would take place in two nights.

# June 1943
# London

After she completed her training, just before she was sent into France, Noor went to say goodbye to her friend Jean Overton Fuller, whom she had met in London and with whom she shared an interest in philosophy and spirituality. It was a little after 11 o'clock at night. Fuller noticed that Noor was radiant and surmised she was in love. Noor told Fuller she was "going on foreign service" and would leave in a few days. "Everything I've always wanted has come at once," she said.

The two friends stayed up all night talking. They began by discussing Noor's horoscope. Noor was a Capricorn. When Fuller observed that Capricorns were supposed to be ambitious,

Noor's **SOE File** photograph

but Noor was not, Noor broke in, squeezing her little fists, "Oh, but I *am*! For the *highest*!"

Noor told Fuller she had read stories about Christian martyrs as a child, and sometimes stayed up at night worrying about whether she would be able to keep a secret under torture. She had thought such matters had ended with the Middle Ages, but now, with the Nazis, they had reappeared. How would she react to being tortured or put in a concentration camp? "I don't see how one can know..." she told Fuller. Then she suddenly drew her nails into her fist with a jerk and said very quietly, "I don't think I would ever speak."

February 25, 1943
Svensbu hut
Hardangervidda
Norway

The day after their reunion at Cousin's Cabin, the Norwegians moved up to a jumping-off position closer to their target, the Vemork heavy-water plant. Jens Poulsson knew of a hut in an area called Fjosbudalen that would be suitable. Knut Haugland and Einar Skinnarland, the intrepid "vacationing saboteur" who had now joined the team, had moved to a different hut from which they would transmit the results of the raid to London.

That left nine men to do the job. As leader of the combined team, Ronneberg divided them into two parties. The demolition party would be composed of Kayser, Stromsheim, Idland and him as leader. The covering party would be led by the thinking man's saboteur, Haukelid, and would include Poulsson, Kjelstrup, Helberg and Storhaug.

Now they had to plan the attack. The Norsk Hydro factory was located in a seemingly impregnable position. It stood on a shelf of rock that had been dynamited out of a nearly vertical mountainside. Below that shelf was a 600-foot drop into the gorge of the Maan River. Above the plant, where a dozen enormous pipes called penstocks carried water down to the turbines, the mountain rose up 1,500 impossibly sheer feet. The only way to reach the plant from this direction was by a steep series of steps, which were mined, booby-trapped and covered by machine-gun nests.

There were only two other ways to approach the plant. One was to cross over a narrow 75-foot suspension bridge that spanned the sheer gorge below the plant, then climb up a steep path to the factory. But crossing the bridge guaranteed a fight. The Norwegians knew that two German guards with submachine guns would be patrolling the suspension bridge. As soon as gunshots rang out, the alarm would be raised, the entire area would be floodlit with spotlights, machine-gun emplacements on the roof of the main building would swing into action, the 30

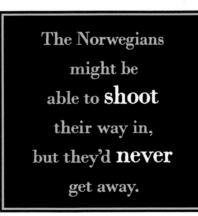

The Norwegians might be able to **shoot** their way in, but they'd **never** get away.

German troops in the barracks outside the building would be alerted and reinforcements from nearby Rjukan would be sent rushing to the scene. The Norwegians might be able to shoot their way across the footbridge, maybe even place their explosives, but it would be virtually impossible for any of them to get away.

That left the last option: to try to climb down the steep gorge somewhere below the bridge, cross the frozen river and claw their way up the even sheerer face on the Vemork side. No one believed that this could be done without climbing equipment. Helberg and Poulsson, who had grown up in Rjukan, thought it was impossible.

Still, the Germans had posted no troops in the gorge itself. And if the team could somehow make it up the sheer gorge, there was a potential weak spot in the German defenses. An old railway line from Rjukan had been cut out of the hillside, and it ran straight to the plant. The Norwegians' inside sources told them the line was unguarded—but that could have changed.

They decided to send Helberg on a reconnaissance mission to Rjukan to find out. Helberg's source in town told him the line was indeed unguarded. As Helberg skied back to camp, he looked down into some crops of pine and birch that were growing in the gorge. That was when the idea first came to him that it might be possible to climb it.

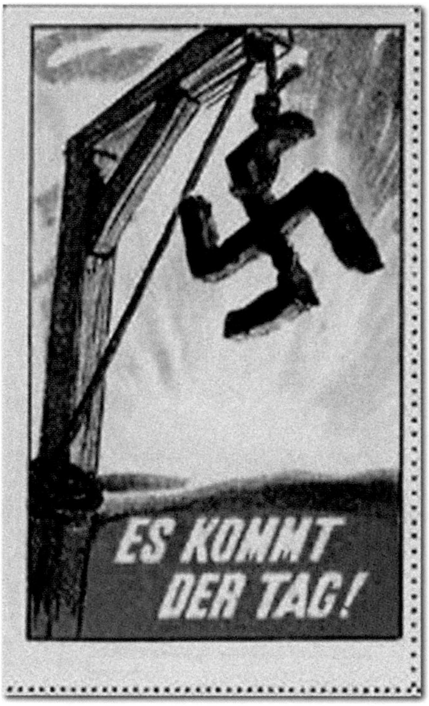
ES KOMMT
DER TAG!

**"The Day is Coming!," a British "black propaganda" sticker intended to degrade enemy morale.**

Helberg returned to camp and gave his report. As they had suspected, crossing the bridge would mean a shootout that would alert the rest of the garrison. "But the gorge itself is not guarded, and neither is the railway leading directly into the plant's yard," Helberg said.

Kasper Idland thought they should attack across the bridge. The only member of the team who was a weak skier, he thought they had little chance to survive and almost seemed anxious to get the whole thing over with.

Helberg and Poulsson disagreed. A firefight, they said, would be disastrous.

Ronneberg pulled out some aerial photos of the area that showed trees and shrubs growing out of cracks in the gorge. Haukelid, whose philosophical bent gave him the aspect of an armed John Muir, looked at the photos. Looking at the pine and birch, he had the same reaction that Helberg did.

"Where trees grow," Haukelid declared, "a man can make his way."

The only way to know if it was truly possible to climb the gorge was to send Helberg back and have him do it. He skied off. When he returned, he was grinning broadly. He had climbed the unclimbable gorge.

## After midnight
## April 17, 1943
## Tarbes, near Toulouse
## France

Harry Ree and his fellow agent, wireless operator René Maingard, sat two feet from the open hatch in the belly of a converted bomber, the static lines of their parachutes connected to the inside of the fuselage. The dark French countryside raced along less than a thousand feet below them.

"Go!" the dispatcher told Maingard. But Maingard didn't hear him. The dispatcher repeated his command. Maingard pushed himself into the hatch and vanished. Now it was Ree's turn. He put his feet through the opening and dropped out of the plane.

For those first terrifying seconds, he fell like a rock. Then the static line released the chute and it opened above him like a flower.

As he dropped through the sky, Ree thought, "Now I have no more links with England."

The ground below was dark. No lights were visible. In just seconds, Ree saw a shadow rushing up at him. An instant later he hit the ground. He was dragged by his parachute and rolled over several times, filling his mouth with dirt.

He had fallen into a small field, bordered by trees on three sides, with what appeared to be a farmhouse on the fourth. A dog began barking in the distance. The shape that had loomed up was a pylon. Ree had missed it by 20 feet.

Footsteps approached. Ree called out quietly, "Maingard!"

"Hello, Harry, is that you?" came the reply. Ree felt a rush of relief: his comrade had found him.

They were supposed to have been met by a reception committee. But because Maingard had not heard the dispatcher and jumped late, they had overshot the rendezvous. Several containers had been dropped with them,

**A C-type supply container. Tens of thousands were dropped behind enemy lines.**

TOI AUSSI !
TES CAMARADES T'ATTENDENT
DANS LA DIVISION FRANÇAISE DE LA
WAFFEN-SS

**A German recruiting poster exhorts Frenchmen to join the French division of the Waffen-SS.**

each eight feet long and filled with arms and explosives. They had to hide them before the Germans found them. And one container was hanging from the pylon and could not be retrieved.

Ree and Maingard gathered their suitcases, including Maingard's wireless set, and set off through the woods to get away from the drop zone. After an hour's walk they crawled into some shrubs and went to sleep.

They hid in the woods for 24 hours. Then they decided that Maingard should leave to go look for an agent named Maurice Southgate, the head of the circuit they were going to join. Ree would stay in the forest.

An entire day passed. As the sun went down, Ree decided to risk getting up to take a little walk. As he was coming back to his clump of bushes, he saw someone approaching. He dove to the ground. Peering out, he realized that the man seemed to be looking toward him.

A few seconds passed. Then the man shouted, *"Je ne vous ai pas vu!"*—"I haven't seen you!"

Ree stood up and yelled that he had lost his way. The man came over, looked Ree up and down and said, "You English? Pilot? Boom boom, shot down, eh?"

Ree said that yes, he was an RAF flier trying to escape. He asked the man for some water. He had drunk nothing for a day and a half. The man nodded and said he would be back soon. Ree wondered if he would come back with the police. Twenty minutes later, the man, an Italian farmworker, returned with wine, bread, cheese and cigarettes.

By the time Maingard finally returned with Southgate and another member of the same circuit, Ree had been hiding in the wood for three days. The four men spent several hours unloading and hiding the containers. Then they split up. Ree and Southgate headed on bicycles toward Tarbes, where Southgate had found Ree a room.

As he cycled through the beautiful French countryside, Ree was suddenly euphoric. The sun was shining, children were scampering in and out of the pink and white houses, he was among friends and would soon have a bath. He was a British agent in enemy territory, and he felt fantastic.

8 p.m.
February 27, 1943
Hardangervidda
Norway

Joachim Ronneberg, Knut Haukelid and the seven men under their command moved out of the Fjosbudalen hut and began their march toward the bottom of the valley, wearing British Army uniforms beneath their snow camouflage suits. They knew the uniforms would not save them from execution, but they hoped to protect the local Norwegians, who would be subject to savage reprisals if the Germans believed that Norwegians were involved in the raid.

The team bristled with weapons. Between them they carried five Tommy guns, two sniper rifles, 10 Colt Revolvers, 10 hand grenades, commando knives, chloroform to use on any Norwegians they might run into and two complete sets of explosives. Each man carried his "L" (for "lethal") cyanide tablet. They had agreed that anyone who was about to be taken prisoner would commit suicide.

The weather had changed dramatically. The snow was melting and the roads were running with water. The frozen river they had to cross twice would be breaking up.

As they descended a mountain and approached a road above the gorge, Haukelid got his first glimpse of the heavy-water plant. In its soaring eyrie, the mighty seven-story building looked like a fortress out of a medieval fantasy. He could dimly hear the hum of the machinery across the gorge.

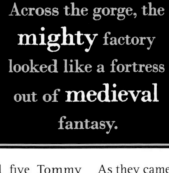

Across the gorge, the **mighty** factory looked like a fortress out of **medieval** fantasy.

The slope down to the road was so steep and covered with wet snow that the only way down was to remove their skis and half-slide, half-climb. At times they sunk in snow up to their arms. As they came slithering down the precipice, two buses appeared on the road, carrying the plant's night shift from the nearby town, Rjukan. The commandos desperately tried to slow their descent as the headlights pierced the darkness below them. As the buses passed, several of the men came crashing onto the road, missing landing on the roof of the last bus by seconds.

They turned onto a smaller, unused road running parallel to the gorge and proceeded along it until they came to the place where

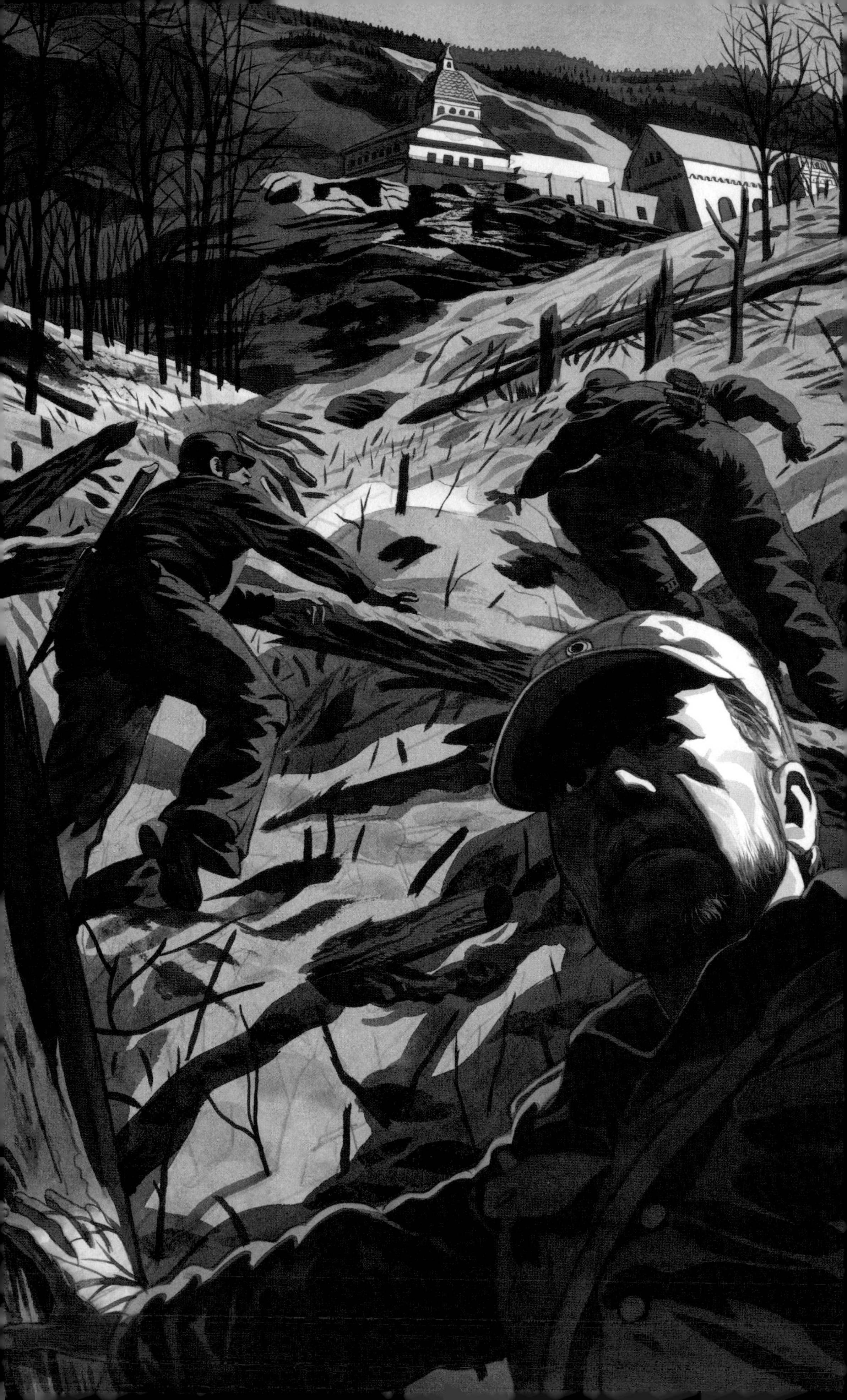

Helberg thought they could make it down. Here they hid their skis and packs, intending to pick them up after the attack, and removed their white camouflage suits.

Ronneberg looked each man in the eye. It was time. One after another, they swung themselves over the edge and vanished into the darkness.

**As he waited, Ronneberg had never felt so close to other human beings before.**

The descent was not too difficult. This side of the gorge was much less steep than the other. But when they got to the bottom, they found that the frozen river was rapidly breaking up. Only one section was still solid, and three inches of water was flowing across it. They crossed one at a time.

Now they were looking up at the sheer wall of the factory side of the gorge, the last physical barrier between them and the plant. Each man eyed the cliff, looking at cracks and trees and ledges, mapping out climbing routes. Ronneberg signaled "Go" with his hand, and they began to climb. The railway was 600 feet above them.

Grabbing at barely visible handholds, feeling with their feet for tiny ledges, they worked their way up the face of the rocky wall. They had been taught in Scotland not to look down. Haukelid was afraid that the others were climbing faster than him, and increased his pace. All the others were doing the same thing, and the whole party climbed faster and faster.

**The nine men worked their way up the sheer 600-foot cliff, never looking down.**

Finally, all nine men made it to the top. They stood, gulping for air, on the shelf of rock along which the railway line ran. The whitish shape of the giant plant loomed less than 800 yards away.

The covering party went first, led by Haukelid. As he walked along the tracks, he was followed by Kjelstrup, Helberg, Storhaug and Poulsson. Ronneberg whispered "Good luck" to the other team as they moved out. They all knew that the Germans had heavily mined the approaches to the plant. Ronneberg and his demolition team waited until the covering party was 50 yards ahead, then started after them, walking exactly in their footsteps, staying well spaced out so a mine would take out only one man.

Haukelid, Ronnenberg and their men made it to a transformer shed halfway down the tracks. It was 11:30 p.m., and they had to wait until the German guards on the bridge were relieved at midnight. So they settled down, nibbling on the food they had brought and chatting about inconsequential things.

Ronneberg had expected his men to be tense, or to make artificial jokes. Instead, they were utterly relaxed, a bunch of friends pointing out familiar lights in the night. The interlude filled him with a quiet confidence. He had never felt so close to other human beings before.

At three minutes before midnight, two German soldiers left the barracks and began walking down the hill to relieve the guards on the suspension bridge. Soon thereafter the two guards who had been relieved came up the hill to the barracks. For the Norwegians, it was surreal watching these tired men trudging along like factory workers at the end of their shift, completely unaware that their lives were hanging by a thread. They felt like they were looking at what they were about to do through the wrong end of a telescope.

Ronneberg told his men to wait another half an hour, to give the two new guards time to relax. He used this last 30 minutes to brief each man again. At 12:30, they moved up to some small buildings 100 yards from the gate. Then he told Arne Kjelstrup, "Go to the gate and cut the chain."

Wielding a heavy bolt cutter he had brought from England, the former plumber sliced through the three-quarter-inch steel chain and pushed the gate open. The covering party followed him inside, taking up firing positions. Meanwhile, Ronneberg's demolition party had cut open another gate as a second escape route and quickly moved to their target, the electrolysis building. They made for the steel cellar door, which an accomplice was to have left unlocked. But he was sick that day and the door was locked. Luckily, Professor

Tronstad in London, who knew every inch of the plant he had designed, had told them about another way to get in, an obscure cable tunnel. Ronneberg, carrying the charges, and Kayser, covering him, found the opening and went in headfirst. The shaft was filled with cables and pipes, but there was just enough room to squeeze in.

Halfway along it, Ronneberg looked down through an opening. Below him was their target: the high-concentration room. In the room sat a lone Norwegian workman, making some notations in a book. Near him they could see two parallel sets of stainless-steel-encased cells, the machinery that converted ordinary water into a type containing hydrogen atoms of double the usual weight—heavy water, the eerily named substance they had come to destroy.

They came to a hole in the tunnel and let themselves down. They were now in a basement room next to the high-concentration room. Drawing their guns, they opened the door.

The **target:** the Norsk Hydro plant illuminated

When they burst in, the terrified man began shaking uncontrollably. "Nothing will happen to you if you do as you are told," said Kayser. "We're British soldiers."

Ronneberg opened his pack and began removing the sausage-shaped plastic explosives. Moving quickly and precisely, he wrapped a charge around each of the 18 high-concentration cells, intricate affairs four feet high and a foot in diameter. He had practiced it so many times he could have done it blindfolded.

As Ronneberg was wrapping a charge around the ninth cell, there was a loud sound of breaking glass. Kayser whirled around, pointing his gun at a window opening onto the back yard. He saw a shadowy face framed by broken glass, struggling to get in. He had just started to squeeze the trigger when he recognized Birger Stromsheim. Unable to find the cable tunnel, Stromsheim and Idland had decided to break in. If Kayser had had a bullet in the chamber, he probably would have killed his friend.

Ronneberg hastily cleared the broken glass from the window frame so Stromsheim could get in, cutting his hand badly in the process. Then, assisted by Stromsheim, he returned to the job. Originally they had planned to set two-minute fuses, but now Ronneberg decided to set thirty-second fuses as well. This diminished the chances of anyone putting out the fuses, but it also diminished their chances of getting away.

As they were about to light the fuses, the workman, who had told them his name was Johansen, suddenly said, "Please, I need my eyeglasses. They're impossible to get in Norway these days."

At any moment, German guards could appear. Ronneberg stopped what he was doing and he and Kayser began looking around the room. After a few moments they found his glasses case and handed it to him. *"Tusan takk,"* Johansen said—"a thousand thanks." Ronneberg turned back, lit another match and was about to light one of the fuses when Johansen suddenly cried out again, "Please, wait! My glasses are not in the case."

Ronneberg blew out the second match, hurried back to the desk, rummaged frantically through the papers on it and found the glasses between the pages of the logbook that Johansen had been writing in. "Here, take them!" he barked. *"Tusan takk,"* the workman repeated solemnly.

Suddenly, they heard footsteps on the stairs. Someone was coming down. Ronneberg was torn. Should he light the fuses now or wait? He decided to wait. The man turned out to be a Norwegian night foreman, who stared wide-eyed at the incomprehensible scene in front of him.

Ronneberg lit the short fuse. Kayser counted to ten, then told the workers, "Run! Run as fast as you can!"

As the Norwegian workers dashed up the stairs, Kayser, Ronneberg and Stromsheim ran out of the room through the steel door leading to the yard, closed it and found Idland outside, waiting for them with his Tommy gun. Ronneberg shook hands with him. Then they all started to run.

They had made it 20 yards when the explosion came. For Haukelid and Poulsson, who had suffered through an agonizing half-hour wait outside with the rest of the covering party, the muffled bang sounded

> They were about to light the **fuses** when the workman cried, "My **glasses** are not in the case."

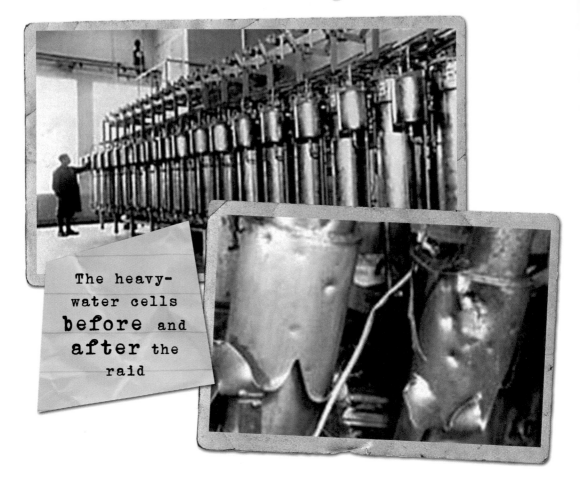

The heavy-water cells **before** and **after** the raid

pathetically weak. Had they come all this way just to make this puny thud?

Taking cover, they waited for the German troops to rush out. But only a single unarmed soldier appeared. He looked up at the tiers of balconies above him, shook his head, tried the steel door to the cellar and went back inside.

Haukelid and Poulsson were about to start heading down the railroad tracks with the others when the German soldier reappeared, now holding a rifle and a searchlight. They knelt down as the soldier walked over in their direction, swinging the light around from side to side. The two Norwegians had their fingers on the triggers of their guns.

The man came closer. Suddenly he aimed his searchlight above them, then onto the ground behind them. If he swung his torch

forward now, to where they were hiding, he was a dead man. But he only looked up once more toward the balconies and went back inside.

The commandos hurried along the railway. Helberg reported that everyone in the party had made it out. The first thought that came into Ronneberg's mind was that now they had to walk all the way to Sweden.

But first, they had to get out of the gorge. Helberg found what looked like the least steep way down and they began half-sliding, half-climbing down, using ledges to slow their descent. When they reached the bottom, they saw that the icy river was breaking up rapidly. As they jumped from one piece of floating ice to the next, a loud sound broke the night: the plant's sirens going off. The hunt was on.

The Norwegians began to climb up the far side of the gorge. After the alarm sounded, the Germans would sweep the area near the plant with powerful spotlights. If they were spotted while making their ascent, there would be no way to escape. They had to get out of the gorge.

As the nine young men climbed with grim concentration up the bank on the other side of the river, they felt true fear for the first time. The commandos had expected to die. Now that they had a real chance to escape, they desperately wanted to make it.

When they reached the road at the top of the gorge, cars and trucks filled with German troops began to pass, headed from Rjukan to Vemork. They ducked down behind a wall of snow thrown up by a snow plow to avoid being seen. But the Germans were convinced the attackers were still in the compound. And certain that the gorge was impassable, they did not think to search it.

After recovering their skis and equipment, the men quickly headed up a steep road that ran next to a cable-car route. The cable car had been installed to allow the local people to enjoy some sunshine during the winter months, when the valley lay in deep shadow all day. If the Germans had thought to commandeer the cable car and send a detachment of men to the top, they would have gotten to the top before the Norwegians. But the cables never moved.

As they **ascended** the gorge, the men felt **true fear** for the first time.

It was a backbreaking three-hour climb before they reached the top of the mountain and saw the Hardangervidda spreading out below them. Miles away in the other direction, the Germans were still running around madly. It was 5 a.m., and the sun had begun to rise.

The men paused for a rest and a little food. They had done it. They had accomplished their mission and gotten out of the valley. The road into the frozen wilderness lay open before them.

It was a moment Ronneberg never forgot. "When you looked across the valley you saw this 2,000-meter-high mountain lit in the morning sun and we had mackerel skies and there was a small bird singing in a tree telling us it was nearly spring," he recalled. "Now we felt the Germans are down in the valley, we don't think of them because now the fight will be between us and the Norwegian nature—and that we knew was a good friend and not an enemy."

Now all they had to do was make it across 250 miles of trackless snow-covered wilderness, with one comrade who could barely ski, with every German soldier in Norway searching for them.

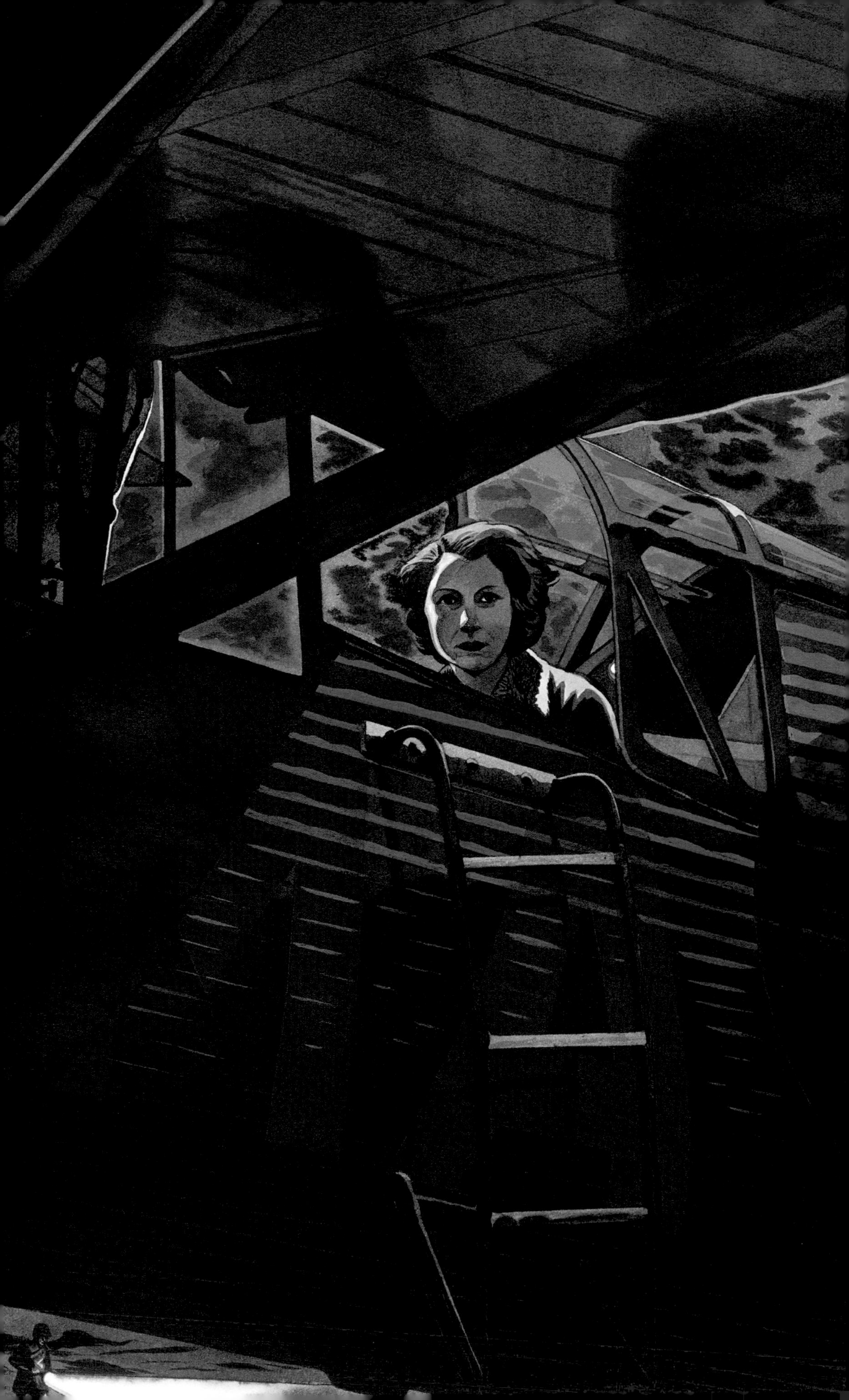

## After midnight
## June 17, 1943
## A field near Angers, France

The Lysander touched down in the dark field, guided by flashlights held by the reception committee on the ground. The pilot slid the cockpit open. Agent Cecily Lefort clambered down the ladder outside the cockpit. Noor handed her their suitcases, stowed some new ones handed to her by the two agents waiting to board the plane and climbed down herself. The two new passengers climbed into the cockpit. Henri Déricourt, the agent in charge on the ground, shouted "OK!" The plane was already facing into the wind. The pilot opened the throttle, put the flaps down and the small plane rose into the air. The entire operation, from landing to takeoff, had taken less than five minutes.

**Three years after she fled France with her family, Noor returned secretly and alone.**

Almost three years to the day since she and her family had escaped on the last boat out of Le Verdon, Noor had returned to France.

Her mission was to work as a wireless operator for an agent named Henri Garry. Garry ran a sub-circuit called Cinema that was part of Prosper, the largest circuit in France, which was headed by a young lawyer named Francis Suttill. His circuit had grown to include 30 agents and hundreds of members of the resistance.

Noor's field name, by which she would be known to other agents, was Madeleine. Her cover name was Jeanne-Marie Renier, her occupation listed as "children's nurse."

As she had been trained to do, Noor buried her pistol in the ground and mounted a bicycle that was waiting for her. She headed for the Angers train station with Déricourt's assistant, Rémy Clément. They planned to take the same train to Paris, traveling in separate compartments for security. Once in Paris, Noor was to call at Garry's apartment.

Noor seemed badly confused. At the station, Clément observed her staring at maps, obviously disoriented. "She was very afraid," he recalled. However, she boarded the train, made it safely to Paris and found her way to 40 Rue Erlanger, in the elegant Auteuil neighborhood in the 16th arrondissement.

Noor mistakenly expected Garry to be an old woman. When she knocked on the door and a young man and his fiancée appeared, she was too nervous to give the password. An awkward conversation followed. When she finally gave the password, they all laughed.

Noor had not eaten since leaving London. She had been too afraid to order food at a café, and had only had a glass of Vichy water. Garry's fiancée made her some food, which she devoured. When she told them she had not made any plans for where to spend the night, they insisted she stay with them. Exhausted, she agreed and was soon fast asleep.

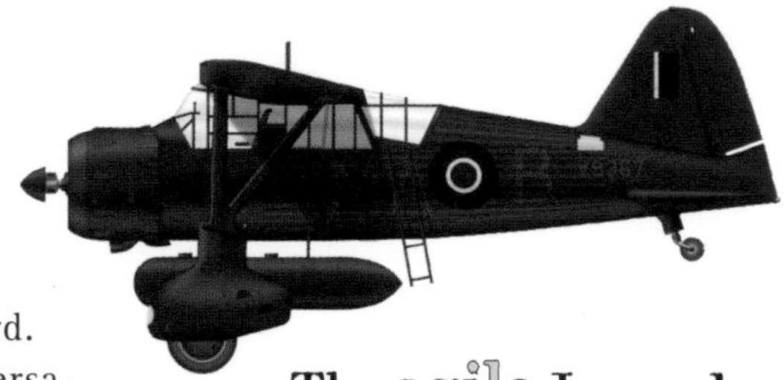

**The agile Lysander was perfect for night landings in tiny fields.**

## June 1943
## Valentigny, near Bensançon
## Franche-Comté, France

Harry Ree had no sooner joined his circuit than his bad accent forced him to head for the hills. He had been sent to the Clermont-Ferrand area to work with Maurice Southgate, instructing members of Southgate's Stationer circuit in sabotage and leading an attack on the Michelin tire factory. But the region was crawling with collaborators and Gestapo, and Southgate was so alarmed by Ree's heavily accented French that he immediately packed him off to a safer region: the Franche-Comté region of eastern France, home of the Jura mountains. There Ree joined the Acrobat circuit, headed by Captain John Starr, whose field name was Bob. Bob was working with wireless operator John Young and courier Diana Rowden, who had been flown in just minutes before Noor, on the same air strip.

**Ree's new mission was to work with the rural resistance—the *maquis*.**

Ree's new mission was to organize the rural French resistance, the *maquis*. Their numbers were swelling. As Germany increased its forced conscription of French workers, more and more young men were fleeing to the hills. Many of them were just trying to avoid forced labor, but others wanted to fight. Posing as a watchmaker named Henri from Alsace—which was supposed to explain his heavy accent—Ree began to recruit potential members, arrange for supply drops, scout out targets for sabotage, give lessons in the use of explosives and organize attacks.

Soon after he arrived in the Jura, one of his men introduced Ree to Rodolphe Peugeot, an amiable young man who was one of the directors of the huge Peugeot auto plant at Sochaux, near Montbéliard. The car factory had been taken over by the Germans and retooled to make tank turrets, military vehicles and parts for aircraft engines. The British military listed it as the third most important industrial target in France. Although Peugeot secretly supported the resistance, and was close to his workers, he was compelled to go along with the Germans.

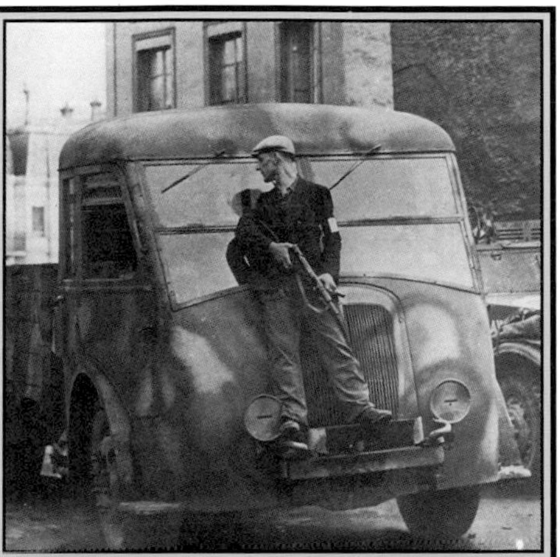

An armed *maquisard* **takes cover** behind a truck.

Ree boldly told Peugeot he was a British agent and asked him for a loan of 50,000 francs, which another agent needed. He promised Peugeot he would be paid back in English pounds—not an uncommon arrangement during the war. Peugeot asked Ree to prove his bona fides by having a prearranged message broadcast over the BBC. Ree agreed and told him to listen between June 12 and June 17. Sure enough, the message, *"La vallée du Doubs est belle, en été"* ("The Doubs valley is beautiful in the summer") came over the air, and Peugeot loaned him the 50,000 francs. After that the sportif young industrialist and the British secret agent became quite friendly.

It did not take Ree long to organize a major strike. In July, he organized an attack on a barn containing 5,000 truck tires. Three of his men overpowered the two French guards and threw six SOE-built firebombs into the barn, causing an enormous blaze that destroyed all the tires.

Within weeks of his arrival, Ree's identity was no longer a secret. He rarely met anyone, even for a few moments, who did not know who he was—"the man who had come from England to help us." Having one's identity widely known was not usually a good thing for an agent, but Ree was fortunate to have landed in a tightly knit area filled with fiercely loyal, anti-German people he could trust with his life. Moreover, his instincts were good: He knew, for example, to be wary of Chou ("the cabbage"), a funny, frightened little alcoholic who meant well but could not keep his mouth shut.

Ree was also shrewd enough to steer clear of some not-so-obvious pitfalls. He avoided getting entangled with the notorious rivalries between different French resistance groups by insisting that he would work only with those groups that would agree to follow his orders. He always represented himself as a low-level British officer, which prevented anyone from expecting too much. And he never encouraged attacks on Germans, because

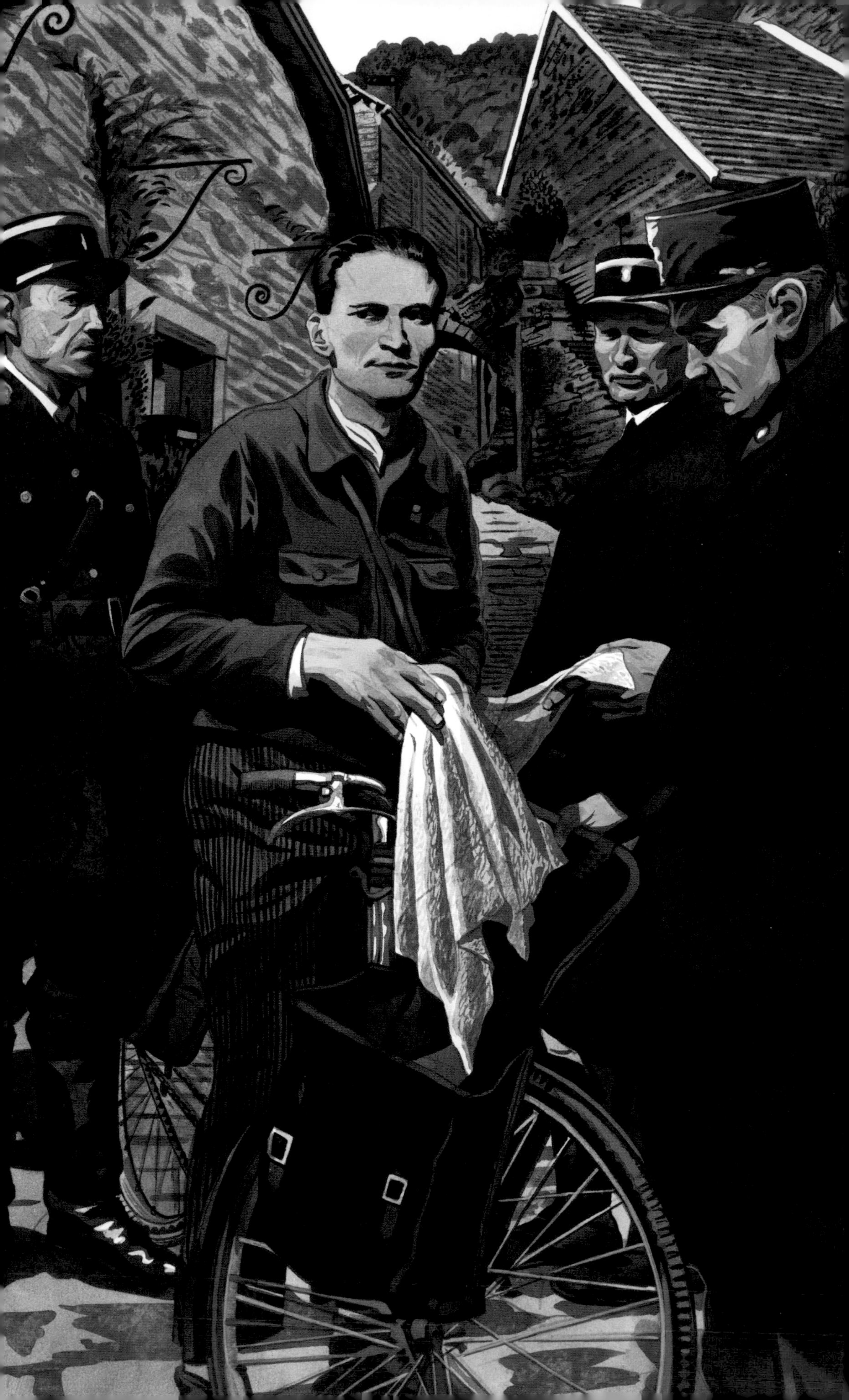

of the harsh reprisals on local people that would follow.

But even more than trustworthy associates and good instincts, what an agent in the field really needed was luck. And despite all his precautions, Ree came within an inch of being caught several times.

Like most agents working in the French countryside, Ree bicycled everywhere. It was the safest and fastest way to get around. Cars attracted attention; walking took too long and if you were stopped, it was hard to explain what you were doing in the middle of nowhere on foot. On a bike, you could use the back roads and avoid being stopped by the police. It was not uncommon for him to bicycle 30 or 40 miles in a day.

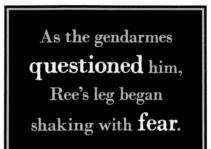

As the gendarmes **questioned** him, Ree's leg began shaking with **fear**.

Ree tried to avoid carrying a weapon or explosives, but there were times it could not be helped. One morning, after showing a barber how to use a sample packet of explosives, he had to take the explosives to another village. He shoved the explosives in his bicycle's saddlebags and was pedaling along when he was stopped by gendarmes. They asked for his identity card and scrutinized it. Then they asked the question he had been dreading: "What have you got in your saddlebags?" He said, "Oh, just a few night things," and reached in and pulled out a towel. The explosives were stuffed down at the bottom. His leg began shaking with fear. One of the gendarmes looked at him and said, "Are you cold?" Ree said, "Yes, it is a bit cold this morning, isn't it?" The gendarme said, "OK, go on."

The young men who helped Ree in the field—as couriers, collecting supply drops, carrying out acts of sabotage—were a fiery, unforgettable collection. One of his favorites was a man named Claude, a bank clerk whose fearless exuberance and Bolshi politics belied his profession. Always cheerful, bursting with energy, Claude became one of Ree's closest associates. Then there was Raymond Lazzeri, a skinny young man who raced around the hilly Jura on an ancient racing bicycle whose chain had a tendency to fly off at the worst moments. Another man, who worked in the local Peugeot plant, was known as *"le bigame"* because he had one girlfriend in France and another in Switzerland. These young men risked their lives every day, and they did so with an élan, a tough innocence, that Ree found deeply inspiring.

He was just as moved by the quiet courage of older people such as the Barbier family, with whom he lived for months. Such people did not blow up bridges, but they opened their doors to Ree, fed him and did everything they could to help him. They knew that if they were caught, they would likely be shipped off to a concentration camp. They received no reward and little acknowledgment for what they did. When asked about it after the war, they typically said that they had merely done their duty.

Ree was less taken with his circuit leader, John Starr, aka Bob, whom he found dangerously boastful and indiscreet. Bob drove around ostentatiously in a car and on one occasion insisted on being introduced to a group of Frenchmen as a chief of the British Intelligence Service. Bob's high-handed manner rubbed some of the locals the wrong way.

The most intriguing of Ree's colleagues was an ex-garage keeper named Pierre Martin. Martin was a local legend, who liked to boast that he had helped Allied airmen escape from France and had himself broken out of a German prison. When he met Ree, he cracked, "I only work for the resistance so that men will talk about me." Ree was put off by this flippant remark, but the Frenchman's high spirits and hard work collecting supplies from parachute drops overcame his reservations.

One day, however, Martin did something that made Ree suspicious. Martin had told Ree that he had conned the Germans into letting him drive around in a car, which was extremely useful in collecting containers after a parachute drop. As Ree and Martin were driving back from a supply drop, some gendarmes stopped them. "Don't you know I drive for the Gestapo?" Martin asked the police. When the gendarmes asked what the containers were, Martin breezily replied, "Haven't an idea. They belong to the Germans, the Gestapo, you know..." The gendarmes hesitated, then waved him through.

Ree found Martin's utter lack of fear disconcerting. Was it the audacity of a hero—or the complacency of a traitor?

## March 4, 1943
## Skrykken
## Hardangervidda
## Norway

On March 2, the Norwegian commandos left Cousin's Cabin and headed for Skrykken, the site where Gunnerside had landed. Claus Helberg had left the party to head back to the Fjosbudalen hut, where he needed to pick up incriminating fake papers and civilian clothes, so there were only eight men on the march. On the way they stopped and hid a message for Knut Haugland and Einar Skinnarland, the two radio operators who had not taken part in the raid and had left to lie low before carrying on resistance work in the area. The brief message concluded: "High concentration plant totally destroyed. All present. No fighting."

Till then, Baker Street had heard nothing from Gunnerside and was racked by anxiety. When Gubbins and the rest of SOE's staff finally received the message, some days later, they were ecstatic. The jubilation reached as far as the prime minister's office. "What rewards are to be given to these heroic men?" Churchill scrawled on the first official report on the raid, signing the note "W.S.C." It was SOE's greatest success to date.

"What **rewards** are to be given to these **heroic** men?" Churchill scrawled.

Soon after the young Norwegians arrived at the hut at Skrykken, it was time for farewells. The band was splitting up. Knut Haukelid and Arne Kjelstrup were going to stay on the Hardangervidda and organize the local resistance. Jens Poulsson and his boyhood friend, Claus Helberg, were going to head to Oslo. But Helberg had not yet returned, and Poulsson and the others were getting increasingly worried about him. The remaining five men—Ronneberg, Stromsheim, Storhaug, Kayser and Idland—would make the long trek to Sweden.

It was "the most splendid coup I have seen in this war."

There were handshakes all around, and then Ronneberg and his charges, wearing British uniforms, set off toward Sweden, 250 miles away. Ronneberg had charted a course that would take them through featureless valleys and hills, away from towns, farms and roads.

They all knew that they had made it past only the first hurdle. SOE had always regarded the escape as the most dangerous part of their mission.

As their five comrades vanished over the horizon, Haukelid, Poulsson and Kjelstrup changed into civilian clothes and buried their uniforms. Haukelid and Kjelstrup loaded a toboggan with supplies for their five-day trek through the Hardangervidda.

"Now it's my turn to leave," Poulsson said. He shook hands first with Haukelid, then turned to Kjelstrup. Poulsson had come to have a deep affection for the broad-shouldered plumber, with whom he had traveled halfway around the world to get to Britain. During their five months together on the Hardangervidda, Kjelstrup had never complained despite a chronic stomach ailment. The two men reminisced about their times together—Kjelstrup walking for miles through a blizzard carrying heavy storage batteries, staggering into the hut looking exactly like a snowman; Haugland sitting by the wireless for hours in thirty-degree-below-zero weather, his frozen fingers on the sending key; Helberg returning from a hunt with 100 pounds of reindeer meat in his pack. The two men had formed a bond few ever experience.

"Well, Arne, good-bye and good luck," Poulsson said. "If we don't meet sooner, we'll meet after the war." He pushed off on his skies heading east, in the direction of Oslo, where he and the missing Helberg had planned to rendezvous in a week. Haukelid and Kjelstrup, feeling very alone, headed off to the west.

While the commandos were going their separate ways, the Germans were mounting a massive search operation. The enraged head of the Gestapo in Norway was certain it was an inside job, and threatened to execute plant workers unless they revealed the culprit. The senior German guard at the plant and several others were sent to the Russian front as punishment. It was only the

and had a regular poker game at the Café Capucines in the Square Clignancourt in Montmartre. Although many waiters were on the German payroll and spies were everywhere, the trio did not always remember to speak French at these gatherings. Worst of all, two German double agents, pretending to be Dutch members of SOE, had recently made contact with them there.

# Did SOE knowingly

SOE agents knew that every day spent in hostile territory was a roll of the dice. They were told that their odds of returning were no better than even. But some authors argue that Britain knowingly sacrificed some of its own agents—either to trick the Germans into believing their radio games had successfully fooled London, or as part of larger deception schemes involving invasion plans for Sicily or Normandy.

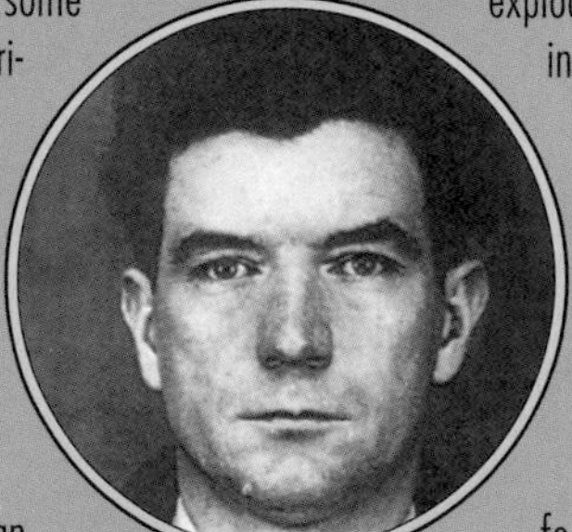
The mystery man: Henri Déricourt

The first person to raise the possibility that SOE betrayed its own agents was Jean Overton Fuller, Noor Inayat Khan's biographer. In her 1954 book *The Starr Affair,* about Noor's fellow prisoner John Starr, she revealed that German counterintelligence officers, including a cunning Abwehr sergeant named Hugo Bleicher and several SD officers at the Avenue Foch, had intercepted SOE agents' mail and were using captured radios to impersonate agents. In her next book, *Double Webs* (1958), Overton Fuller went further, writing that SOE's air movements officer, Henri Déricourt, was the person who had intercepted the mail and given it to German counterintelligence officers. The real bombshell, though, was Déricourt's claim that he had acted on orders from London. Déricourt was highly untrustworthy, and the truth about who he was working for has never been established. But it was the testimony of Nicholas Boddington, one of SOE's senior officials, that helped exonerate Déricourt when he was tried for treason after the war.

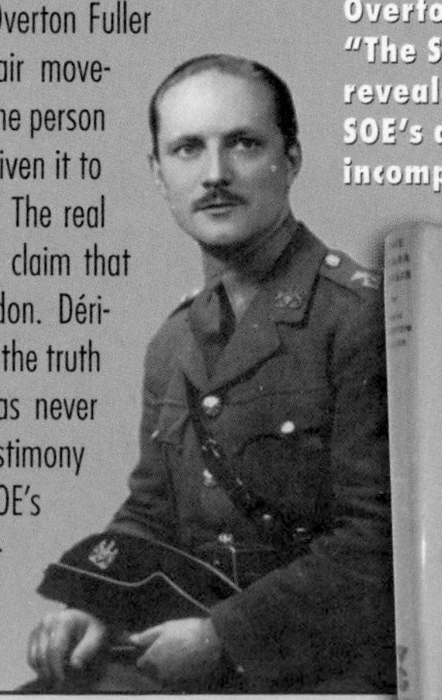

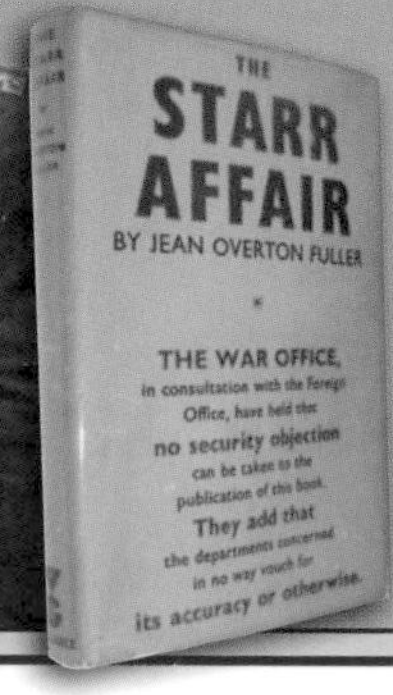
THE
STARR
AFFAIR
BY JEAN OVERTON FULLER
THE WAR OFFICE, in consultation with the Foreign Office, have held that no security objection can be taken to the publication of this book. They add that the departments concerned in no way vouch for its accuracy or otherwise.
Overton Fuller's "The Starr Affair" revealed SOE's deadly incompetence.

The same year that Fuller published *Double Webs,* journalist Elizabeth Nicholas's *Death Be Not Proud* caused the issue of SOE's incompetence, or downright villainy, to explode onto front pages across Britain. Pursuing the truth about the death of her childhood friend Diana Rowden, Nicholas put forward a "truly dreadful theory": that top British officials offered up SOE agents' lives in a scheme to deceive Axis leaders. "London knew very well that Poste Madeleine had been taken over by the Germans and was busily feeding to it false information to deceive the enemy. More than this...London had prepared to send agents deliberately to a reception committee organized by the Germans so as to maintain the deception." Nicholas admitted that such action "would demand a logical and cruel recklessness such as the British never employ, even in war," but claimed that a number of SOE officers believed it to be true. Nicholas also charged that the British government had covered up the truth about the deaths of Rowden and six other female SOE agents.

The secrecy-obsessed British government did nothing to help its own case. For more than 15 years after SOE shut down in 1946, the government refused to acknowledge its existence. Officials were happy to as-

Prosper was likely doomed in any case. But there was another factor. Henri Déricourt, the SOE air movements officer who had greeted Noor when she landed, was secretly working for the Germans. (See sidebar.)

The thread snapped the day after Noor's lunch with her comrades. On June 21, two newly arrived Canadian agents, Ken Macalister and Frank Pickersgill, were arrested by the Gestapo at a roadblock. Two established

## sacrifice its own agents?

sist with hagiographic accounts of SOE heroines like Odette Sansome and Violette Szabo, but closed the door on any inquiries that might lead to awkward conclusions. Whitehall's stonewalling aroused public suspicion that it had something to hide.

The first authoritative book about SOE, Bickham Sweet-Escott's *Baker Street Irregular,* was written in 1954 but its publication was forbidden until 1962, when the government finally caved in. And it was not until Dame Edith Ward, a Conservative MP, joined Nicholas and Overton Fuller in demanding answers that the British government finally commissioned the organization's first official history, *SOE in France* by Oxford historian M. R. D. Foot.

In his heavily researched 1966 tome, Foot rejected the idea that SOE had intentionally betrayed its agents, arguing that incompetence in London, penetration by German agents and bad security by agents in the field were solely responsible for the 1943 Prosper disasters in France and other security debacles.

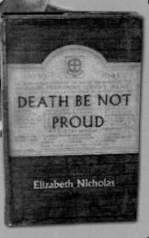

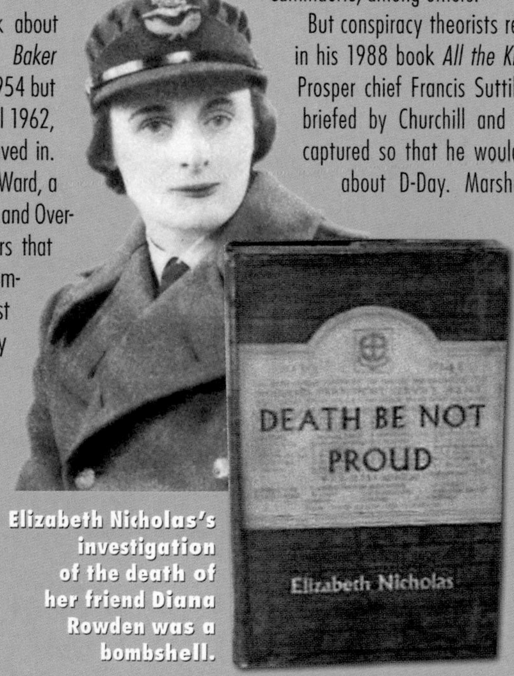

In a later edition, Foot addressed the charge that the alleged betrayal was part of the Allies' vast deception scheme that successfully misled Hitler about D-Day. He argued that it would have been highly unlikely that the Allies would have relied on fallible agents for such a crucial mission.

Considering the government auspices of Foot's research, some skeptics find his conclusions predictable. Nonetheless, Foot's explanation has the virtue of simplicity and is shared, with some reservations, by top SOE historian David Stafford, investigative reporter Sarah Helm (author of the stunning *A Life in Secrets*), and former agent Francis Cammaerts, among others.

DEATH BE NOT
PROUD
Elizabeth Nicholas
**Elizabeth Nicholas's investigation of the death of her friend Diana Rowden was a bombshell.**

But conspiracy theorists remain. Robert Marshall, in his 1988 book *All the King's Men,* claimed that Prosper chief Francis Suttill was personally (mis) briefed by Churchill and then sent back to be captured so that he would mislead the Germans about D-Day. Marshall also asserted that Déricourt was being run by Claude Dansey of SIS. One of SOE's top officials, Harry Sporborg, corroborated part of Marshall's theory, saying that he was certain Déricourt was working for SIS and that the spy agency would not have hesitated to "sacrifice some of our people" if it suited their purposes. (Decades after the fact, F Section head Buckmaster also suddenly remembered that Déricourt was a double agent working for a higher Whitehall power, but his own addled memories of SOE make his testimony suspect.) Rita Kramer, in her 1995 book *Flames in the Field,* is agnostic, but concludes that if SOE did betray its own, the move was morally justifiable in the fight against Hitler.

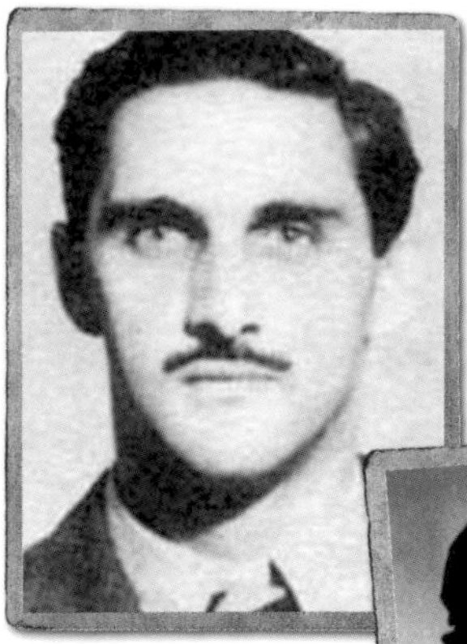

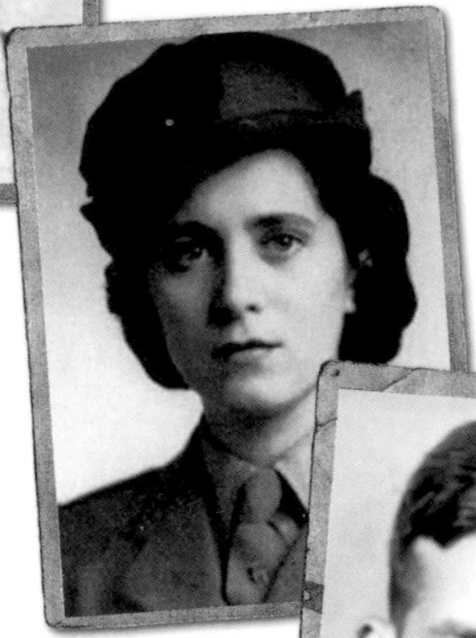

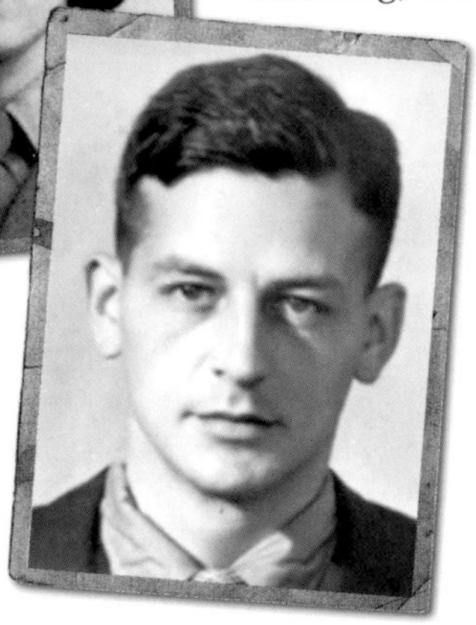

**Three doomed agents: Gilbert Norman, Andrée Borrel, and Francis Suttill**

SOE operatives, Pierre Culioli and SOE's oldest female agent, a tough 46-year-old grandmother named Yvonne Rudellat, tried to flee but were wounded in a gunfight and captured.

The arrests had catastrophic consequences. The Gestapo recovered Macalister's wireless set and messages in clear (i.e., unencoded) intended for agents in Paris. In Culioli's briefcase, the Germans found the addresses of Norman, Borrel and other key members of Prosper.

Two nights later, just after midnight, the dread knock on the door sounded at the apartment where Norman and Borrel were staying. The Gestapo burst in and arrested them. Suttill was traveling, but the Germans waited at his apartment and arrested him the next day.

Norman and Suttill were subjected to severe interrogation at the Nazi Security Service (SD) headquarters on Avenue Foch in Paris. Suttill's arm was broken and he was beaten unconscious. The Germans forced Norman to send a wireless message to London. When he deliberately omitted his true security check to alert SOE that he had been taken, F Section head Buckmaster actually sent back a message chiding him for omitting it. Norman later told another prisoner that Buckmaster's folly so disheartened him that he began to collaborate with the Germans.

Norman claimed his collaboration was limited and denied he ever made a deal with them. But either Norman or Suttill—it has never been established which, although it was probably Norman—apparently did make such a deal. Whether beguiled by skillful handling, broken by rough treatment, or both, one of the two men agreed to reveal the time and location of SOE supply drops to the Germans, in exchange for a written promise that no other agents or resistance members except them would be executed. As a result of this deal (which the Germans failed to honor) and of Baker Street's continuing failure to realize that Norman and the two Canadians had been taken, 27 SOE agents and at least 400 (and perhaps as many as 1,500) members of the resistance were arrested, and huge amounts of arms and explosives seized.

Noor, of course, knew none of this. Staying in Grignon, she was warned about the arrests by an anonymous phone call on June 25. She quickly buried her radio set under a bed of lettuce and returned to Paris. There she got in touch with Garry and Major France Anthelme, a Mauritian SOE agent in his 40s who quickly developed a keen—perhaps romantic—attachment to her. Anthelme ordered Garry to change houses and found a place for Noor to stay at One Square Malherbe.

As ordered, Noor lay low for a few days. But on July 1, anxious to transmit to London, she returned to Grignon. She rode up to the school on her bicycle, leaned it against a wall and quietly entered the grounds. But some sixth sense warned her that something was wrong. As she approached the building, she realized it was infested with SS men. Leaving her bike behind, she jumped on a passing bus and took the train back to Paris.

The smashing of Prosper meant that Poste Madeleine was now F Section's only underground wireless link in Paris. Buckmaster, realizing Noor was in mortal danger, offered to fly her back to London. Noor refused. Buckmaster agreed to let her stay, but told her to avoid transmitting for the present. (In later years, Buckmaster claimed that he ordered Noor to return. But Buckmaster's recollections of SOE are filled with glaring errors, and there is no evidence for this claim.)

F Section head
**Maurice Buckmaster**

Noor followed Buckmaster's advice for only a few days. Although suffering from a severe cold, she began looking for a place to transmit, ideally an apartment with a tree outside to which she could attach her wireless set's aerial. She began regularly meeting three French agents at a park bench in the Tuileries, collecting their information to send to London. One of the agents would sometimes drive with her out into quiet lanes in the suburbs, where she would put up her aerial and transmit. The French agents had lost their wireless operators in the big Gestapo sweep, so she was their only link to London. Among other important tasks, she arranged for de Gaulle's Free French headquarters to send them a million francs.

In mid-July, Noor found an apartment. It was in Neuilly, in one of several huge, identical white apartment buildings on the Boulevard Richard-Wallace, opposite the Bois de Boulogne and just yards from the bridge across the Seine that led to her childhood home. Her apartment was a tiny room on the ground floor. There was a tree outside to which she could attach her aerial, but it was on the street, and the building was filled with SS officers. Noor used the apartment mainly as a letter drop. She never slept in it and avoided transmitting from there.

One night, however, Noor needed to make a transmission and decided to risk it. It was dusk. She dropped the aerial out the window, went outside and tried to connect it to the tree, whose lowest branches were just within her reach. As she wrestled with the branches and the aerial, she heard footsteps behind her. "Mademoiselle!" To her horror, she found one of the SS officers from the building standing next to her.

The German asked, "May I help you?" Trying to compose herself, Noor replied, "Thank you, I should be glad if you would." She gave him the aerial, which he attached to the tree. Then he gave a little bow, said, "At your service, Mademoiselle," and went into the building. Noor told a friend later that the chivalrous SS man must have assumed she was listening to the radio for entertainment. What British agent would be so idiotic as to put up an aerial in plain view?

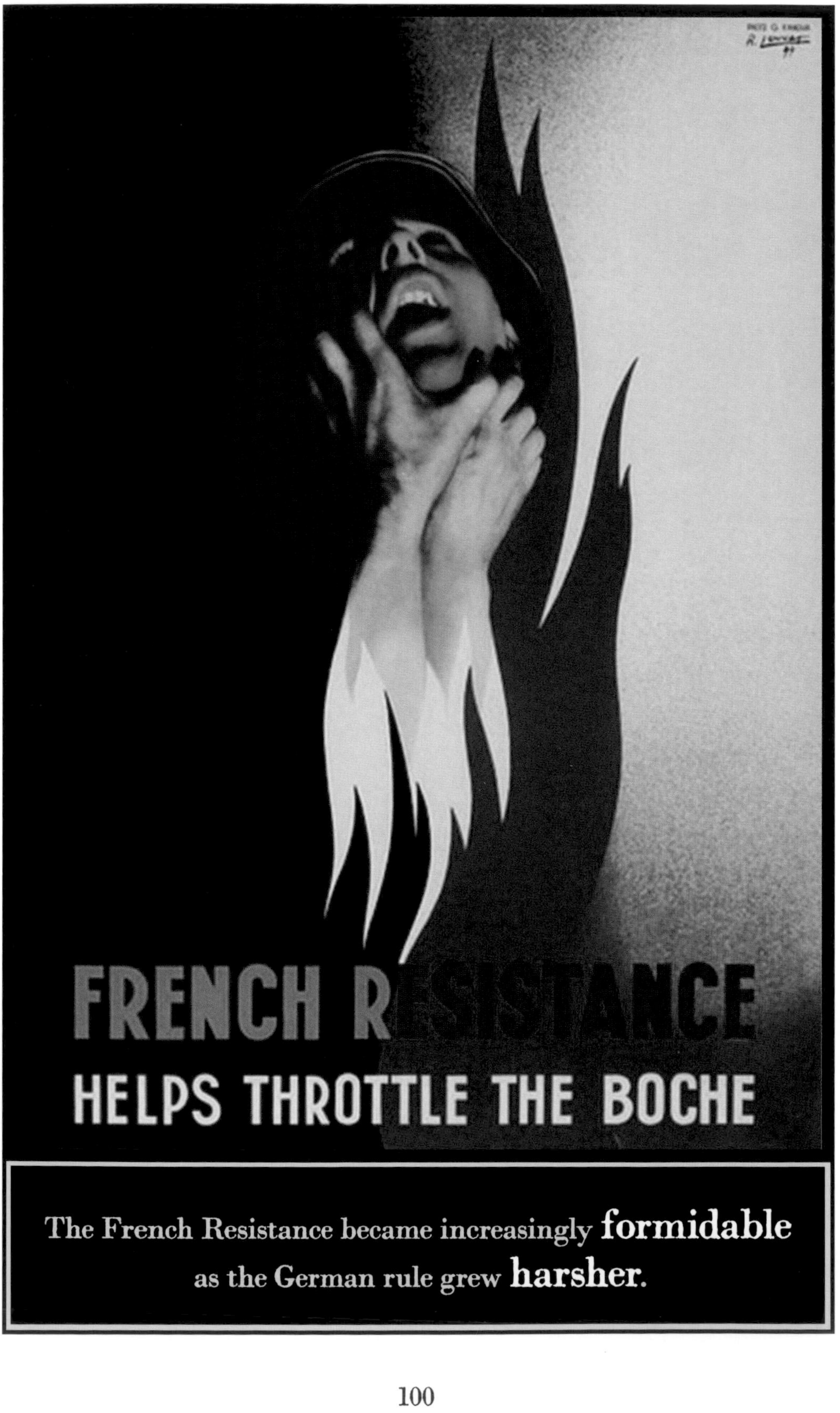
FRENCH RESISTANCE
HELPS THROTTLE THE BOCHE

The French Resistance became increasingly **formidable** as the German rule grew **harsher.**

# Summer 1943
# London

As Prosper collapsed, Claude Dansey, Stuart Menzies's number two at SIS, waltzed into the office of his boss's assistant. "Have you heard the news? SOE's in the shit," he gloated. "They've bought it in France. The Germans are mopping them up all over the place."

SIS had already suspected that the Germans had penetrated SOE's Dutch circuits and were running a radio game, luring unsuspecting agents to their doom. With the fall of Prosper, they had become virtually certain of it. And now suspicions also fell on SOE's shaky Belgian circuits.

Dansey hated SOE even more than Menzies did. After the war, Dansey is said to have threatened to blackball any SOE member who was proposed for membership in the venerable London men's club Boodles. He and his boss now had a perfect opportunity to shut SOE down for good. Menzies sent a damning report about SOE's compromised networks to the Joint Intelligence Committee.

The success of the Vemork heavy-water raid had only briefly silenced SOE's enemies in Whitehall. Tensions were also running high with the RAF. SOE wanted more planes, both to support the guerrillas waging open warfare in Yugoslavia and to drop supplies to the growing resistance movement in France. The RAF reluctantly offered a few more bombers for the Balkans, which the military Chiefs of Staff had designated SOE's top priority, but refused to budge on Western Europe.

The furor forced Churchill to call an August 2 meeting of the Defence Committee, where the adversaries went at it. Selborne vigorously insisted that resistance movements in Europe were growing and desperately needed arms if they were not to fade away. RAF chief Portal stuck to his guns: he could spare no bombers from his campaign against German cities. Menzies demanded that SOE either be placed under his control or killed off.

Churchill sided with Selborne—up to a point. The prime minister acknowledged that SOE's sponsorship of covert attacks on the Germans had resulted in harsh reprisals against civilians. But then, in classic Churchillian fashion, he pronounced that "the blood of the Martyrs is the seed of the church" and declaimed that the reprisals had made the Germans "hated as no other race had ever been hated." SOE would not be shut down or handed over to SIS. But Churchill refused to allocate more planes for SOE.

Another crisis soon followed, this time over SOE's involvement in Greece, where the resistance movement was rancorously split between royalists and Communists. Fearful that Greece might fall under Soviet control, the Foreign Office and Churchill thought SOE tilted too much toward the Communists. As the dispute over Greece came to a boiling point, Churchill became so angry at SOE that he considered dissolving it altogether.

At a tense meeting of cabinet ministers on September 30, Churchill saved SOE. But its hand was slapped hard. It was ordered to coordinate more closely with the Foreign Office and report to a political guidance committee for the Balkans. The chief of SOE's Middle East headquarters in Cairo was replaced.

Claude Dansey
hated SOE.

SOE had been firmly rebuked. But the changes actually made it more effective. The shake-up in Cairo smoothed relations with the Foreign Office. And when Allied commanders decided not to invade the Balkans, opting instead for France, SOE's role in Greece and Yugoslavia was strengthened. Guerrilla warfare, SOE's specialty, was now the only kind of war being waged in the Balkans.

But the most crucial change came at the top. SOE's executive director Charles Hambro, smarting from the rebuke, offered his resignation. Selborne did little to dissuade him. Hambro, who had replaced Frank Nelson in 1942, had done a creditable job under impossible circumstances, but with the European invasion looming, Selborne believed that SOE had reached the stage where it would be best led by a professional soldier. With Churchill's approval, he appointed Gubbins as the third and final executive director of SOE.

At age 47, Gubbins was now formally in charge of a three-year-old operation with hundreds of agents in the field around the world and a total staff of thousands. He was responsible for the well-being not just of those agents, many of whom he knew personally, but of the countless thousands of men and women who were working with the resistance across Europe and elsewhere. He had to negotiate the treacherous political shoals of the Balkans, wrangle more planes out of the RAF, get to the bottom of the ominous mess in Holland and deal with the Medici-like intrigues in Whitehall. And he had to do all this while dealing with the pain brought on by the recent end of his marriage, which had not survived the secrecy and all-consuming nature of his job.

But the one thing that kept Gubbins up at night was the approach of D-Day. Throughout 1943, Allied High Command had hinted that it might launch the long-awaited invasion, code-named Overlord, that year. The prospect deeply worried Gubbins. Allied commanders were counting on the French resistance to rise up and wreak havoc in the enemy's rear during the invasion. But he did not think they would be ready for another year.

The days when SOE could justify itself with isolated acts of sabotage were over. It was now a legitimate piece on the strategic chessboard. If SOE failed at this climactic moment, all of its other successes would mean nothing.

"Strategically, France is by far the most important country in the Western Theatre of War," Gubbins wrote to Buckmaster. "I think therefore that SOE should regard this theatre as one in which the suffering of heavy casualties is inevitable."

The coming year would bring triumph to SOE. But it would also bring shattering personal tragedy to Gubbins.

## Morning
## July 16, 1943
## Besançon, France

Besançon had been hit hard during the night. Streets were smashed, ruined buildings gaped over burned-out cars. Ree had taken shelter under a peach tree as the bombs exploded. The RAF had made a thorough job of it, Ree thought now as he walked through the streets. Noticing SS men moving around, stopping people at random, he headed quickly to a safe café.

When he sat down, the proprietor came over to him. "Do you trust Pierre Martin?" he asked Ree. The Englishman thought about the flashy Frenchman who had boasted about driving for the Gestapo. "Not much," Ree replied.

"Well, I think he has betrayed Bob," said the patron, referring to John Starr, the Acrobat circuit chief, by his field name. "Look at this! It's for you. I got it this morning." He handed Ree a note from Martin.

The note said that Martin and Bob had been arrested the day before. The Germans had let Martin go, but had thrown Bob into prison at Dijon. "Can't understand how they got me and Bob, nor why they released me and not Bob. Are you being followed? Be very careful. Meet me Friday afternoon in the waiting-room of the Dijon station. Yours, Pierre."

Ree was stunned. From friends in Dijon, he was able to put together more or less what happened. Martin had asked Bob to accompany him to look at a potential dropping ground near Dole. Just before they left, Martin said he had to make a phone call. Soon after they drove out of Dijon, they rounded a corner and came upon several cars blocking the road and a squad of SS men armed with automatic weapons. Both of them were hauled off to prison, but Martin was released that afternoon.

**Ree had an urgent task: kill Pierre Martin.**

Ree knew that the Gestapo would be trying to break Starr. Agents had been trained to hold out for at least 48 hours, which would give everyone who knew them time to scatter. But not everyone could hold out for that long. Ree had to warn everyone who had come into contact with either Martin or Starr. The two people in the greatest danger were Starr's courier, Diana Rowden, and his wireless operator,

John Young. Ree sent word for them to hide in a sawmill.

He also had another urgent task. He had to kill Pierre Martin.

Ree and local resistance men came up with a plan. Ree would send word to Martin that he was in hiding and wanted to turn over his circuit to him. A trusted lieutenant, Andre van der Straaten, would guide Martin to Ree's hideout in a ruined cottage in a clearing in the woods. Once Martin arrived, Ree would knock him out by hitting him on the head, then shoot him with a muffled pistol. They would dump his body in an unused well.

Waiting in the roofless cottage, Ree was tortured by the thought of what he was about to do. He had never killed anyone. What right did he have to take another man's life? He told himself it was war, and he was doing it in self-defense. But he wasn't going to kill Martin the way a soldier kills an enemy soldier. He was going to murder him in cold blood. Yes, Martin was a traitor. But who was Ree to judge him? What would the Lord Chief Justice say? What about the *Manchester Guardian*?

Finally a line from *Rough Justice,* a novel by C. E. Montague about the First World War, came into Ree's mind: "Revenge is a kind of Rough Justice."

His conscience now clear, Ree lay down in the dewy grass to wait. He heard footsteps approaching. He hid behind the cottage wall. But when Andre appeared, he was alone.

Martin was on to them, Andre told Ree. When Andre had gone to the café where he was to meet Martin, two big men at another table had stared hard at him. Soon thereafter a big, closed car pulled up. The waitress whispered "Gestapo," but Andre already knew. He quickly walked through the kitchen and out to his bicycle,

**Devastated Besançon after the RAF bombed it.**

which he had left behind the café. As he pedaled off, he saw Martin sitting in the backseat of the car, reading a paper.

Martin's mask was off. He was now openly working with the Germans. Andre and Ree had to get away. For four hours they pushed their bicycles through the woods, carrying them when the thickets were too dense. Finally they made it to a village where they could hide.

Safe for the moment, Ree began plotting his biggest attack yet: on the giant Peugeot works owned by his young friend Rodolphe. The same night the RAF bombed Besançon, it also hit the Peugeot works. Ree had taken the 30-mile train trip from Besançon to Montbéliard and saw the damage with his own eyes. Dozens of civilians had been killed, homes and businesses wrecked, but the plant was hardly damaged. Ree was disturbed by the devastation. And he also knew that high civilian casualties angered the French and decreased support for the resistance.

Now an idea came to Ree. He paid a call on Peugeot and made him a proposal. If Peugeot would agree to let Ree's men sabotage the plant, Ree would ensure that the RAF would not bomb Sochaux again.

Peugeot was not only anti-German, he also wanted his factory and its 60,000 jobs to survive the war. He knew that targeted sabotage would leave most of the plant untouched, while RAF bombing could destroy everything. He replied, "Fine."

Peugeot gave Ree a diagram of the factory and put Ree in touch with Pierre Lucas, the chief electrician at the plant. Ree contacted Buckmaster in London, who convinced the RAF to suspend their bombing if Ree could demonstrate his sabotage was successful.

One afternoon, Ree met Lucas at a café outside the plant. The foreman gave Ree a pair of overalls, which he put on in the bathroom of the café. Then, under the eyes of the German security police, the two "workmen" took a leisurely tour of the plant, looking closely at machines and transformers. The foreman pointed out exactly where Ree's men should place the charges to cripple the plant's turbine compressors and other crucial machines.

Soon afterward, Ree got catastrophic news. The Gestapo had swooped down and made mass arrests, including the local priest, Abbé Schwander, the leader of the Gaullist resistance in the area. After being horribly tortured, Schwander died of suffocation on the train to Buchenwald.

The Peugeot sabotage was off. Ree was in extreme danger. He had to get out of France. But first he had to try to save his circuit. He met with Schwander's successor, a local schoolteacher named Roger Fouillette with whom he had become close. He wrote a letter to be delivered to his fellow agents John Young and Diana Rowden, telling them to keep lying low, and wrapped up other business.

On August 1, Ree—led by two *passeurs,* cross-border guides, one a 16-year-old boy—hiked through the woods, avoiding the regular German patrols, and crossed into neutral Switzerland. Ree was immediately detained, but the Swiss turned a blind eye to British agents and he was soon turned over to the British legation in Berne. He sent letters to London explaining the debacle and asking to be allowed to return to France to continue his work.

Four weeks after he had escaped to Switzerland, Ree slipped back across the border into France, a marked man.

# An unimaginable epic of Survival

Of all the tales of survival to emerge from World War II, none is more incredible than that of SOE agent Jan Baalsrud.

Baalsrud and a party of other Norwegian agents had been dropped by boat in northern Norway in March 1943 and immediately were betrayed by a nervous shopkeeper to whom they had revealed their identity. Baalsrud's three companions were gunned down by German troops as they attempted to swim from their boat to the shore of a small island. Pursued by Germans as he climbed a snow-covered ridge above the harbor, Baalsrud hid behind a boulder, shot a Gestapo officer at point-blank range, wounded another German and managed to slip out of sight as his pursuers took cover.

ACE 35¢ BOOK
"An epic story of a man's staggering feat of endurance . . . puts fiction to shame."
WE DIE ALONE
DAVID HOWARTH
Complete and Unabridged

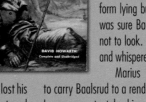

Half of his big toe had been shot away and he had lost his boot. But knowing the Germans would find him if he stayed on the island, Baalsrud swam through ice 50 yards to a small rock and hid. He managed to elude the confused Germans, but he knew that if he spent the night there he would freeze to death. His only chance was to make it to a larger island in the opposite direction from the Germans, 220 yards away. His body suffered agonizing cramps during the icy swim and he almost drowned, but he made it to the shore.

Two little girls found Baalsrud lying on the beach and brought him to their nearby homes. Their mothers risked their lives to warm him, feed him and hide him for the night. Baalsrud walked 30 miles to the other end of the island in rubber boots, once marching for 28 consecutive hours. As he skied over a mountain, he was buried by an avalanche. Snow-blind, he wandered in circles for three days before stumbling upon a log cabin, home to a man named Marius. The semiconscious Baalsrud was afraid the stranger would betray him. Realizing this, Marius—an editor who had been waiting for an opportunity to prove his patriotism—leaned over and said to him, "If I live, you will live, and if they kill you I will have died to protect you." Baalsrud spent a week in Marius's barn, then a horrible week alone in an abandoned farmhouse, racked by pain in his severely frostbitten feet.

Marius and three other men built a sledge. In an unimaginable feat of strength and will, they carried Baalsrud 3,000 feet up a sheer mountain. But the party they were to rendezvous with did not show up, and they were forced to leave him alone on a plateau, in a hollow next to a boulder. There Baalsrud lay for 27 days, five of them buried in the snow, alone.

When Marius and a local girl named Agnethe returned to the plateau, they found a motionless form lying buried deep in the snow. The editor was sure Baalsrud was dead and told Agnethe not to look. But then Baalsrud opened his eyes and whispered, "You can't kill an old fox."

Marius and Agnethe recruited villagers to carry Baalsrud to a rendezvous point near Sweden, where Lapps were to take him across the border. Once again a blizzard forced them to leave Baalsrud in the snow. Three weeks passed, and still the Lapps did not come.

Baalsrud feared he was going to die of gangrene. Lying in the snow, he amputated his remaining nine toes with his pocket knife, using brandy for an anesthetic. After cutting each toe off, he placed it on a ledge where he could not see it. The grueling surgery took three days.

When Baalsrud had abandoned all hope, he opened his eyes to find a Lapp looking down at him and a wild sound of snorting and shuffling. The Lapps, and their great herd of reindeer, had come for him at last. That night he listened to the eerie sound of the Lapps singing drunkenly—an ancient rite called yoicking. Two days later, on a sledge pulled by a team of reindeer, Baalsrud and the Lapps outraced Germans firing rifles at them and crossed a frozen lake into Sweden.

**A Lapp-led team of reindeer pulled Baalsrud to freedom.**

## 8:15 p.m.
## March 18, 1943
## Near the Norway-Sweden border

For two weeks, Joachim Ronneberg and his men had been slogging through desolate valleys and across scrubby hills, dragging a backbreaking toboggan and stumbling under the weight of their heavy packs. The trek had taken twice as long as they planned. The weather was dreadful, the snow was slushy and they had almost run out of food. They had gotten lost repeatedly and burned up precious energy going the wrong way, sometimes for miles. They had had to sleep out in the snow repeatedly, getting wet to the bone, and the cold, physical exhaustion and hunger had pushed them to the edge. But so far, they had avoided German patrols. And Sweden was almost within sight.

Could the **trolls** of Norway save Ronneberg and his men **one more time?**

Kasper Idland, who could barely ski, struggled desperately to keep up with his comrades, never once complaining or asking them to slow down. The quiet postman had not expected to survive the mission, and Ronneberg knew that if it came to a crisis, he would insist that the others leave him behind. His teammates knew that they would never do that.

Finally they made it to the Glomma River, the last natural barrier between them and Sweden. They were only 40 miles away from freedom. They expected the big river to be frozen over. But to their despair they found that it was ice free. They knew there were German patrols in the area, searching for refugees trying to cross the border. Would they be captured now, with the promised land so close?

Hans Storhaug set off to contact a local patriot. A few hours later he returned with a boat he had stolen. The five men clambered into it, quickly rowed across the river and hurried into the forested hills on the other side. There were no huts in the area and they had to spend two more nights in the open. They were so hungry and cold they were unable to sleep.

The last miles of the march were brutal, a maze of thick woods and stony,

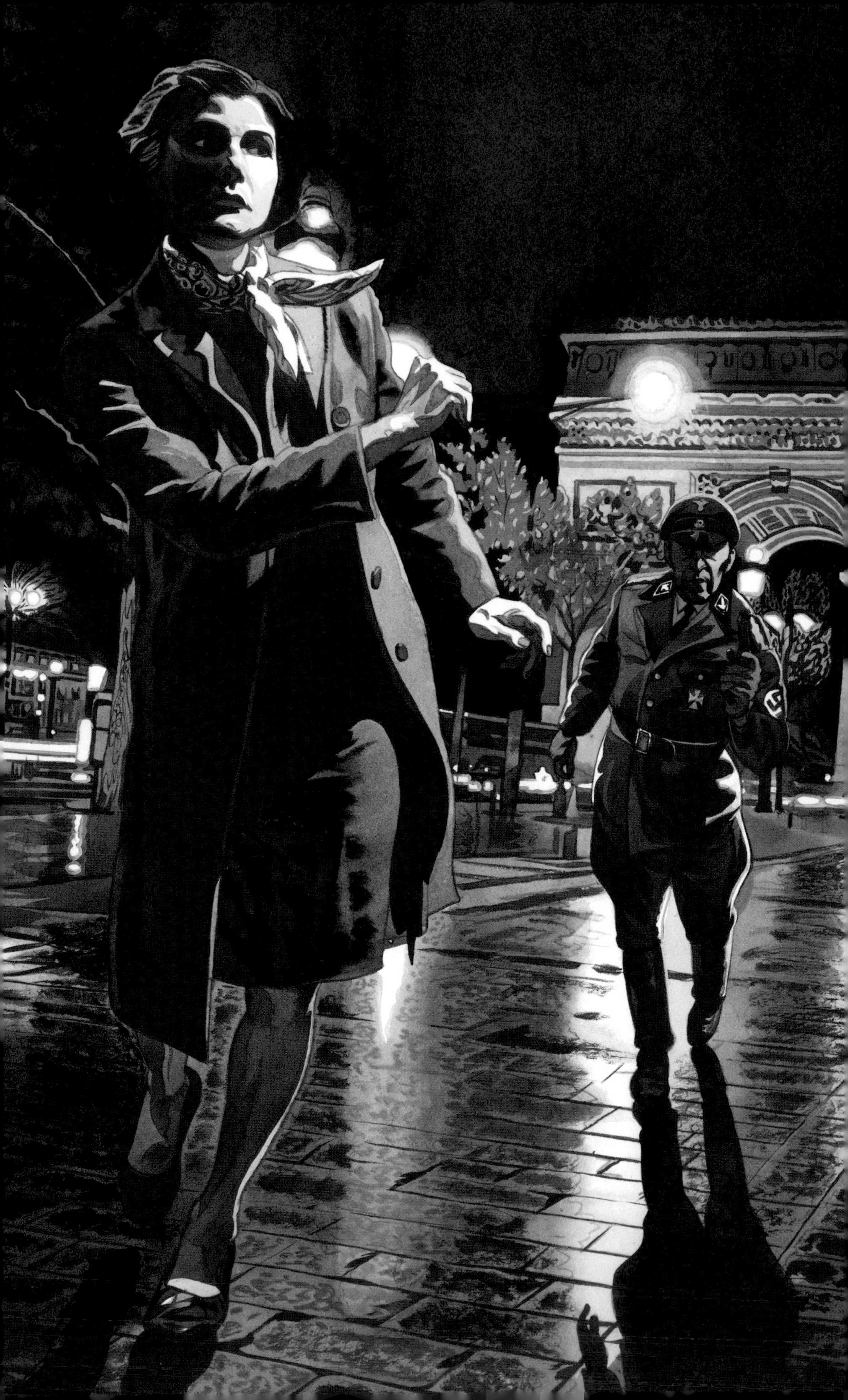

scrub-covered hills with no visibility. But the end finally came. A little after 8 p.m. on March 18, 1943, Joachim Ronneberg, Kasper Idland, Hans Storhaug, Fredrik Kayser and Birger Stromsheim stood on neutral Swedish soil. Against all odds, 18 days and 250 miles after they had set out from the Hardangervidda, they were free. The trolls of Norway had saved them.

And yet they could not fully celebrate. Their joy was tempered by the fact that they did not know the fate of the rest of their comrades. For all that they knew, they were in the hands of the Gestapo.

## September 1943<br>98 Rue de la Faisanderie<br>Paris

Noor had dyed her hair so many times it had become stiff. One old friend who saw Noor on the street was alarmed to see her with a bright red coif, which combined with her olive complexion gave her a look found nowhere in nature.

"Noor," her brother Vilayat once said, "is a deer." Now the deer was being hunted by a pack of bloodhounds.

The Germans knew her code name, Madeleine. Their direction-finding units were working 24 hours a day, trying to locate her places of transmission. Plainclothes police were everywhere. She refused to wear a waterproof cape because it would slow her down if she had to sprint. Once she actually had to run away from a Gestapo man when he began to follow her.

**Noor's foot speed saved her when a Gestapo man began following her.**

It was too dangerous to stay in any one place, so she was constantly moving, meeting contacts and transmitting. She took the extremely risky step of returning to her old neighborhood in Suresnes, where everyone knew her, and convinced an old family friend to let her transmit from her house, which was just up the hill from the Fazal Manzil. Noor sent messages from at least five different places, taking Métro trips from literally one end of Paris to the other. She trekked from Bondy in the east to Neuilly in the west, 29 stops each way with a change at Bastille, always lugging around her 30-pound transmitter.

On one trip, Noor observed two German soldiers looking at her, and at her suitcase. They began conferring, still looking at her. She was terrified. There was no way to get off the train until the next station.

The soldiers walked up to her. One of them asked her, "What do you have in that case, Mademoiselle?"

"A cinematographic apparatus," she replied.

After a pause, the still-suspicious soldier asked, "May I see it?"

"Certainly," Noor replied. She opened the lid and raised it partway. Some of the machine was still in shadow.

The two soldiers peered at the machine. Noor realized they did not recognize it. She said in an impatient voice, "Well, you can see what it is. You can see all the little bulbs."

The soldiers continued to stare at the machine. Finally one said, "Excuse me, Mademoiselle. I thought it might have been something else." They walked off.

Her places of refuge were disappearing. The Germans intercepted a phone call that alerted them to her address on the Boulevard Richard-Wallace. They stormed the apartment, but Noor had smelled danger, paid the rent and left. She soon found a new apartment on the Rue de la Faisanderie, half a mile away from the dread SD headquarters on the Avenue Foch. From the street in front of her building, the roof of the building was faintly visible to the north.

The trap was closing on her. Noor was exhausted, at the end of her rope. But she kept transmitting.

Noor arranged supply drops. She helped other agents in the field, arranging for them to get identity cards and other papers. She kept London informed about the circuits around Paris. Under extreme duress, Poste Madeleine sent more than 20 messages to London from July to October.

The sending key was her weapon, and she would fire it until the end.

# November 5, 1943
# Montbéliard, France

After Ree returned to the Jura, he was made head of a circuit renamed Stockbroker. It was an ironic name for a *réseau* led by a leftist, he thought.

Ree continued his work in the field. But the Gestapo was closing in. They had already inflicted heavy damage on the local resistance, and on October 20 they struck their most devastating blow yet. Ree reported to SOE that "Gestapo made descent in the night, arresting 160 people in the Belfort Montbéliard area, and all but decapitating French organizations. They had names of all chefs de groupe." His close friend Roger Fouillette, the local resistance leader, was taken away. Ree himself was a target, and they knew his code name: The Germans told a man with whom Ree had stayed, "You sheltered a certain Monsieur Henri."

The mass arrests had severely demoralized the fighters in the region. To restore their fighting spirit, Ree and the resistance men who were left decided they needed to "make bangs and fires everywhere as soon as possible."

Like countless such decisions made by SOE agents and resistance fighters during the war, it was an act of great and unnoticed courage. Ree and his men had no officers ordering them to charge, no battalions of troops at their side. They made the decision—and suffered the consequences—alone.

The target would be the big one: the Peugeot plant.

The attack was scheduled for November 3. Ree had assembled a team of six men who worked in the factory, including Andre van der Straaten, who had become Ree's lieutenant and who had tried to lure the traitor Martin to his doom. They made their way to the transformer house, their pockets crammed with explosives and guns. One of them had forgotten to get the key, and they sent someone to get it.

While they waited, the others started playing a game of soccer with the German guards. In the middle of the game, a clam bomb dropped out of Andre's pocket onto the ground. One of the German guards pointed it out, saying, "You've dropped something, I think, sir." Andre put it back

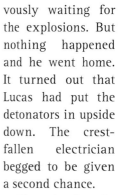

The Peugeot plant after the RAF **bombed** it. Despite appearances, it was largely undamaged.

in his pocket, mumbling something about electric fuses, and continued the game.

While his men were placing their charges, Ree himself was riding around the outside of the factory on a bicycle, nervously waiting for the explosions. But nothing happened and he went home. It turned out that Lucas had put the detonators in upside down. The crestfallen electrician begged to be given a second chance.

They struck again two days later, on November 5—Guy Fawkes Day in Britain. The anniversary of history's most famous failed explosion did not prove an ill omen. This time Lucas put in the detonators correctly and slipped out.

The timed detonators went off and a series of explosions rocked the factory. When the Germans rushed in, they saw that a huge hole had been blown in the side of the crucial turbo compressor and its precision-engineered blades twisted beyond repair. High-voltage engines were destroyed and other key machines and tools smashed. The plant would not be operational again for five months, and continuing sabotage of the factory by Ree's men ensured that it never again reached any more than a fraction of its operating capacity. It was one of the great industrial sabotage coups of the war.

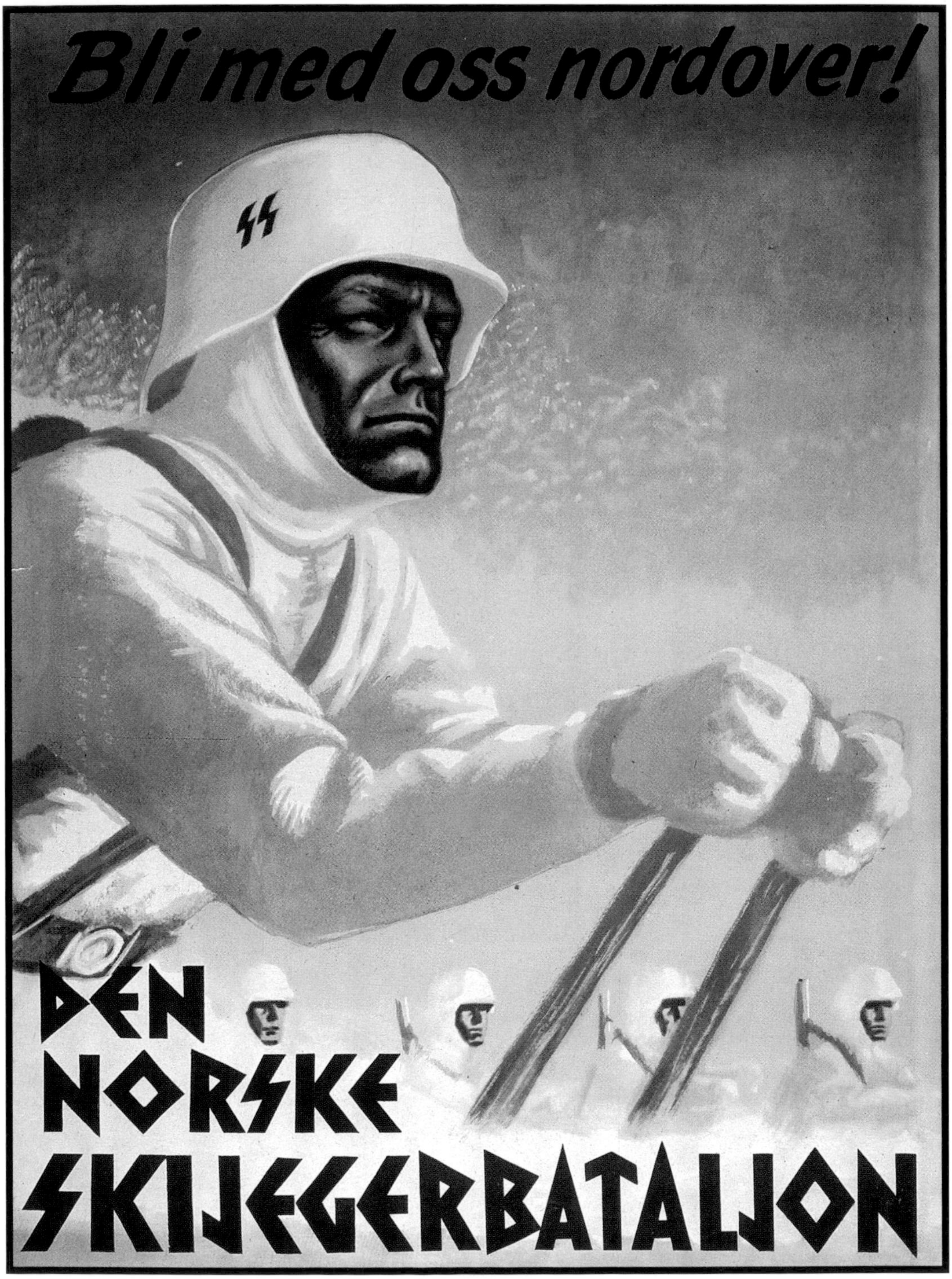
Bli med oss nordover!
DEN NORSKE SKIJEGERBATALJON

The Germans recruited Norwegians for their "Ski-hunter" batallion.

The enraged Germans dispatched an SS regiment to the scene but never found the perpetrators. Andre van der Straaten escaped to Switzerland on a route prepared by Ree, made it to Britain, was trained by SOE and parachuted back into his native France after D-Day.

Ree himself lay low for a while after the attack. In the report he mailed to London, he said he was "very tired." But he was still thinking about his friends in the Jura. At the bottom of the page, he scrawled and underlined the words, "Do your best to keep RAF away!!"

One British agent and a small group of courageous Frenchmen had done what repeated raids by squadrons of heavy bombers had not and might never have achieved. Harry Ree never fired a shot. But every Panther tank that was missing from the Panzer divisions racing to Normandy, every Messerschmitt that never shot down an Allied plane, could be chalked up in part to the bookish schoolteacher from Manchester.

## Morning
## October 13, 1943
## 98 Rue de la Faisanderie
## Paris

The spider's web the Germans had spun for Noor and her fellow agents went much further than London realized. The Germans had been successfully playing back the radio sets belonging to the two Canadians and Gilbert Norman. Despite unmistakable evidence that the agents had been captured, including omitted security checks and different "fists," or Morse sending styles, F Section head Buckmaster—who an SOE officer claimed "never wanted to believe anyone was captured"—insisted on sending agents to meetings that were in fact arranged by the Gestapo.

Sometime in late September, Buckmaster ordered Noor to go to the basement of the Café Colisée on the Champs-Élysées and meet with the two Canadian agents, Ken Macalister and Frank Pickersgill, who unbeknownst to London had been captured soon after their arrival. Buckmaster saw this meeting as a crucial first step in rebuilding the Prosper circuit. Noor dutifully complied—and sat down with two German agents. The Germans, hoping to reel in all her contacts, did not attempt to arrest her at the time. They tailed her after she left the meeting, but Noor managed to shake them off.

The strain of knowing how close she was to doom pushed Noor to the edge. At the house of an old family friend, she broke down. Covering her face with her hands, she sobbed, "I wish I were with my mother."

Finally, even Buckmaster had had enough. He ordered Noor to leave. But she refused to go until a replacement was found for her. It was only after he assured her he had found another wireless operator that she agreed to fly back to London. She was scheduled to depart by Lysander on October 14.

Around this time, the SD's top counter-intelligence officer, *Sturmbahnführer* Josef Kieffer, received a telephone call from an anonymous Frenchwoman. The woman, who gave her name only as Renée, told him she had an important proposition to make.

The woman was Émile Garry's sister, Renée. She betrayed Noor out of jealousy: she was in love with France Anthelme, and was convinced Noor had stolen his affections.

Renée Garry came to SD headquarters on the Avenue Foch. The German officer who met her described her as about "30 years old with dark hair and fairly corpulent." Ushered into Kieffer's office, Garry told him that she needed money and would deliver Madeleine to him for a price. Garry gave an accurate description of Madeleine and the address of her apartment on the Rue de la Faisanderie. Kieffer agreed to pay her 100,000 francs and dispatched some officers to put Noor's house under surveillance.

Mademoiselle Garry was not only a Judas but an incompetent one. The going rate for betraying a British agent was a million francs.

The morning of October 13, Noor came out of her apartment and went into the baker's, which was in the same building. When she left the bakery, two German officers who were shadowing the building recognized her and started trailing her. But she turned around, realized she was being followed and quickly vanished around a corner. The two agents searched the area for her for hours, but could not find her. Kieffer sent one of his subordinates, Ernst Vogt, and a French "V-man" (traitor; from the German word for "trusted man," *Vertrauensmann*) named Pierre Cartaud, to the Rue de la Faisanderie. Using a key provided by Renée Garry, Vogt let Cartaud into Noor's apartment.

Noor was taken to **Gestapo** headquarters at 84 Avenue Foch.

Sometime later that day, Noor made the grave mistake of returning to her apartment. When she opened the door, Cartaud jumped out from behind it and seized her hands. Noor fought back ferociously, biting his wrists. Bleeding badly, Cartaud was forced to release her. He tried to handcuff her, but she continued fighting so fiercely he was unable to. Finally he drew his gun, told her he'd shoot if she moved and telephoned Kieffer.

When Vogt and several other SD men arrived, they found Cartaud with his gun drawn in a corner of the room while Noor, sitting bolt upright on the couch, clawed at the air in helpless fury. She looked, Vogt thought, exactly like a tigress.

When the men from Avenue Foch entered the room, Noor hurled a torrent of abuse at them, calling them *sales Boches* ("dirty Germans"). "This would happen at the last moment!" she wailed in anguish. "Another few days and I should have been in England!"

Noor finally stopped fighting after Vogt told her that if she did not go quietly, he would be forced to arrest the friend in whose apartment she was staying. They escorted her out and put her in a car. A few minutes later, she was taken up the stairs of 84 Avenue Foch.

## Night
## March 25, 1943
## Vrajoen Lake
## Hardangervidda
## Norway

Claus Helberg realized he had made a terrible mistake as soon as he opened the door of the old Jansbu hut. The place was trashed. The table and chairs had been thrown aside, mattresses cut open, cupboards ransacked. The Germans had been here.

He could hardly believe it. In all the months he had been on the Hardangervidda, he had never even seen the enemy. The great white plateau had been an invincible barrier, a loyal friend that he had believed would always protect him. No more.

> **Helberg could not outshoot the Germans. His only hope was to outski them.**

Fearing the Germans were still in the vicinity, he dashed outside. When he looked to the mountains to the east, his fears were confirmed. A group of German soldiers were skiing hard toward him. They were less than half a mile away and spreading out, trying to surround him.

After the raid, Helberg had hid out in Oslo for a while, but then returned to the Hardangervidda to collect a cache of arms. A resistance contact had erroneously told him the Telemark area was safe. He had stopped off at the old hut to get something to eat and have a rest.

Helberg always wriggled out of trouble, but he had never found himself in a fix like this. He knew he could never shoot it out with the Germans—all he had was a Colt .32. His only hope was to outski them.

Helberg put on his skis and pushed off. Looking up, he saw that his pursuers had not managed to surround him yet. There was a gap between two of the men he thought he could get through. He headed toward it as fast as he could, into the sun, making himself a harder target.

Helberg was not frightened until the first shots rang out. As the bullets whizzed past him, he thought, "This is the end for me." At least he and his friends had accomplished their mission, he told himself.

But the Germans, shooting into the sun, missed again and again, and in a few seconds the shooting stopped. He glanced back. They had decided to try to run him down.

They were in the mountains of Telemark, where competitive skiing was born, where

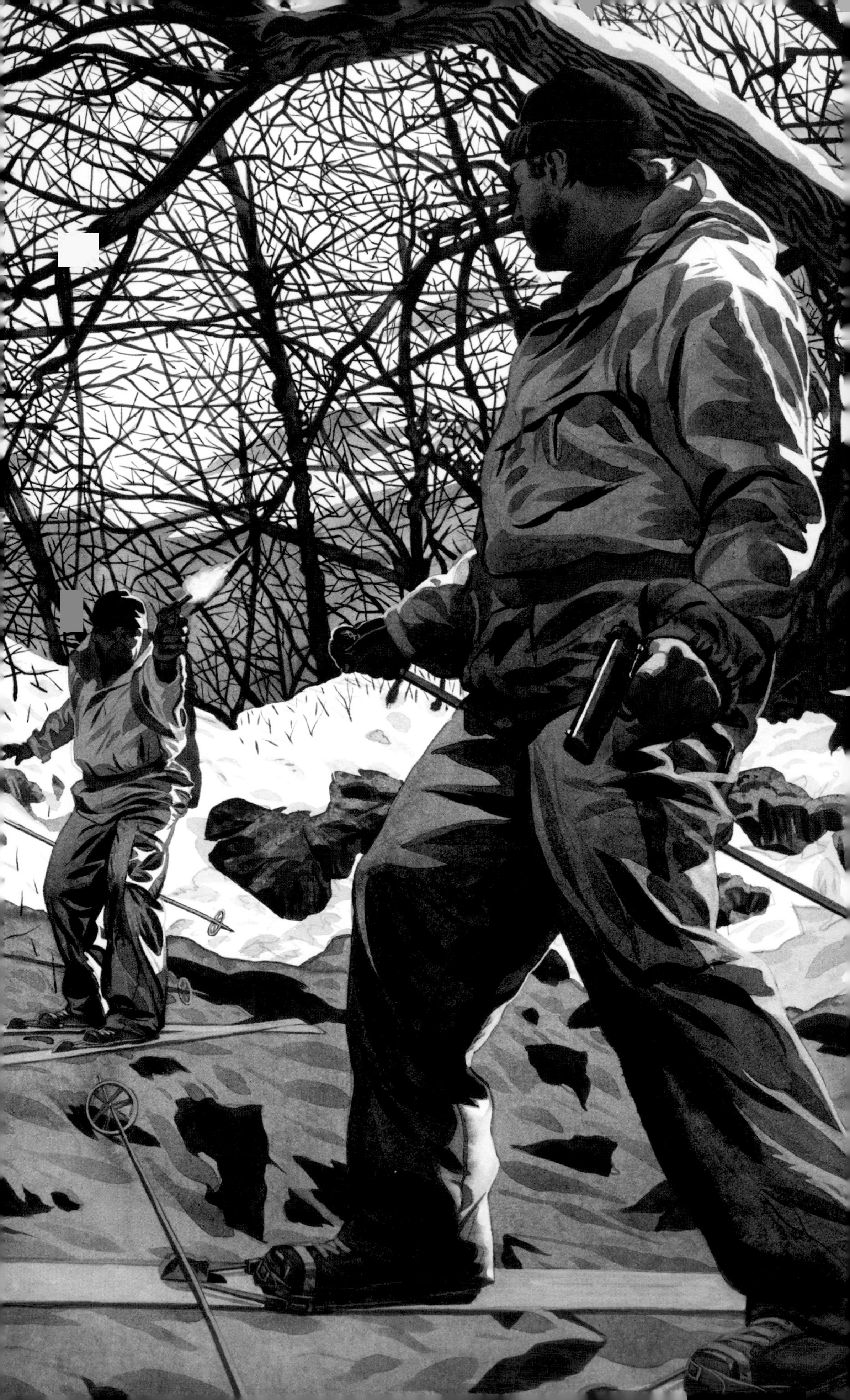

Helberg had won medals as a Nordic racer. But this race would be for his life.

The Norwegian drove ahead, using his flexible bamboo poles to propel himself forward, his powerful thighs and shoulders moving in the swinging, fluid rhythm that was as familiar to him as breathing. Past hillocks and huge rocks, frozen waterfalls and scrub brush he glided, knowing that if he made a mistake and fell, the enemy would be upon him. He wondered if he would have time to take his cyanide pill.

After an hour, several of the Germans began to fall behind. One by one, they slowed down and finally abandoned the chase. But two men were still coming doggedly after him.

The chase went on, three specks moving across the vast white desert, the only sound the harsh rasping of Helberg's breath and the shushing of his skis. Three miles, five miles, eight miles, and still they came after him. Finally, after they had done ten agonizing miles, one of the two remaining Germans dropped out.

But the last German kept coming. And he did not appear to be tiring at all.

Helberg was 24 years old and in superb condition. But he had already skied 30 miles before the chase began. The German was fresher, and Helberg could tell he was a top-notch skier. There was nothing to do but push himself until he got away or the German killed him.

The race went on and on for an hour, maybe two hours—Helberg lost track of time. The distance between the two men never varied by more than 30 or 40 yards.

As the young Norwegian labored up a hill, he realized that every time he climbed, he gained ground on the German, and every time he went downhill, he lost ground. He quickly altered course to head for the nearest hill. He climbed it, then set course for another. But after he reached the top, he saw that there were no more ridges. There was nothing but downhill ahead.

Desperately, Helberg skied downhill as fast as he could, using every trick he knew to outdistance his implacable adversary. But after 15 minutes, he began to hear the dread sound of the German's skis and poles. Then his pursuer yelled out, "Hands up!"

Helberg turned to face the man, his Colt in his hand. They were about 40 yards apart. The German, holding a Luger, stiffened when he saw the gun.

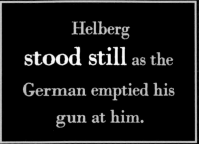

**Helberg stood still as the German emptied his gun at him.**

Helberg fired once—and missed. He realized that whoever emptied his magazine first would lose. He knew how difficult it was to shoot accurately in the mountains, with rays of light distorting objects and exhausted muscles and sweat-filled eyes making it difficult to aim. Even with a rifle it was not easy. So he stood there, offering himself as a target at 40 yards range. It was the ultimate biathlon event: the silver medalist would die.

The German fired back at Helberg and missed. Then he took careful aim and fired again. The bullet whizzed next to Helberg's ear. He fired again and missed again.

As he stood waiting for the next shot, Helberg suddenly wondered if he should move an inch or two to the side. Before he could decide, the next bullet sped past his arm. If he had moved that way two inches it would have hit him.

The German fired his fifth shot and missed. Helberg was shaking with fear

# Shadow Knights

and tension as he waited for the final shot. Crack! The bullet zipped past him and ricocheted off a rock.

Now the tables were turned. The German had an empty gun. Helberg had five rounds. And the chase would now be uphill, not down.

Realizing the desperate plight he was in, the German began skiing uphill as hard as he could. Helberg knew that if his enemy could make it to the top, he'd be unable to catch him, since the German was faster going downhill. And the Norwegian did not dare chase him back in the direction of the other Germans.

King Haakon to all Norwegians:

"Fight as proudly and resolutely in the new year as you have in the old."

Helberg hesitated for a moment. Then he set off after the man at top speed.

The German was climbing the hill fast, but Helberg began gaining on him. He fought off the impulse to fire. After the nerve-racking ordeal he had just been through, he wasn't sure if he could concentrate well enough to hit him yet. And the German's frantic movements gave Helberg confidence that he could gain more ground.

Just before his adversary reached the top of the hill, 30 yards ahead of him, Helberg stopped. He aimed at the center of the man's back and fired several times. The man staggered and then stopped, leaning down over his ski sticks.

Helberg did not wait to see any more. The other Germans could appear at any moment. He turned around and skied away.

As he pushed himself on through the moonless night, Helberg fought off exhaustion. He knew he had to cover his tracks. The other Germans would be able to follow him easily. Helberg headed for a nearby lake, Vrajoen, where he could ski on ice that would leave no tracks.

As he skied along next to a ravine near the lake, Helberg realized that his memory of the duel with the German, in which it seemed to go on for a long time, had been delusional. The German had actually fired all his shots within the span of five or six seconds.

Helberg was skiing along on autopilot, thinking about this strange phenomenon, when he found himself flying off a cliff.

He was in the air a long time before he smashed into a snow-covered hill below. He slid and rolled down, finally coming to a stop in a snowbank. He lay in the snow in shock, too exhausted to get up. A throbbing pain announced itself in the vicinity of his left shoulder and arm. When he tried to move his arm, a sharp pain stabbed him and the limb didn't react right. He looked at his arm. It was visibly broken. He had fallen 120 feet.

**Evening
November 9, 1943
Café du Belfort, Hôtel Terrace
Besançon, France**

Harry Ree's comrade Claude was itching to kill Pierre Martin. On Ree's instructions, the young bank clerk had put together a three-man team to shadow the traitor. They had been following him for more than a month. But Martin was too cautious to ever appear in public without a bodyguard, and his house was patrolled by armed men with dogs.

One of the things Ree had liked about Martin was his enjoyment of fine food and wine. He was also something of a womanizer. Claude and Ree were hoping that Martin's appetite for the good life would make him careless.

On the evening of November 9, one of Claude's team reported that Martin had left his house alone and was driving into Besançon, presumably on a date. Claude, who had been resting after his shift tailing Martin, began whistling merrily when he heard the news. "We'll find him at any one of the expensive joints in town," he said. "It's just a question of whether we can get to the right one in time." They began making the rounds.

> Claude was **itching** to kill Pierre Martin.

Claude and a comrade found Martin at the Hôtel Terrace. They sat down and ordered some food, watching him the entire time. At around 7:50 p.m., Martin finished his meal and got up to leave. At that moment, they pulled out their revolvers, walked up to him, and opened fire at point-blank range. Bullets ripped into the traitor's head, chest and abdomen and he collapsed to the floor, bleeding heavily. In the confusion that followed, they slipped out into the street and ran away. Martin died 20 minutes later.

Claude made it safely away and sent a letter by courier to Ree, who was temporarily hiding in Switzerland. "Don't forget to bring a few presents and some chocolate," the elated Claude wrote Ree. "That's really why I am writing you this letter! Your pal until death, Claude."

Ree never saw Claude again. The light-hearted bank clerk went to ground for a while, then returned to the field, carrying out sabotage attacks and working with the *maquis*. In late January or early February 1944, Claude was sitting in the Café Grangier in Sochaux when a squad of SS men burst

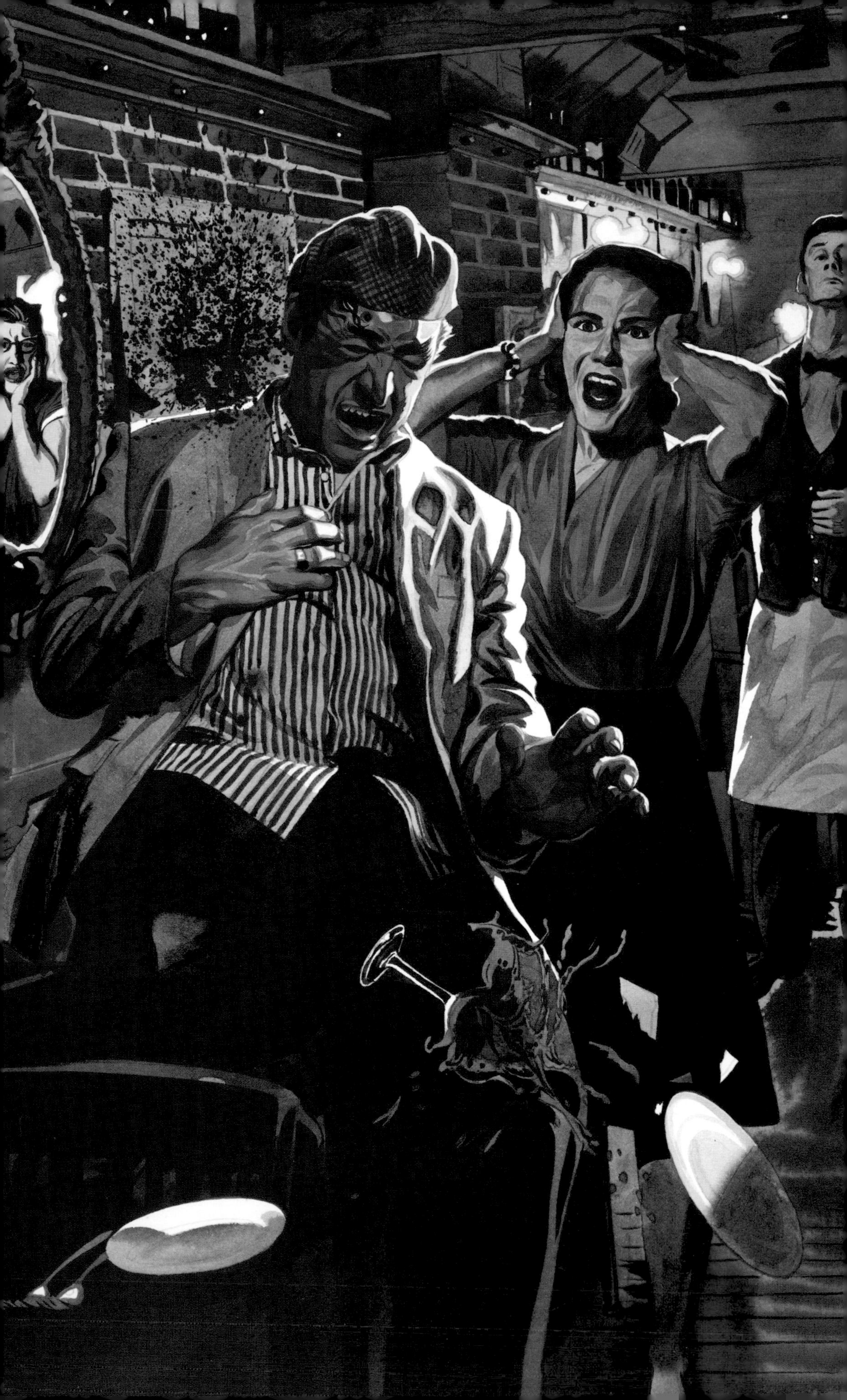

in and surrounded him. He pulled out his gun and opened fire, killing one SS man and wounding two, until he was cut down in a hail of bullets. He was 29 years old.

For the rest of his life, Ree remembered something Claude once said to him. It was a hot summer day, they had been bicycling for 25 miles, and they were famished. They stopped for lunch at a village wine merchant's house. The merchant laid out a sumptuous feast, which in true French fashion they lingered over all afternoon. Finally, at about five o'clock, over liqueurs and coffee, Claude pushed back his chair, looked at his friend and quoted the famous last line of *Les Croix de Bois,* a French novel about World War I.

"You know," Claude said, "after the war we'll say, 'They were good times after all.'"

## Shortly after midnight November 25, 1943 84 Avenue Foch Paris

The Germans escorted Noor up to the fifth floor of 84 Avenue Foch. Before her interrogator, Ernst Vogt, had a chance to ask her a single question, Noor said to him, "You know who I am, and what I am doing. You have my radio set. I will tell you nothing. I have only one thing to ask you. Have me shot as soon as possible!"

**Bullets fired at point-blank range ripped into Martin's head, chest and abdomen.**

Vogt assured her that he would not have her shot. Then he began asking her questions. Noor refused to answer. She did not speak a word. After an hour, he gave up and decided to send her to her cell. She asked if she could take a bath. Suspicious, Vogt agreed, but her guards left the bathroom door ajar. Noor furiously insisted that they close it so she could undress. Vogt agreed and the door was closed. But he went to another bathroom from which he could see her window.

The door to her bathroom was no sooner closed than Noor climbed out the bathroom window and began nimbly walking along a narrow gutter. She was making for a triangular roof over the room Vogt was in, the only place from which she could climb onto the roof and escape.

Vogt looked out the window and was shocked to see Noor coming toward him. Afraid that if he yelled at her she would

YOUR TALK
MAY KILL YOUR COMRADES

**Servicemen were constantly warned not to blab.**

least cooperative prisoner he had ever encountered.

One of Noor's fellow prisoners on the fifth floor was none other than John Starr, "Bob," the agent who had worked with Harry Ree before being betrayed by Pierre Martin. Starr had become a sort of jail trusty, who was given special privileges by his captors because they valued his skill as an artist. Starr saw Noor taken into Vogt's office the day she was arrested. He heard the Germans speaking of her ferocious spirit with admiration. He learned a few other details about her, including the fact that she had asked for large quantities of writing paper.

Starr saw Noor when she came into the guard room, where he had a worktable set up to do illustrations for the Germans. He was able to exchange a few friendly words with her, but never in private. She always appeared calm when he saw her in the day, but at night he could often hear her crying in her bed. Once she sobbed through the entire night.

One day Starr managed to smuggle a note into her cell, reading, "Cheer up. You're not alone. Perhaps we shall find a way to get out of here." Noor answered that she was happy to get his note and that she had already made contact with the prisoner in the next cell, a Frenchman named Colonel Faye. Faye and Noor exchanged messages by tapping in Morse code.

The three prisoners began to plan an escape. Their cells were simply converted rooms and they all had the same weak point: skylights secured with iron bars. The bars in Starr's room were attached to a wooden frame and could be easily unscrewed. The bars in the other rooms were attached to the wall and would be more difficult to remove, but it was still possible.

fall to certain death, he waited until she was almost directly in front of him, then said quietly, "Madeleine, don't be silly. You will kill yourself. Think of your mother! Give me your hand."

Noor froze, hesitated, then took his outstretched hand. He pulled her back in through the window.

Back in her cell, sitting on her small folding bed, Noor began to weep bitterly. "I am a coward!" she cried. "I ought to have let myself fall." She was inconsolable. "I don't know what I took your hand for," she wept. "It was just because you held it out."

For five weeks, Vogt tried to get Noor to talk, but nothing worked. She was the

# Shadow Knights

They began to work late at night, using a purloined screwdriver and filling the holes around the bars with face powder Noor asked her captors for. The laborious process went on night after night. Noor's bars took the longest to loosen, but finally she messaged them that she was ready. They decided to go at midnight, after the guard turned off the lights.

At the appointed time, Starr climbed onto the chair, removed the bars and climbed into the skylight. Faye was already on the roof and helped him up. But Noor was not there.

"Where's Madeleine?" asked Starr. Faye didn't know. They made their way to the skylight of her cell. Below, to their dismay, they saw her still working away on the bar. Afraid that it would fall out and she would be unable to replace it, she had not loosened it enough. Faye leaned down to help her and they began desperately trying to free the bar. It seemed to take forever.

Finally Faye freed the bar, took it out and pulled Noor onto the roof. They had made it. In his excitement, Faye hugged her and gave her a kiss. They picked up blankets they had brought to use as ropes, hung their shoes around their necks and moved quickly across the roof.

The roofs of most of the buildings around theirs were inaccessible. But on the far side of the courtyard there were some flat-roofed buildings from which they could descend to the street. To get there, they had to walk along a narrow strip of roofing that sloped downward, five stories above the ground. They managed to negotiate it. Now they had to get down to the roof below. Calculating the drop, they tore up some blankets,

The improvised rope held. Faye could not restrain his joy. "We're free!" he exulted. "We're away!"

knotted them together and slid down one at a time. The improvised rope held. Faye could not restrain his joy. "We're free!" he exulted. "We're away!"

At that moment, an air-raid siren began to shriek.

It was the worst possible thing that could have happened. During every air raid, the guards immediately searched their cells. They had to get off the roof and away before the Germans had time to throw a cordon around the neighborhood.

Antiaircraft fire erupted from German positions in the Bois de Boulogne and searchlights swept the sky, looking for the Allied planes. Then, to their horror, more searchlights began sweeping the roofs from a lower-floor window in the Avenue Foch. They fell flat, hoping they would not be seen. The torches stopped sweeping after a few moments and they jumped up and ran to the edge of the roof.

The only place they could land was a narrow ledge one story down, below a window. They feverishly tore up more blankets to make another rope and lowered themselves down. Faye went first. He reached the ledge, broke the window with his elbow and let the others in.

They were standing in pitch darkness on a landing. They expected the inhabitants of the house to come out, but no one stirred. They quietly slipped downstairs and gingerly opened the front door.

Their hearts sank. The street was a cul-de-sac, and SS guards were marching back and forth at the open end.

They quickly conferred. Faye wanted to make a break for it. They agreed and moved toward the opening, keeping in the

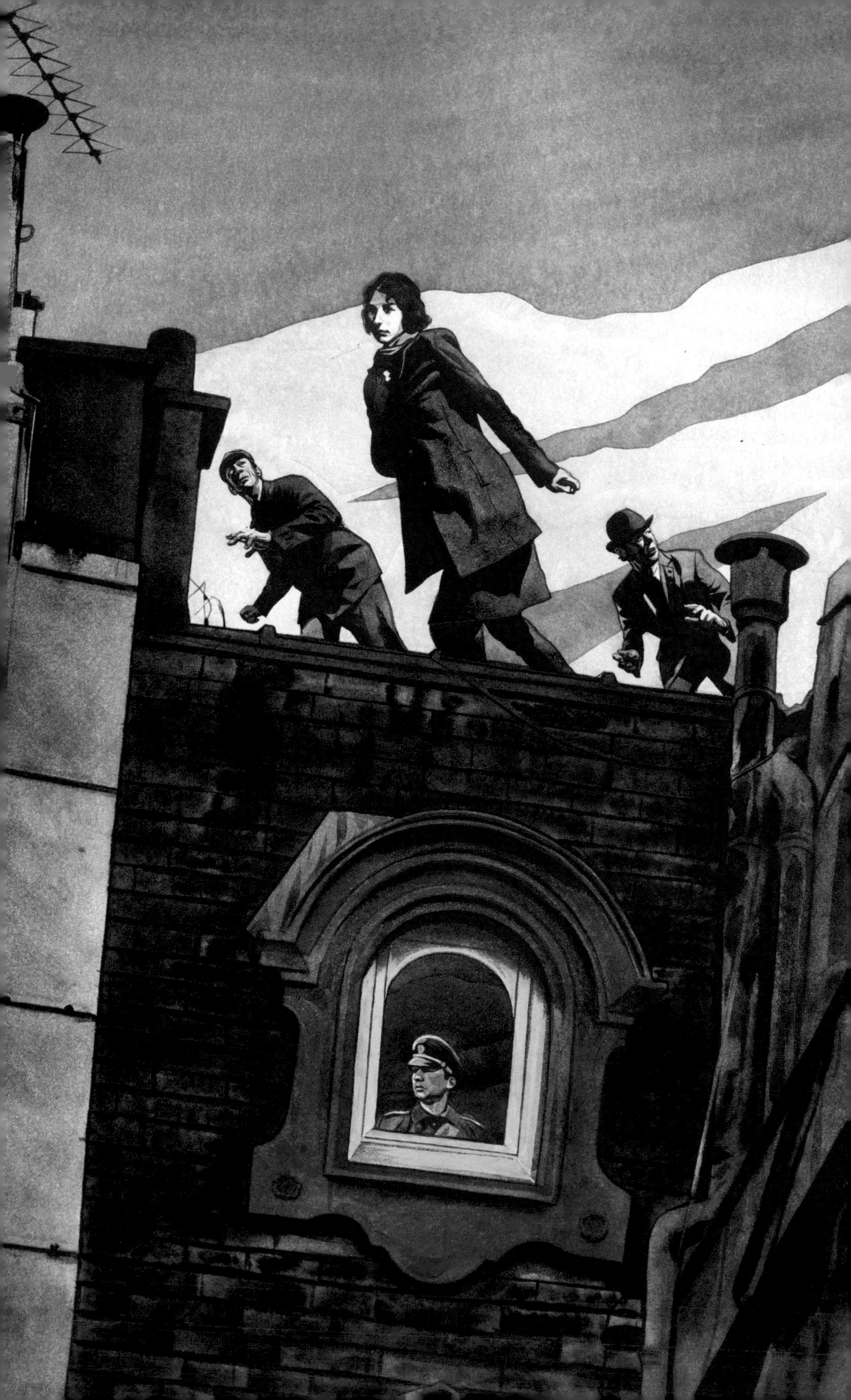

shadow of the wall. When they reached the corner, Faye started sprinting. There was a burst of automatic weapons fire and Faye was seized by SS men and hauled away.

Noor looked at Starr, not sure what to do. He pulled at her sleeve and said, "Come back." They went back into the house and walked aimlessly up the stairs to the first floor. They pushed open a door and found themselves in a living room. They felt their way in the dark, sat down on a couch and began talking. Asked after the war what they talked about, Starr did not remember.

> **As Noor and the others ran across the roof, an air-raid siren began to shriek. It was the worst thing that could have happened.**

A woman's voice suddenly said, "What's going on? Are you thieves?" Starr and Noor turned to look at the woman, who was leaning over a banister. Noor said to her, "We're not thieves! We're escaped prisoners!" She was weeping.

Heavy boots pounded outside. A troop of SS men burst into the house, raced up the stairs, switched on the lights and seized Starr and Noor. As they marched them back to captivity they began beating and kicking their prisoners.

When they arrived at the Avenue Foch, *Sturmbahnführer* Kieffer was in a towering rage. "You're all three going to be shot!" he screamed. He ordered SS men to stand the three agents against a wall. Faye cried out, "I have only done my duty!" A guard hit him in the mouth.

Kieffer was clearly trying to decide whether to have them executed then and there. As he stared at them, a guard showed him a photograph found in Starr's pocket. It was a photograph of Kieffer himself, which he had given Starr to use to paint a portrait of him. "What were you taking my photograph away for?" Kieffer asked Starr. "A little souvenir," replied Starr. A tiny twitch of a smile appeared for a moment on Kieffer's grim face, then vanished.

Kieffer made up his mind not to shoot them. He told the guards to take them upstairs.

Later that night, Kieffer came to visit Noor in her cell. He asked her to give her word of honor that she would not attempt to escape again. If she signed a "parole," a declaration to that effect, he promised her that she would be kept at the Avenue Foch under the same conditions. If she refused, he told her, he would be forced to resort to the harshest measures. Noor refused to sign.

Kieffer sent an immediate telegram to Berlin informing them that Madeleine was incorrigible and he lacked the facilities to detain her. He requested that she be transferred to prison in Germany.

Berlin sent a return telegram approving Noor's transfer. That very day, Noor and Faye, who had also refused to sign the parole, were put on a train to Germany. Noor was the first female agent to be sent there.

Noor was classified as a "Night and Fog" prisoner. According to an order issued in late 1941, captured resisters and spies fell into the *Nacht und Nebel* category, which meant their return, in the bland language of the Nazi bureaucracy, was "not required." They were to vanish without a trace, as if they had disappeared into night and fog.

On the wall of her room, the guards found that Noor had drawn a *V* and the bull's-eye device of the RAF. They also looked through the sheets of paper on her desk. They were covered with little poems and stories about animals and children.

# March 28, 1943
# Road to Grini concentration camp
# Near Lier, Norway

Claus Helberg's shoulder and arm throbbed with pain, but his legs were working and his skis were unbroken. Using one arm, he skied in the direction of a farm where he knew a friendly family. But when he got there, his hosts warned him that 50 Gestapo and Hird men had commandeered a neighboring farmhouse. Helberg devoured some food, shoved more in his pockets and skied on toward the town of Rauland. When he arrived, he discovered that the town was swarming with German troops and Gestapo men, all searching for the "terrorists" who had destroyed the heavy-water plant. He found a shopkeeper he knew and collapsed on the kitchen floor. He had been on his skis for 36 hours and had covered 112 miles.

When Helberg woke up the next day, he decided his only hope was to brazen it out. He went up to a group of German troops, found one who spoke Norwegian, showed his London-made identity card, and introduced himself as a local man who had injured himself in the mountains searching for the terrorists. The sympathetic Germans not only bought his story, they ordered two soldiers to take him to a field doctor, who dressed his injury and arranged for him to be taken by ambulance to the town of Dalen. Helberg hid his revolver in his jacket pocket while the doctor was treating him.

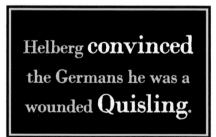

> **Helberg convinced the Germans he was a wounded Quisling.**

When the ambulance dropped him off in Dalen, Helberg headed for the town's hotel. He desperately needed more food and rest. He was no sooner ensconced in a comfortable room than he heard loud voices and the sound of boots. To his dismay, he realized that the hated *Reichskommissar* (military governor) of Norway, Josef Terboven, and his entourage had arrived to command the search for the saboteurs and were requisitioning rooms. There was no way to escape: every exit was guarded. Helberg's identity papers passed inspection again, and he went down to the dining room, where he ate a heavenly meal of fried trout,

potatoes, carrots, local cheese and wild strawberries.

As Helberg was drinking his coffee, Terboven and his party came into the room and sat down at two tables by the fire. As wine was served, Terboven's lascivious eye fell upon a beautiful Norwegian girl at a nearby table, and he ordered her to join them. She refused, coldly complying only when the order was repeated. She turned out to speak perfect German, which delighted Terboven until she proudly informed him that her father was a colonel in the Royal Norwegian Army who had escaped to England. His lust undeterred, Terboven suggested that she go upstairs with him. When she laughed in his face, he was enraged and ordered her to leave.

Terboven's public sexual humiliation proved to have serious consequences. At 5 a.m. the next morning, the Norwegian guests in the hotel were summoned to the lobby. Because of their impertinent attitude toward *Reichskommissar* Terboven,

they were told, they were all under arrest. A bus would soon arrive to take them to Grini concentration camp for questioning and possible internment.

Helberg was not sure what to do. Should he repeat the same story he had told the Germans in Rauland? Or would that be too risky? He decided his best move would be to get on the bus and try to somehow escape on the way.

Helberg had hoped to take a seat at the front of the bus, near the door. But he was ordered to go to the back. He assessed the situation. It was bleak. An armed guard was sitting next to the front door, and three more armed guards on two motorcycles with sidecars were escorting the bus, one riding 15 yards ahead, one the same distance behind.

Helberg found himself sitting next to the same beautiful young woman who had rejected Terboven. He struck up a lively conversation with her, hoping to attract the attention of the guard by the door. Sure

Joseph Terboven reviews troops. He **blew** himself **up** at the end of the war.

enough, in a few minutes the guard made his way to the back of the bus and joined in the conversation, obviously smitten with the Norwegian beauty. Soon he suggested that he and Helberg switch seats.

Helberg was now by the door, which was controlled by a lever next to the driver. He had very little time; as soon as they got near Grini, the guard would resume his seat. But he needed to find the right spot. He stared out the window tensely. As the bus came to the top of a hill, the woods came close to the road. There was only a small field to get across. He stood up, reached across the astonished driver, pulled the lever and tumbled out into the road as the guard at the back of the bus began angrily shouting.

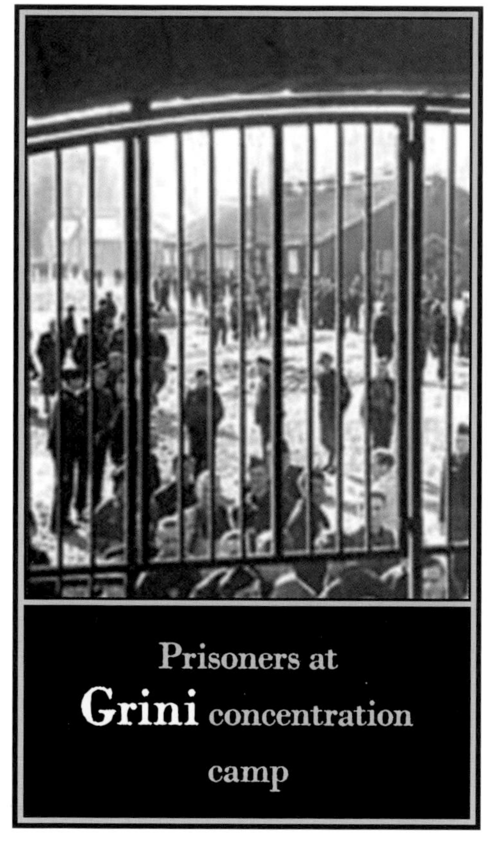

Prisoners at **Grini** concentration camp

As the bus shrieked to a stop, the guards riding in the rear motorcycle and sidecar braked, dismounted and were about to grab him when he took off sprinting toward the woods. Bullets thudded into the ground next to Helberg as he zigzagged toward the trees. He had just made it across the field when deafening explosions erupted around him: hand grenades. He hit the ground as shrapnel flew through the air. Helberg got up and kept running. He had just reached the deeper woods when he felt a grenade hit him right in the middle of his back. He hurled himself into the brush, waiting for the explosion that would tear him apart, but the grenade never went off and he ran deeper into the woods. The Germans fired a few more shots but then called off the search.

Fighting through exhaustion, hunger and the excruciating pain from his injured shoulder and arm, Helberg stumbled on through the woods. He knew that there was an insane asylum in the town of Lier where the staff would be friendly. At one in the morning, he knocked on the door. The staff, two men and two women, were having a party. They opened the door to behold a wild, gaunt figure, bleeding, with torn clothes and a swollen arm. The Norwegians took Helberg in without any questions, fed him and gave him clean clothes before sending him to a local hospital, where he stayed for 18 days.

The Germans never launched a manhunt for Helberg. The guards probably told their superiors they had killed him, to avoid being punished. After being discharged from the hospital, Helberg was driven by an escape organization to a location near the border. With borrowed skis, he crossed the hills into Sweden. On June 2, 1943, he boarded a plane to London, where he had a joyous reunion with Joachim Ronneberg and the others.

The irrepressible tomcat had used up every one of his nine lives. But he had survived.

## November 27, 1943
## Charmont, near Besançon
## France

Harry Ree's luck was running out. His fellow agents John Young and Diana Rowden had been arrested. On November 15, the Germans had swarmed in and seized them at the sawmill where they had been hiding. They were the latest victims of one of Berlin's radio games.

Ree should have immediately left for Switzerland. The Germans had circulated a "wanted" leaflet with his photograph on it. But he decided to stay a little longer to finish some work for the circuit, delegate authority and help his friends avoid being captured.

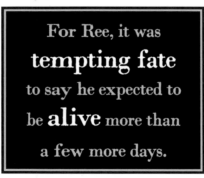

For Ree, it was **tempting fate** to say he expected to be **alive** more than a few more days.

A couple of weeks after the arrest, Ree rode his bike out to the home of the Barbiers, the family with whom he had lived for much of his six months in the Jura. He was keeping a promise.

When he first met Madame Barbier in May, Ree was a raw agent whose French was barely passable. They had talked all afternoon long—not about politics or war, but about their families. For Ree, it was wonderful to be able to forget his mission and talk about his wife and family with this plump, motherly Frenchwoman. At the end she asked Ree when his birthday was, and insisted that he must spend it with the Barbiers. "If I'm still alive," Ree replied. "Don't say things like that, it's unlucky," Mme Barbier said. "Just promise to come."

Ree promised he would try. He did not tell Mme Barbier that he thought it was tempting fate to say that he ever expected to live more than a few more days.

Ree was tied up on his birthday, so the celebration was postponed. But on November 27, although he was too worried to be in the mood to celebrate, he bicycled over for his birthday party. Monsieur Barbier brought out his best bottle of wine, the son scared up a turkey for which he had traded some bicycle tires, and they had a wonderful meal. After they finished their coffee, Ree bid them farewell. He had to visit a schoolteacher named Jean Hauger to whom he had given some explosives. Hauger had organized his students into a resistance group.

It started to rain, and it was an hour's ride against the wind before he arrived at the schoolteacher's house. He leaned his bike against the stone steps and rang the doorbell. It took a long time for anyone to answer and he peered into the dark hall, trying to see who was coming. Finally the door opened and a man wearing a green trilby hat appeared. Taking him for a friend of the family, Ree asked, "Is Jean at home?"

The man said, "Put up your hands." Ree noticed he was pointing a pistol at him.

Ree was irritated. Members of the resistance were always fooling around with guns, showing off in a juvenile way. "Don't be an ass," he said. "It's dangerous to play with firearms. Is Jean in?"

Maquis are instructed in the use of the **Sten gun.**

"Put up your hands," the man repeated.

Now really angry, Ree said, "Don't be a bloody fool! Put that thing away."

Keeping his gun trained on Ree, the man fumbled in his coat, pulled out a small book and showed it to Ree. Inside it was an identification card with the words

GEHEIME FELDPOLIZEI printed in large Gothic letters. German secret police.

Ree shot up his hands. "Oh, I'm so sorry," he said. "What's been happening here?"

"Step inside. Move it!" the man said sharply. "And keep your hands up."

Ree walked into the room. The man searched him. Ree was not worried about the search: he never carried a gun or any incriminating papers. After checking him, the Gestapo man relaxed and asked Ree to sit down. He asked Ree why he had come to see Jean. Ree said he had come to borrow a book. "But what's happened to Jean Hauger?" he asked.

"He was arrested this morning," the Gestapo man said. "He is a terrorist. We found arms concealed in the house."

"Good Lord!" Ree replied in apparent shock. "I had no idea Jean dealt in that sort of thing." He asked politely what the man planned to do with him. "You see, I'm a watchmaker and I'm meeting a customer in a café at four o'clock. Can I go now, please?"

"No, you can't," the Gestapo man said. "You'll wait with me here until five o'clock. Then you'll go along to the Gestapo office to have your identity card checked. If what you say is true, you'll be allowed to go. It's a mere formality."

Ree knew that once they checked his ID, he was done for. He had to get out before the other Gestapo men arrived in 45 minutes.

Ree decided to strike up a friendly conversation. Lighting his pipe, he asked the man what he thought of the war. The man said he couldn't stand it and wished he could go home. Ree agreed. The man asked whether Ree was a Gaullist. "Everyone in France is a Gaullist," he said bitterly. Ree reassured him that there were plenty of Frenchmen like him, who didn't care about politics and only worried about how to get something to eat and smoke and drink.

"Oh, by the way, how about a drink?" Ree said. "There must be a bottle somewhere in Mother Hauger's cupboard."

```
2:30 p.m.
November 27, 1943
Pforzheim Prison
Near Karlsruhe
Germany
```

**W**hen Noor arrived at Pforzheim, guards put her in a cell, manacled her hands and her feet, then ran a chain between them. The manacles were never removed. The cells on either side of hers were emptied. She was never to see or be seen by other prisoners. She was fed garbage: watery "soup" made of potato peels, rutabagas or a kind of paste made of sour cabbage. When she ate, she could barely lift the spoon to her mouth. A female jailer, who was forbidden to speak to her, had to clean her.

Pforzheim was a civilian prison, and Noor was its first political prisoner. When the prison's 72-year-old warden, Wilhem Krauss, went to see her in her cell, he was appalled by what he found. In his 50-year career he had never heard of any prisoner, even a murderer, being kept in such conditions. He ordered that her chains be removed and that she be allowed to walk around the courtyard once a week. But the head of the Karlsruhe Gestapo overruled Krauss and ordered Noor to be put back in chains.

> Noor looked **tormented,** wild-eyed, as if she were undergoing a spiritual **crisis.**

Krauss thought Noor looked tormented, wild-eyed, as if she were undergoing a spiritual crisis.

Krauss visited Noor regularly in her cell, sitting down next to her on her little iron bed. She did not speak German well so their conversations were halting, but she confided in him that she was a British agent, that her father had been a kind of priest and that she had visited India and studied philosophy and literature. She never complained to him, and he realized she did not hold him responsible for the harsh conditions of her captivity. He came to think highly of her.

Noor revealed things about her father to Krauss that she had never told Ernst Vogt or even her colleagues in the resistance. Perhaps she felt that now that she had endured what she feared most, interrogation by the Gestapo, she had no reason to hide anything. Perhaps talking to this kindly old man reawakened memories of her beloved father. As time passed, she seemed to Krauss more at peace than when she arrived.

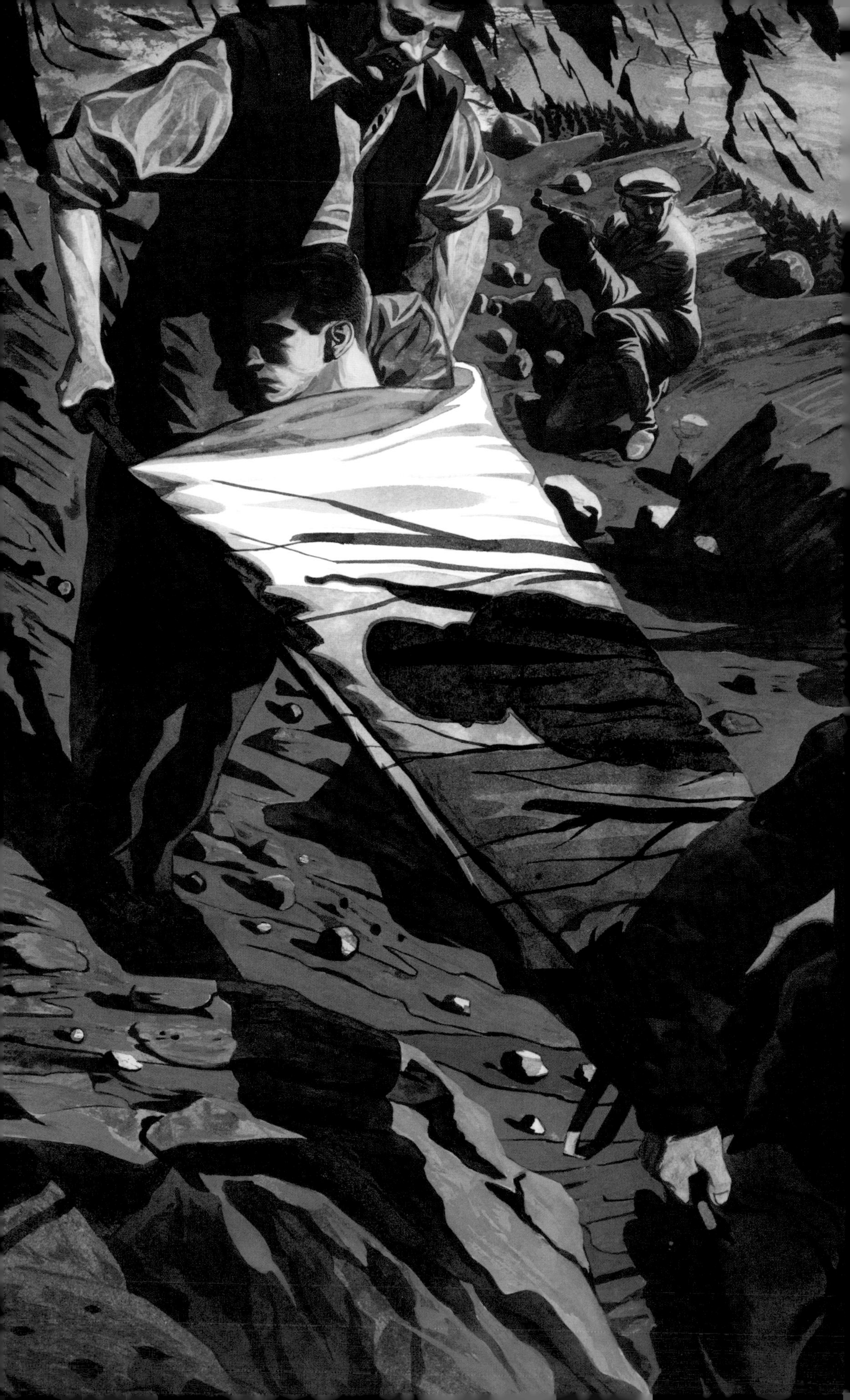

## Late afternoon
## December 3, 1943
## Near Thiancourt
## France

Harry Ree had battered the Gestapo man to the ground, leaving him crumpled on the floor in Jean Hauger's cottage. But he had been shot six times during the desperate struggle. Miraculously on his feet, he had staggered down to the edge of the river, the blood from his wounds running down his chest and into his pants. The river was 15 yards wide and turbulent from the rain. Now, as Ree waded out into the churning water, the current hit him hard and carried him downstream. He seized a hanging willow branch and held on, exhausted. After resting for a few moments he let go and swam to the other side.

He began walking toward the village of Étupes, where he had friends. He staggered through a long plowed field. The earth was muddy and huge clods of dirt stuck to his shoes with each step. He was suffering from loss of blood and shock, barely able to stand. But he could not stop. By now the SS would be turning the area upside down looking for him.

**Resistance men carry the gravely wounded Ree over the Swiss border to freedom.**

Somehow he made it the three miles to the village. It was almost dark. He stumbled to the home of Madame Bourquin, a 70-year-old widow whose son-in-law, Marcel Hosotte, was a member of the resistance who had worked with Ree.

Marcel took one look at the bloody, filthy visitor at his door, took him inside, laid him on a couch, undressed him and covered him with hot towels. Hosotte's wife gave him hot brandy and sent her 16-year-old daughter biking off to get a doctor.

When the doctor, whose name was Petrequin, arrived, he discovered that Ree had sustained two serious gunshot wounds, one bullet piercing his lung and the other missing his heart by a few millimeters. He also had four minor bullet wounds in his side, shoulder and arm.

Dr. Petrequin could not believe Ree had walked four miles and swum a river in his condition. In amazement, he murmured, *"Ah, les anglais, les anglais..."*

Petrequin dressed Ree's wounds and gave him tetanus injections. Ree urgently needed to go to the hospital, but the Germans would be searching there.

Ree stayed at the widow's house for

three nights. The Germans were offering a large reward for the capture of the "terrorist." Many local people knew where Ree was, but no one betrayed him. Still, it was too dangerous for him to stay put.

The director of the Peugeot works, Monsieur Sire, heard of Ree's plight, sent his car and moved him to the château of an aristocratic resistance family. Ree stayed there for four days, tended by Dr. Petrequin. On his last visit, the doctor told Sire that Ree was declining and needed to be taken to a hospital in Switzerland where they could operate on him. "He won't last longer than two days," the doctor said.

They had to find a *passeur* to take Ree over the border. The best man for the job was a baker named Marcel Poète, a resistance leader who was part of a fabled Jura *passeur* network, led by three nuns, that helped more than 14,000 refugees cross to safety in Switzerland.

Poète had just carried out a sabotage operation and was hiding in a friend's house when they heard someone tap at the window. They knew it could not be the Gestapo, because they didn't tap—they just kicked in the door. They opened the door and found Sire and three other people, including a doctor, standing there.

"I have Henri in the car," Sire said. "He is very badly wounded. You must take him immediately across the frontier so he can get hospital treatment."

"What, Henri, the English captain?" asked Poète. He went out to the car. Ree was wrapped in blankets. He was very pale but calmly puffing on his pipe. He gave Poète a smile and a wink. "What happened?" Poète asked. Ree whispered, "Ah well, I've been hit. Don't worry, I can take it..."

**Harry Ree was awarded the Distinguished Service Order.**

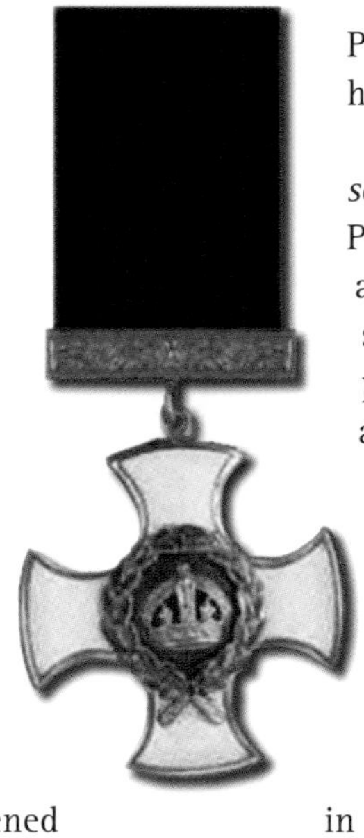

The doctor told Poète that Henri might last until tomorrow, but he had to cross the frontier that night. Poète told him this was a tall order, because he was on the run himself and did not have his men with him. Henri would have to be carried on a stretcher, which would require at least six men—two to carry the stretcher and four to cover them with Sten guns. But they would have to manage somehow, Poète said. They couldn't let their Henri die.

It did not take long for Poète to find helpers. As soon as the local people heard that *le copain anglais* needed help, Poète had so many volunteers he had to turn men away.

Sire dropped Ree and the *passeurs* at Delle, near the border. Poète and his men hoisted him up and set off through the night, constantly on the lookout for German patrols. They were forced to make a long detour because they could not climb over the rocks with the stretcher and had to take a footpath. But at last they came to the large white stone they had been waiting for, the one bearing the word *SUISSE.*

Ree spent two weeks recuperating in a hospital in Switzerland before being sent into the country. He had to go through France to cross the Spanish border. In Spain, he was interned at a purgatorial detention camp called Miranda, where the unfriendly Spanish government sequestered SOE agents and other escapees from occupied Europe. Finally he was put on a plane to London.

Upon his return, like all agents who made it back, Ree was debriefed at Baker Street. It was an invaluable process that allowed SOE to evaluate methods and equipment, kept it abreast of conditions in the field and helped future agents avoid mistakes. During the interview Ree told his superiors that he was willing to go back into the field. But as the officer debriefing him noted in his file, Ree "let drop the remark that he doubts if he would have as much luck next time as last time, and I personally feel that this is the correct reading of the situation. I think he should now be allowed to develop along different lines." Now promoted to captain, Ree worked at SOE headquarters for the rest of the war, assisting in the training of Jedburgh teams, three-man units (normally made up of one French, one American and one British officer) that were dropped behind German lines in France around D-Day.

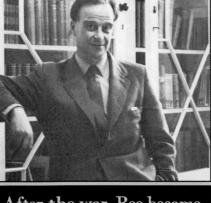

After the war, Ree became the first **professor** of **education** at the University of York.

Soon after the German surrender Ree returned to France, playing himself in a fictionalized RAF documentary about SOE called *School for Danger* (later retitled *Now It Can Be Told*). When he returned to the Montbéliard area to look up his old comrades, he discovered that many of them had been taken away or killed. He was especially worried about the schoolteacher Roger Fouillette, who had been seized in the big Gestapo sweep of October 1943.

Ree learned that soon after Fouillette was arrested, the Gestapo had taken him back to his home for a meeting with his wife. The couple had two children, aged 12 and nine. "We've heard that you've had a happy family life, and we don't want to destroy it," the Gestapo told Madame Fouillette. They told her they intended to shoot her husband, but would spare his life if she told them where the English Captain "Henri" was.

Madame Fouillette asked her husband what she should do. He said, "Follow your conscience."

She told them that she knew Henri but did not know where he was, that he had fled. It was a lie; she knew where he was. Roger Fouillette was sent to Buchenwald.

Now, wearing battledress, Captain Ree tracked down Madame Fouillette and knocked on her door. It was dark. The eldest daughter, now 15 years old, opened the door, took a step back and said, "Papa!" Ree had never wished more that he was somebody else.

The Fouillette family had had no word of the fate of Roger. With a heavy heart, Ree returned to England. Four weeks later, a letter from France arrived. When he opened it, he read, "My dear Henri, I am alive. I am home."

Twenty-five years after the end of the war, Ree told an audience in his native Manchester that his attachment to Roger Fouillette was the deepest one of his life.

Harry Ree was awarded the Distinguished Service Order and the OBE. Back in civilian life, he returned to teaching and went on to become the first professor of education at the University of York. He never lost his fierce individualism, his hatred of war or his self-deprecating sense of humor. He refused to glorify anything he had done.

# Exploding Turds and One-Man Submarines

## SOE's Secret Weapons

From James Bond's passenger-ejecting Aston Martin to the *Mission Impossible* team's array of fiendishly lethal devices, outlandish gizmos are an essential part of secret agent mythology. But long before 007 blasted his first supervillain with a weapon concealed in his sunglasses, SOE inventors had created an entire catalog of deadly devices. Working out of clandestine locations that included the basement of the natural history museum in South Kensington, a team of innovative SOE scientists and engineers came up with a plethora of weird and ungentlemanly gadgets, from self-igniting briefcases to itching powder designed to be sprinkled in German undergarments to a tiny, single-shot gun disguised as a fountain pen.

Some of the more exotic devices were not exactly practical. Fashioning statues of the Buddha out of plastic explosives was a clever idea, but the figurines do not seem to have ushered any Japanese troops into a state of permanent nirvana. There is no record of any agent using SOE's tiny knife hidden inside a coat lapel to slash an enemy's jugular vein. The Welman, a one-man submarine that carried 550 pounds of explosives and was capable of submerging to 350 feet, failed in the only mission it attempted. And it seems unlikely that the variety of exploding turds, rats and vegetables served up by SOE's scientists caused much damage to the Axis.

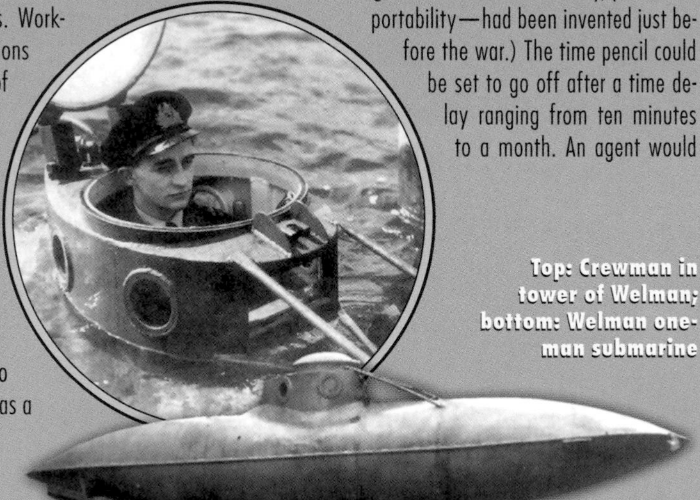

**Top: Crewman in tower of Welman; bottom: Welman one-man submarine**

But many of SOE's less sexy weapons and devices proved invaluable. SOE's most significant invention was probably the "time pencil," a simple, portable fuse in the shape of a pencil that could be embedded in an explosive charge. (Plastic explosives—which revolutionized sabotage because of their stability, power and portability—had been invented just before the war.) The time pencil could be set to go off after a time delay ranging from ten minutes to a month. An agent would simply press a ridge on the pencil to release acid that ate through a wire; when the wire snapped, the explosives detonated. The 12 million time pencils SOE manufactured were used in every theater of the war.

Another crucial weapon was the Sten gun, a submachine gun invented in 1941 by two British engineers. Simple in design, water- and dirt-proof and absurdly cheap (it cost just a pound and a half to manufacture one), the Sten was the guerrilla weapon *par excellence.* Useless at any range longer than a few yards, and prone

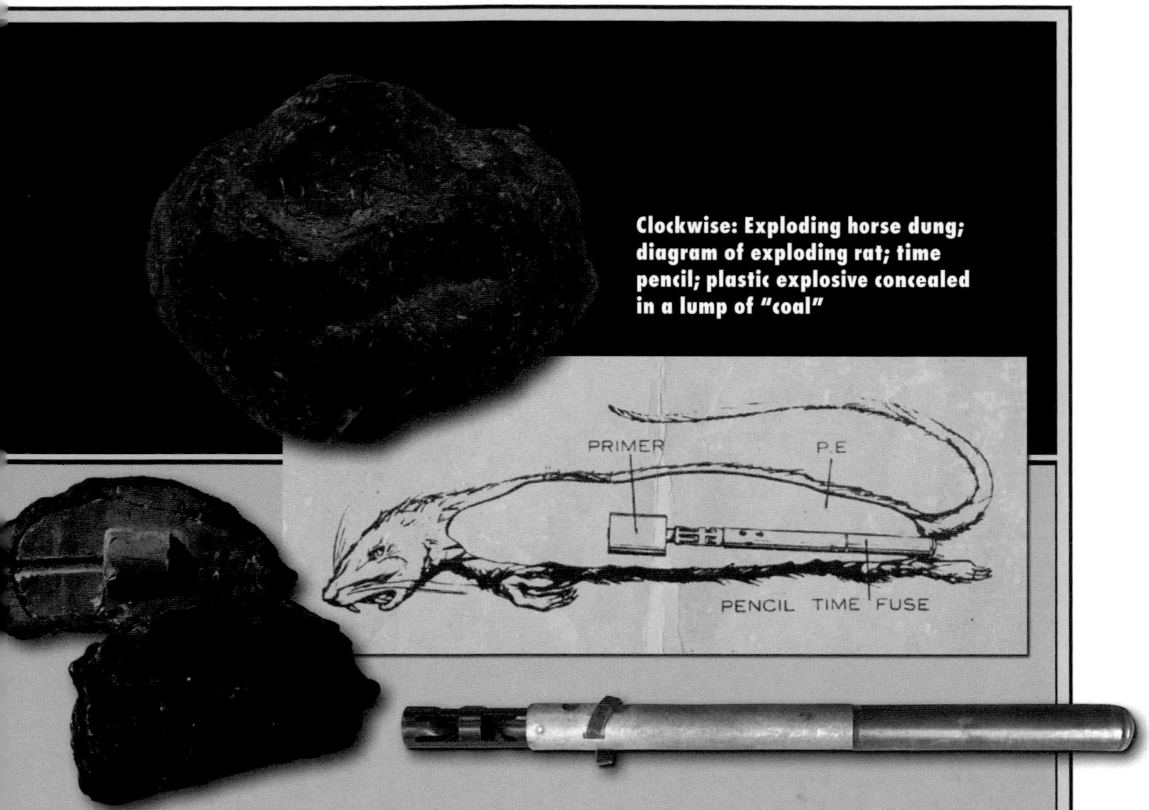
PRIMER
P.E
PENCIL TIME FUSE

Clockwise: Exploding horse dung; diagram of exploding rat; time pencil; plastic explosive concealed in a lump of "coal"

to jamming, going off when jostled or exploding when first fired, the Sten was nonetheless a deadly weapon when used in an ambush at close quarters. SOE passed out more than a million Stens to guerrillas around the world.

The caltorp, an updated version of a medieval device used against cavalry, also delivered a lot of bang (literally) for the buck. It consisted of a tripod of three two- or three-inch steel prongs and a fourth that aimed upward. Hurled onto roads, it proved extremely useful in puncturing enemy tires.

The same care that went into SOE's high-tech weaponry and gadgets went into ensuring the authenticity of its agents' clothes, papers and possessions. SOE hired an old German tailor, who could tell at a glance if a suit came from Czechoslovakia or France, to cut suits to Continental patterns. Every trace of anything British was removed, right down to the manufacturer's name on zippers, which were removed with a dentist's drill. The clothes were aged by being worn constantly, even to bed, and then repeatedly treated with Vaseline and rubbed with sandpaper to get rid of all newness. Money was aged by being handled and walked on. Papers and documents were turned out by a virtuoso forging operation.

Before agents went into the field, they were carefully inspected at the airstrip, to make sure nothing incriminating was in their pockets. An old Tube ticket or an English cigarette could mean death. Not until they passed muster were they allowed to board the plane. Once in the field, they would have to rely on their wits—and the skill and ingenuity of the craftsmen and inventors who worked tirelessly to make sure they had a fighting chance.

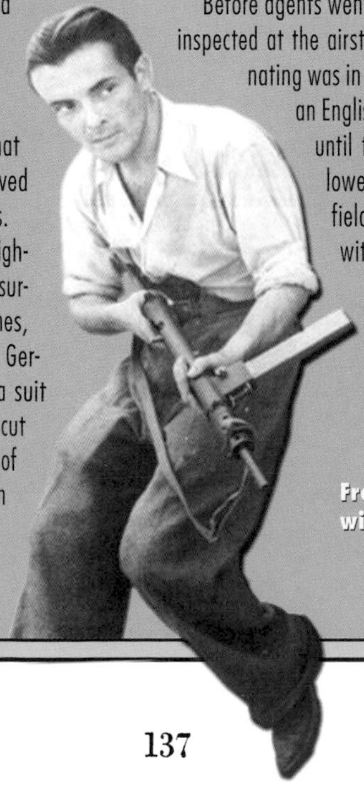

French resistance fighter with Sten gun

## 4:30 p.m.
## February 6, 1944
## Anzio, Italy

The oldest of Colin Gubbins's two children, Michael, was an officer with SOE's Italian section. Michael accompanied the unit when it landed at Anzio. In early February, the unit lost touch with Rome, and it was decided to send a messenger. An Italian courier was found, but to contact him, it was necessary to cross an exposed strip of no-man's-land. Michael did not need to go, but craving excitement, he insisted on accompanying another SOE officer, Michael Munthe.

The two men set out about 4 p.m. on February 6. When they emerged from a roadside ditch they found themselves in an exposed roundabout, and German machine guns and mortars opened fire on them. They took cover in a slit trench, but Munthe was seriously wounded and Michael was hit by a mortar and killed instantly. Stretcher bearers managed to evacuate Munthe under fire, but what was left of Michael had to be abandoned. His body was never recovered.

Gubbins searched in vain for his son's body.

The duty officer at Baker Street that weekend, who did not know Gubbins very well, saw the telegram announcing Michael Gubbins's death. He marked it "deepest sympathy" and placed it at the top of Gubbins's in-tray. Gubbins came in early that Monday morning to prepare for an important meeting with the Chiefs of Staff, so neither his military assistant nor his personal secretary was

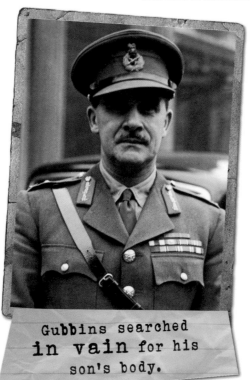

there to soften the blow. Gubbins picked up the telegram himself. Overcome by grief and remorse, he somehow managed to get through the meeting.

Some months later, Gubbins went to Italy and spent the day looking at graves, fruitlessly hoping to find a trace of his son. A friend was distressed at Gubbins's bottomless grief, but could do nothing except pull out a prized bottle of Johnny Walker Black, which the two men shared. Later, at SOE's Middle East headquarters in Algeria, Gubbins was seen wandering back and forth in the sand dunes, despairingly murmuring to himself "so useless, so useless."

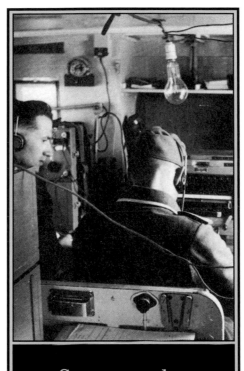

Gestapo members playing a ***Funkspiel*** (radio game).

Gubbins's loss made it hard for him to carry on. The wiry Highlander had always insisted on developing personal relationships with the men and women who were risking their lives for his organization. He made a point of meeting with his agents, both before and after they went into the field. He briefed himself thoroughly in advance on each agent's mission, discussed possible problems they would face, and within the limits of security even talked about the larger strategic implications of their missions. The old soldier was a born leader, and he inspired tremendous loyalty among the young people who were, in effect, his troops. But each interview exhausted him. And after his son's death, the process of dispatching these brave young men and women into the jaws of the Third Reich seemed to take even more out of him.

Gubbins was not the only member of SOE's staff who had to cope with dread about their comrades' fate. SOE code-master Leo Marks was certain that Noor had been taken.

Marks had taught Noor to use only an 18-letter key phrase in her coding if she had been captured. The first transmission London received after Noor was captured, sent by the Germans, contained 18 characters. Marks went immediately to Buckmaster, but the ever-credulous F Section head said he intended to continue replying to Poste Madeleine. The Germans continued the successful *Funkspiel* for months, and more agents were sent to their deaths.

The usually wisecracking young code maker was devastated at the thought that this gentle, innocent girl was in the hands of the Gestapo, and he sent out a silent prayer for her. "Please God...can anything be done to help Noor, who knows you by another name? I can feel her pain from here, and I know how much worse it must be for you."

# Spring 1944
# Pforzheim Prison
# Near Karlsruhe
# Germany

In January, a group of French political prisoners, all women, were brought into Pforzheim. They soon realized that one prisoner was being kept in isolation and treated much worse than the others. One of the new prisoners, a young Frenchwoman named Yolande Lagrave, the only one who was to survive the Nazi death camps, remembered her as an "English parachutist who was interned and very unhappy."

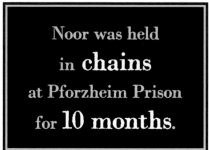

Noor was held in **chains** at Pforzheim Prison for **10 months.**

The new prisoners were forbidden to speak to Noor, but they figured out a way to communicate with her by scratching on the bases of their food bowls with knitting needles. "There are three Frenchwomen in cell no. 12," they scratched. When the clean bowls came back to them, Noor had scratched, "You are not alone, you have a friend in cell 1."

So started a laborious communication between Noor and the French prisoners. Sometimes it took days for the bowls to come back, but they kept scratching away. Her fellow prisoners tried to cheer up Noor, saying the war would soon be over and they would drink champagne.

Noor tried to rally. On U.S. Independence Day, she wrote on her bowl, "Here's to the 4th of July." On Bastille Day she scratched, "Long live free France, for that keeps us together," and added a drawing of an English and a French flag. But the other prisoners knew she was suffering terribly. One bowl came to them inscribed, "Keep me in your thoughts, I am very unhappy." Another bowl instructed her fellow prisoners never to tell her mother she had been in prison.

Once, two of Noor's fellow prisoners gave her some news by singing as they passed her cell. A guard heard the singing and began shouting at Noor. The two women heard him open Noor's door, hit her and take her down to the basement, where they were forced to listen to her cries as he beat her.

Another time, the Frenchwomen heard a prison official screaming at Noor because the peephole in her cell was open. She replied proudly to him in German, holding her head high as he insulted her. She continued to defy him even after he slapped her across the face. Later, they heard her sobbing in her cell.

One day, as summer approached, they all heard RAF planes flying overhead and the sound of bombs exploding. The Allies were getting closer.

## 10:45 a.m.
## Sunday, February 20, 1944
## Ferry Hydro
## Lake Tinnsjo
## Norway

The commando raid had dealt Hitler's heavy-water program a serious blow, but it had not killed it. The Germans immediately threw enormous resources into repairing the damage and getting the plant up and running again. Einar Skinnarland, SOE's intrepid mole, reported to London that full production would probably resume in August 1943, six months after the raid.

After the Germans strengthened the plant's defenses, Allied commanders ruled out another ground attack. Desperation led them to approve a massive bombing attack. They did not inform the Norwegian government of the impending raid. On November 16, 300 U.S. B-17s and B-24s dropped their payloads on the plant, but the bombs failed to destroy it and killed 22 civilians, including one unlucky man who was skiing alone on a desolate mountainside miles away. The failed mission enraged the Norwegians and succeeded only in convincing the Germans to move their entire heavy-water operation out of Norway, to Germany.

A U.S. bombing raid on the Vemork plant failed to destroy the heavy water.

On February 7, 1944, Skinnarland wired London that the heavy water would be shipped to Germany in a week. It would be taken by train to a ferry, ferried across

Lake Tinnsjo, loaded on to another train, shipped to a port and then put on a ship for Hamburg.

Allied commanders replied that under no circumstances was the heavy water to be allowed to leave Norway. It must be destroyed, even if the attack led to reprisals against civilians. The Norwegian government, although still furious about the bombing raid, gave permission for an attack even if it led to the deaths of innocent people.

Only one member of the Gunnerside team was still in the area: Knut Haukelid. SOE quickly recruited him to lead the attack. The philosopher-saboteur had one week to figure out how to blow up the heavy water.

For most of the previous year, Haukelid had been living a solitary existence. While he was hiding with a friend in Oslo after the Vemork raid, his father unexpectedly came to visit. Haukelid hid behind the door while his friend hastily got rid of him. Every member of the underground knew they must never contact family members: doing so could endanger both the agent and his or her next of kin. So Haukelid forced himself to remain silent.

It turned out to be the last time Haukelid ever saw his father. Soon after, the Germans discovered that the elder Haukelid had a cache of wireless sets hidden on his property and sent him to the concentration camp at Grini. The father was made of the same iron as his son; the old man died that summer without betraying the resistance.

Haukelid abandoned Oslo for the Hardangervidda, feeling more secure in its wild and frozen expanse. He and Arne Kjelstrup built a hut and named it Bamsebu, or Little Bear, after a cute elk-hound puppy they acquired. After Kjelstrup had to return to Britain because of his health, which had never recovered after his months of near-starvation, Haukelid and Einar Skinnarland lived in the hut, organizing

local resistance groups. The two men had no coffee, sugar, tea or tobacco, subsisted almost entirely on reindeer meat and fish and during the warm summer months went about almost naked. But they were happy. "We again realized that civilization was a mass of superfluities," Haukelid said of his year on the great plateau.

As Haukelid plotted his second strike on Hitler's heavy-water cache, he weighed where he should strike—at the plant, on either of the trains, on the ferry, on the dock. After studying the various options, Haukelid and London decided the only viable option was to try to sink the ferry as it sailed across Lake Tinnsjo, the deep, narrow lake into which the Maan River flowed after passing by the Vemork plant. His plan was to sneak aboard the ferry before it sailed, time the detonators so that

the ferry would sink in the deepest part of the lake and place enough charges to sink it quickly.

Haukelid was a stoic man, but he had a lot on his mind as he prepared for the job. He needed to find reliable helpers. He didn't have detonators or fuses. He had very little time to do reconnaissance. And he had just received a letter from his wife, who had fled to Sweden, asking for a separation. His wife's letter, he noted laconically, was a "hard blow." He had not been home in three years.

But above all, Haukelid was worried about the innocent Norwegians who would certainly die as a result of his sabotage. This was a moral problem he had never faced before, and it haunted him. But he was a soldier in a war, and he had orders to carry out.

After shaving off his bushy beard, Haukelid left the Bamsebu hut on February

The ferry "Hydro" at the rail terminus

13 and headed for Rjukan. He quickly recruited three Rjukan men to help him and contacted friendly workers at the plant to ensure that the heavy water would be loaded on the Sunday ferry. On Sunday, there would be fewer passengers, and there was only one ferry, so the Germans could not postpone the trip. He considered trying to convince the Norwegian crew to let him sabotage the ship, but decided they would never agree to anything that would almost certainly kill local people. He would have to do it himself.

Dressed as a workman, carrying a Sten gun wrapped in a sleeping bag and a couple of hand grenades in his rucksack, Haukelid boarded the ferry and made the trip across Lake Tinnsjo. He calculated that it took 20 minutes for the ship to get to the deepest part of the lake. The best place to hide the charges, he decided, would be in a watertight compartment near the boat's bow. The explosion would cause the ship to tip forward, and the railroad cars carrying the heavy water would slide into the lake. The 500-ton ferry had to sink quickly, within five minutes, or it might be possible to beach her in the narrow lake. After spending hours calculating, he decided he would need enough explosives to blow a hole four feet wide.

When Haukelid returned to Rjukan, the Germans were stopping everyone suspicious and checking their papers and packages. With his sunburned face and dirty clothes, he would be arrested immediately. Looking around, Haukelid noticed that he was surrounded by a crowd of well-dressed musicians carrying their instruments. There was a big concert in town. He hastily borrowed a blue suit and a violin case from one of the musicians and put his Sten gun in the violin case. The Nazis must not have watched enough bad American gangster films, for he walked through the town without being questioned.

Just after midnight on Sunday, the day the ferry was to sail, Haukelid and his three

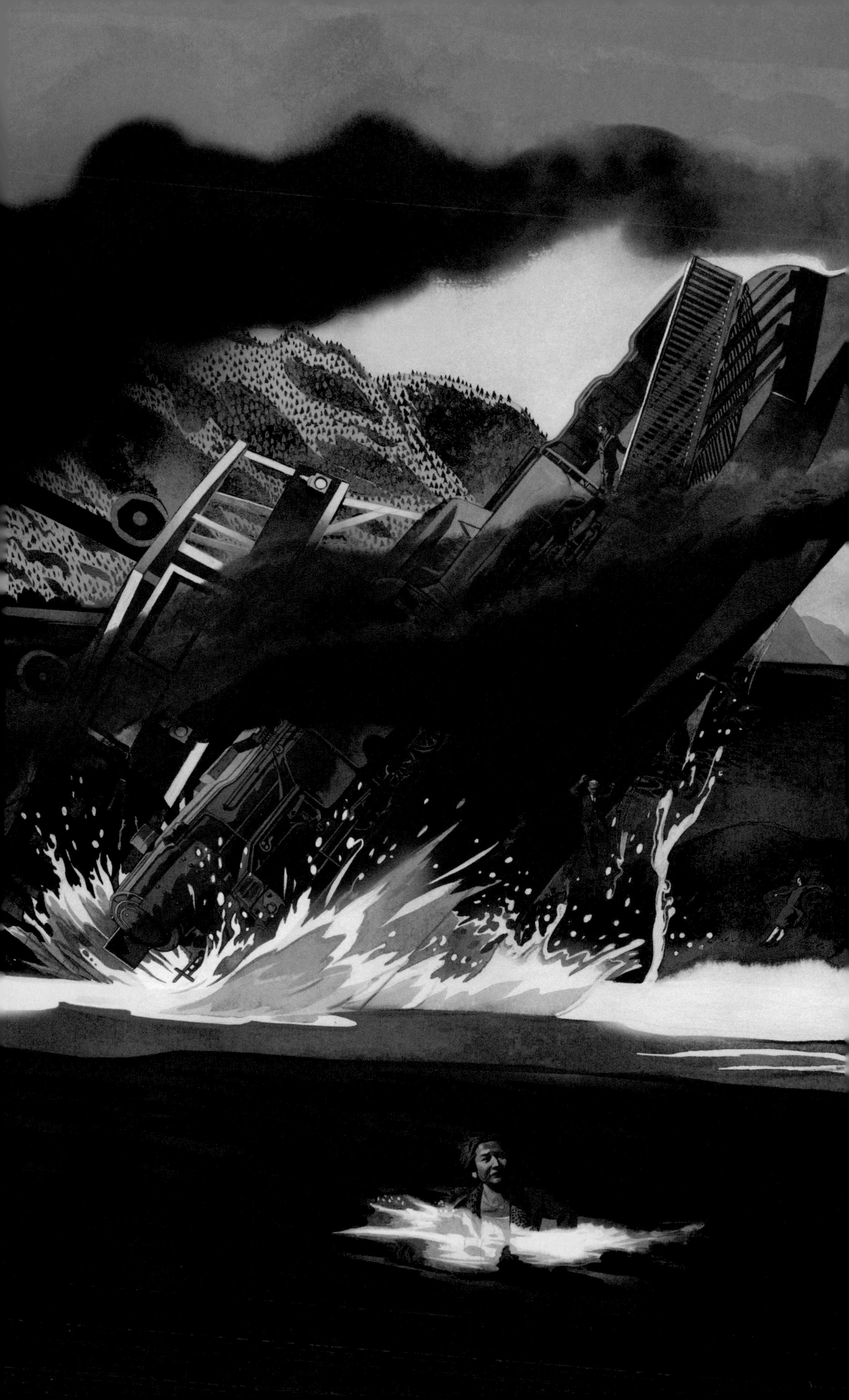

accomplices drove from Rjukan to the ferry port. They left the car off the road with the driver and one member of the team, telling them under no circumstances to wait more than two hours. The three men walked down to the ship, carrying the explosives and homemade timers made using alarm clocks. They were armed with Sten guns, grenades and pistols. Although the trucks carrying the heavy water were guarded, the Germans, incredibly, had omitted to guard the ferry itself.

Haukelid and his men stole on board, observed only by a stoker who said nothing. When they approached the crew's quarters, they heard voices; some kind of party was in progress. They were about to go through a hatchway down to the bilges when they were suddenly accosted by a watchman, who had heard noises and left the party to investigate.

Haukelid told the man they were on the run from the Gestapo and needed somewhere to hide. The man turned out to be a good Norwegian. He told them they could hide down below.

Leaving one of his men behind to talk to the watchman, Haukelid and his remaining accomplice quickly descended to the third-class deck and squeezed through a hole in the floor into the bilge. Standing in a foot of water in the cramped compartment, they carefully placed their explosives: 19 pounds in the shape of a sausage. Rigging the detonators and timers was a painstaking and dangerous job with the hammer on the alarm clock only a third of an inch away from the detonator. Finally they finished, clambered back above, bade farewell to the watchman and hurried back to the waiting car. They barely made it: It had taken them two hours, and their driver had been about to leave.

> The *Hydro*'s stern **rose** into the air and she headed straight to the **bottom.**

On Sunday morning, several dozen Norwegians and a few Germans boarded the *Hydro* for the short ride across the lake. Among them were a couple from the nearby town of Notodden and their three-year-old daughter, and two brothers, 14 and 15 years old. The poorer Norwegians headed below deck to the cheaper seats. The ferry cast off and began steaming peacefully across the beautiful lake as it had done so many times before.

At 10:45, Haukelid's alarm clocks went off. An enormous explosion ripped through the forward bow. The *Hydro* listed heavily to port. In just a few minutes it was flat on its side. Then its stern began to rise out of the water, its propellers still turning in the air. The people on the top decks had a chance to jump into the water, but most of those in the lower decks were trapped. In less than five minutes, the *Hydro* went straight to the bottom, 1,000 feet down. Fourteen Norwegians and four Germans drowned, including the family from Notodden and the two young brothers. Nineteen were saved. All the heavy water, except a few barrels that were less than half full, was lost forever.

On the train to Oslo with one of his accomplices, Haukelid looked at his watch at 10:45. If everything had gone according to plan, the ferry would be sinking to the bottom of Lake Tinnsjo, taking with it the precious heavy water—and many innocent Norwegians. He thought about all the people who had already died to prevent Hitler from creating a doomsday weapon: the 43 Englishmen who perished in the glider mission, the civilians killed by the bombing raid. He himself had sacrificed almost a year and a half of his life on the Hardangervidda, along with the comforts of home and family. He had done his job, but there was nothing to celebrate.

Haukelid, and the rest of the team that took part in what military historians regard as the exemplary sabotage mission in the annals of war, survived the war. Claus Helberg went on to design Norway's network of year-round mountain trails, including self-service log cabins stocked with food and firewood. Knut Haugland took part in another legendary exploit, serving as radio operator on Thor Heyerdahl's balsa-wood raft, the *Kon-Tiki,* during its 4,300-mile voyage from South America to Polynesia.

All of the men became, and remain, national heroes in Norway.

The sinking of the *Hydro* spelled the definitive end of Hitler's ambitions to make an atomic bomb. The nuclear physicist in charge of fission research for Germany's War Office, Kurt Diebner, said after the war, "[I]t was the elimination of German heavy-water production in Norway that was the main factor in our failure to achieve a self-sustaining nuclear reactor before the war ended."

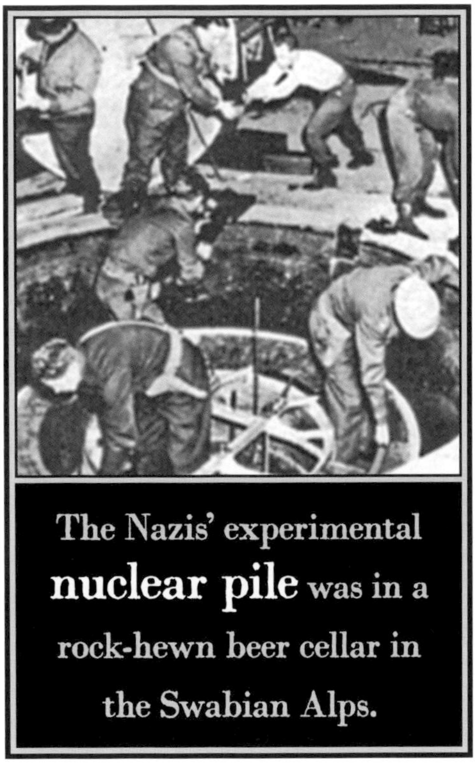

The Nazis' experimental **nuclear pile** was in a rock-hewn beer cellar in the Swabian Alps.

In fact, we now know that the Nazis' atomic-bomb program was not nearly as advanced as the Allies believed it was. Starting in 1942, Hitler's physicists had directed most of their energy toward trying to create nuclear-driven machinery, not bombs. Even with unlimited stocks of heavy water, it is unlikely Germany could have built an atomic bomb by 1945.

But neither the Allies nor the Norwegians knew that. They simply knew that if the Nazi regime had any chance of building a doomsday weapon, they must do whatever they could to stop it.

Perhaps there are quantum effects in the human realm just as there are in sub-atomic physics. The true meaning of a deed is not always measured by its observable effects. We do not know for certain how to measure the impact of the raids on the Vemork plant and the ferry. But the young Norwegians climbed a different mountain, one not shown on any map. Asked to sacrifice their lives for a greater good, they unflinchingly agreed. Asked to achieve the impossible, they did. Perhaps their most fitting tribute can be found in the words a poet gave to another exile who, after great trials, returned in triumph to his home.

*Death closes all: but something ere the end,*
*Some work of noble note, may yet be done,*
*Not unbecoming men that strove with Gods.*
. . .
*that which we are, we are;*
*One equal temper of heroic hearts,*
*Made weak by time and fate, but strong in will*
*To strive, to seek, to find, and not to yield.*

–From "Ulysses," by Alfred, Lord Tennyson

# Evening
# June 5, 1944
# France

At 9:15 p.m. on the evening of June 5, 1944, a diminutive English WAAF named Annette Cormeau turned on the radio set in her bedroom in a farmhouse in the village of Castelnausur-l'Avignon in Gascony in southern France and heard, through the crackle of static, the BBC announcer say, *"Il a un voix fausset"* ("He has a falsetto voice").

She went downstairs, where George Starr, field name Hilaire, was sitting in the kitchen with the members of the Laribeau family, in whose house the two agents were living. She told Starr what she had heard. The hard-bitten engineer from Staffordshire—and brother of John Starr, who had almost escaped across the Parisian roofs with Noor—smiled, said, "That's it, then," got up and went out to summon his men. In a few hours, the sound of explosions ripped through the night as the local railway lines came under attack.

CHAQUE FRANÇAIS
EST UN SOLDAT DE LA
LIBERATION!
DERAILLER LES TRAINS NAZIS
PLACEZ LA TETE D'UN CRAMPON DANS L'ESPACE OU LES DEUX RAILS SE JOIGNENT--DE PREFERENCE DANS UN VIRAGE OU EN VOIE DESCENDANTE.
DIRECTION DU TRAIN →

**Even matchbooks had intructions for sabotage.**

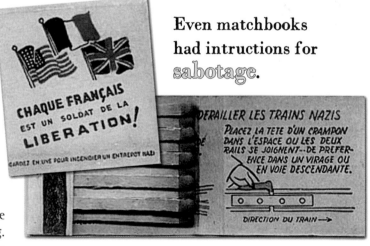

All night, more men of Starr's Wheelwright circuit kept arriving in the village, some on foot, some on bicycles, some in the smelly, charcoal-driven cars called *gazogènes*. They broke out the Brens and Stens that had been hidden in the church and passed them around. Then they headed out into the night.

What Cormeau had heard was an "action message" announcing that Operation Neptune, the assault phase of Overlord, the code name for the invasion of France, was under way. The task of Starr's men, and the thousands of other lightly armed, largely

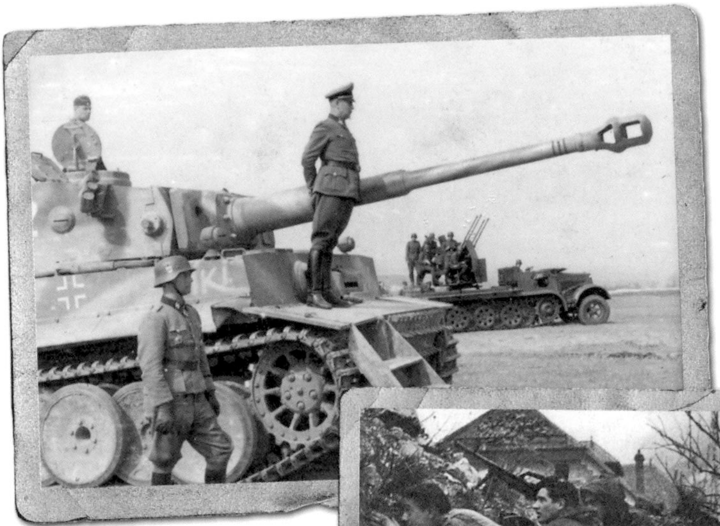

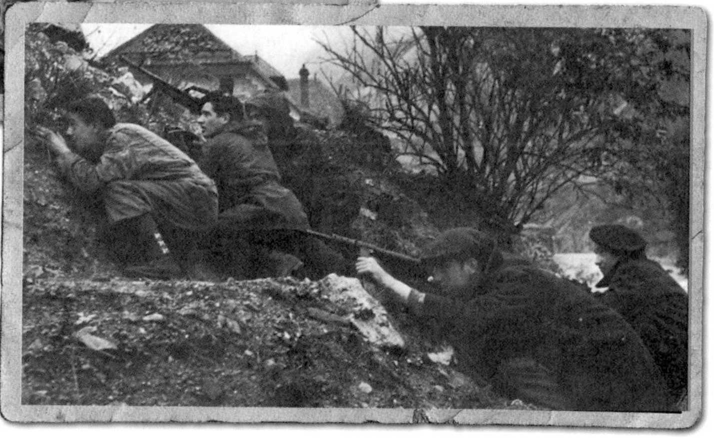

**Das Reich (left); *maquisards* firing from cover (right).**

untrained *maquisards* across southern and central France, was to somehow slow down the mighty German Panzer divisions that would soon be rushing toward the Normandy bridgehead, trying to drive the Allies back into the sea.

For the Allies, for SOE, for France—for the world—the moment of truth had finally arrived.

SOE's mission was to disrupt communications and railways, slowing German reinforcements moving toward Normandy and creating diversionary threats that would tie down additional enemy forces. In the Marseilles area, the head of the Jockey circuit, Francis Cammaerts (an old friend of Harry Ree's and a fellow former conscientious objector), organized attacks on dozens of rail lines and power stations. Farther north, *maquisards* of Pearl Witherington's Wrestler and René Maingard's Shipwright circuits made no less than 800 railroad attacks during June. Of the 1,050 railroad interruptions planned for that night, SOE circuits chalked up 950, and made 2,000 more rail cuts in the next three weeks. They blew up hundreds of electrical transformers, telecommunications centers, bridges and other vital targets. Saboteurs misrouted trains, gave German motorcyclists wrong directions, switched road signs and scattered tire-busters on the roads. French railroad workers helped gum up the works with slowdowns and intentional mistakes.

In a château packed with *maquis* above the Dordogne River, Jacques Poirier heard his message: *"La girafe a un long cou"* ("The giraffe has a long neck"). The young French head of the Digger circuit, known as Commandant Jack, had survived a dozen close calls that spring. Many of his friends were not so lucky. When one captured comrade refused to talk, the Germans had thrust his hands into the charcoal furnace of a *gazo* car, then held him against the burner until he died.

Now the 22-year-old Poirier had the chance to hit back at the men who had wrecked his country and killed his friends. He got into his car and drove like mad through the woods from one *maquis* camp to the next, telling his men to "make as much mess as you can."

On the morning of June 6, while Allied troops were fighting their way ashore on Omaha and Utah and Juno and Sword and Gold beaches, the Second SS Panzer Division, stationed in the town of Montaubon in southwestern France, received a signal: "Since the early hours of the morning, the invasion has been taking place on the Channel coast. Preparations are to be made for a march."

Hitler's SS divisions were the elite of his superb army. They were brutal, ruthless, maniacally devoted to Hitler, viciously anti-Semitic—but they were unsurpassed soldiers. The Second SS Panzer Division was one of the top units which Hitler had been holding in reserve, ready to rush

forward to the front lines after the Allied invasion. "Das Reich," as the division was called, was not the invincible fighting machine it once was. It had been savaged on the Eastern front, where war was waged with such ferocity and in conditions so appalling that France seemed to German troops like paradise by comparison. But it was still a formidable unit, with 15,000 troops led by battle-tested officers, 209 tanks and assault guns and 1,200 other vehicles. British intelligence assumed that Das Reich could make it to Normandy by D+3 —three days after D-Day.

The Allies' brilliant deception scheme, code-named Fortitude, had tricked the Germans into believing that the landings in Normandy would only be a bluff and the real attack would fall on the Calais area. Confused and indecisive, German commanders did not order Das Reich to begin moving north until June 7, and it was not

**Allied troops fight their way ashore on Omaha Beach.**

# A Seductive Spy

Of all SOE agents, the beautiful and enigmatic Christine Granville may also have been the most absolutely fearless. There's a reason why the Polish countess's exploits read like they're torn from the pages of a James Bond novel. Bond creator Ian Fleming allegedly had an affair with Christine, and she is said to have inspired the sexy double agent Vesper Lynd, who steals 007's heart in *Casino Royale.* (Fleming was well aware of SOE because of his position as personal assistant to the Director of Naval Intelligence, and borrowed much material from the secret agency: Bond's improbable array of deadly gadgets and weapons was based on SOE's dirty-tricks R&D "toy shop" in the basement of the Natural History Museum in South Kensington.)

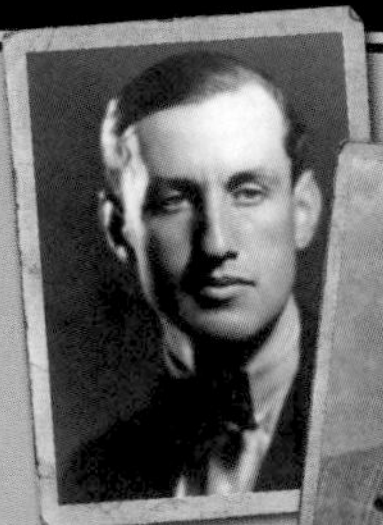

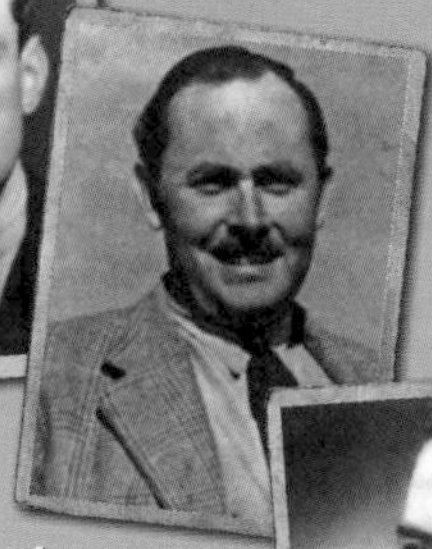

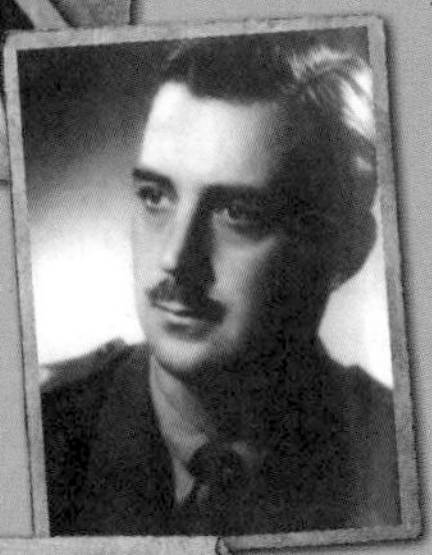

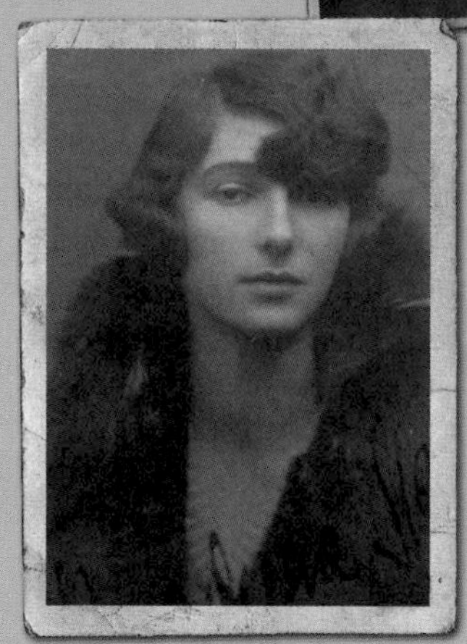

**From top: Ian Fleming's muse, Andrew Kowerski's lover, Francis Cammaerts's savior. Below: Christine Granville.**

Christine was born Krystyna Skarbek, the daughter of an impoverished aristocrat father and a wealthy Jewish mother. After Germany invaded Poland, she fled to England and, at age 25, began doing undercover work for the Foreign Office, working out of Budapest. An expert skier, she repeatedly braved the mountains between Hungary and Poland, running an escape network for Poles and British prisoners, spreading anti-German propaganda, organizing resistance movements and bringing back intelligence. When the Gestapo hauled her in for interrogation, she managed to avoid being arrested by biting her tongue until it bled copiously and claiming she had tuberculosis.

She had to get out of Hungary immediately. The British embassy provided her with a false passport under the name Christine Granville, and she made it to Yugoslavia, then Turkey and finally Egypt, careening across the Eastern Mediterranean in a redoubtable little Opel.

Christine radiated sensuality. When not defying death, her favorite pastime was lolling in the sun like a cat. Among her many virtues, Christine could not include a gift for monogamy. Although she was married to a hot-tempered Polish writer, Jerzy Gizycki, the love of her life was a fellow Polish agent, Andrew Kowerski. She also left a long trail of other lovers in her wake, including one SOE agent who was so smitten that he tried to commit suicide by throwing himself into the Danube. (As a letter in her SOE file drily notes, "it was frozen.")

On July 7, 1944, Christine parachuted into southern France. She was to work as the courier for the great SOE agent Francis Cammaerts, head of the Jockey circuit. But the Germans had arrested Cammaerts and two other agents, and their executions were imminent. Realizing a direct assault on the prison was hopeless, Christine decided her only chance was to bluff the Germans into releasing the agents. Brazenly walking into a Gestapo officer's office, she told the German that she was the niece of the legendary British general Bernard Montgomery, hero of El Alamein. Waving some broken radio crystals to convince him she was a British agent, she warned him that he would be executed by the advancing Allies if they were not freed. She also offered him a huge bribe. If her gambit had failed, she would have been shot on the spot. But her bravado worked: The German officer freed the agents just hours before they were to be killed.

Just before the end of the war Christine asked SOE to parachute her into camps in Germany so she could free more prisoners "just before they get shot," writing, "I should love to do it and you know I like to jump out of a plane even every day."

Lost in peacetime, Christine ended up working as a steward on an ocean liner. In 1952 she was stabbed to death in her hotel by a pathetic little man whose advances she had rejected. It was a sad fate for the woman who had stared down the Gestapo.

until dawn on June 8—D+2—that the vast convoy got under way.

Das Reich's Panther IV and V tanks and its fearsome self-propelled assault guns should have been shipped north by rail. Tanks are not designed to be driven long distances. Their treads constantly break, requiring time-consuming repairs, so driving takes much longer. But because of SOE's sabotage of the railroads, the heavy armor had to drive.

At 8:30 a.m. on June 8, outside Groslejac, a tiny hamlet on the Dordogne River in one of the most beautiful parts of France, Das Reich first came under fire.

Early that morning, word trickled into Groslejac that the Germans were heading in their direction. The village mayor, a stonemason named Marcel Vidal, began knocking on doors. At a hasty meeting, a dozen or so villagers tried to decide what to do. Some wanted to fight. De Gaulle had ordered every Frenchman to do everything in his power to fight the Germans. But others thought it might not be worth it. How many Germans would there be? Were they just in trucks, or were there tanks? Would there be reprisals? Still arguing vehemently, the 15 *maquisards* nonetheless got out their guns and began walking toward the old bridge across the Dordogne. The town's butcher, a radical socialist named Marcel Malatrait, assumed command. None of them had ever been in a battle before.

When the German half-tracks swung onto the village street and into view, the little group of Frenchmen opened fire with their bolt-action, single-shot rifles. The convoy ground to a halt. German infantrymen jumped out of the troop carriers, quickly working their way around to the *maquisards'* flanks. In moments, they poured a torrent of automatic weapons fire upon the exposed villagers at the bridge. When the nearby Hôtel Jardel was hit by cannon fire and began to burn, a group of guests tried to run out the front door and were cut down by a hail of bullets. The surviving *maquisards* ran away. The skirmish had lasted 20 minutes and left five French fighters and five civilians dead. The Germans suffered no casualties.

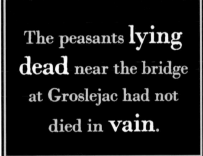

> The peasants **lying dead** near the bridge at Groslejac had not died in **vain.**

No bard has sung the praises of these embattled farmers. The shots they fired, far from being heard around the world, remain unknown to anyone except their fellow villagers, who later erected a plaque next to the bridge. But the *maquisards* of Groslejac, like the countless other resistance fighters who rose up across France on D-Day, deserve a place of honor in the annals of the war. They did not and could not do any real damage to the mighty Wehrmacht. But by provoking top German commanders into taking them much more seriously than they deserved, the ragged, underequipped *maquis* had the same effect as divisions of Allied troops.

For Groslejac was not alone. The heads of German Army Group G in Toulouse, whose 17 divisions were responsible for southern France, received a torrent of panicky messages from isolated German garrisons warning of a mass uprising by "terrorists" and "bandits." The German brass should have simply ignored the reports and moved at all possible speed to Normandy. They could easily have smashed the resistance later, after disposing of the mortal threat in the north. But

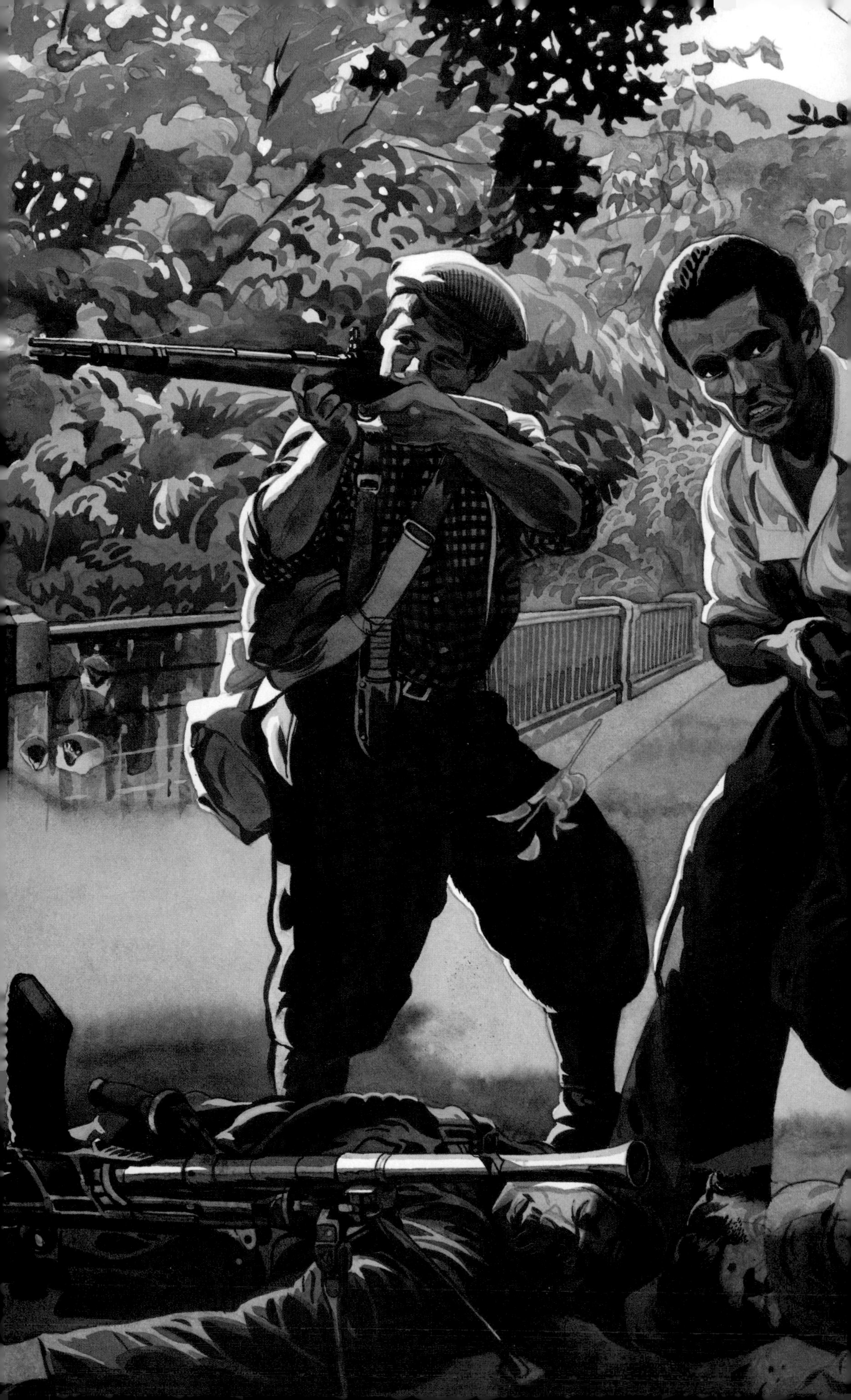

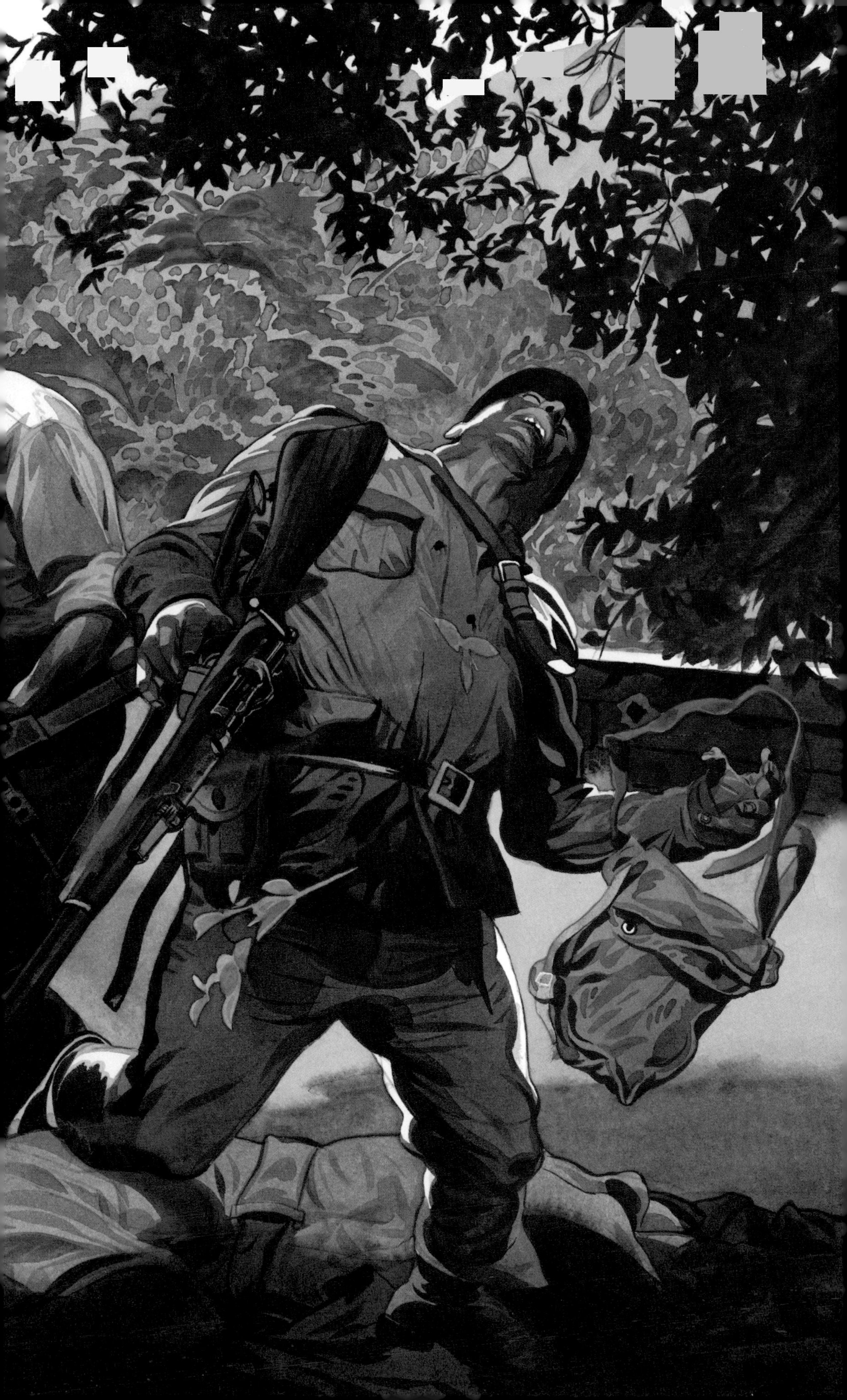

# Shadow Knights

in an act of supreme folly, they decided they needed to remove the threat to their rear immediately, and allocated an incredible eight divisions to fight small bands of untrained men in berets wielding jam-prone Sten guns that could not hit anything more than 50 meters away.

Like many conventional forces facing insurgencies before and after them, the Germans had been tricked into defeating themselves. The peasants and shopkeepers lying dead near the bridge in Groslejac had not died in vain.

As Das Reich rumbled north, suffering an ambush here, a man or two killed there, the division's soldiers and officers grew more and more enraged by the "terrorist" attacks. They began to employ the kind of brutal reprisals they had used in Russia. In the picturesque town of Tulle, Das Reich troops rounded up the citizenry and methodically hanged 99 innocent local men from lampposts.

The division kept laboring north, removing fallen trees, being harassed by hit-and-run attacks. When a popular German major was captured by resistance fighters, the Germans snapped. On June 10, troops of Das Reich herded the entire male population of the town of Oradour-sur-Glane into garages and barns and machine-gunned them. Then they forced more than 400 women and children into the local church, closed the doors and set it on fire, killing those who tried to escape with grenades and machine-gun fire. In all, 642 people, including 190 schoolchildren, were killed, almost the entire population of the village. It was one of the worst atrocities of the war.

Leaving this terrible charnel house behind them, Das Reich moved north again—only to face new attacks. Ninety-three multinational, three-man Jedburgh teams led resistance fighters in guerrilla attacks. British SAS commandos brought their formidable fighting skills to the fray.

But the real devastation came from above. After Das Reich and other German units crossed the Loire, they were savaged by Allied fighter-bombers, which enjoyed virtually unchallenged dominance of the air. Burned-out German tanks and half-tracks littered the roads of northern France. Gen. Erwin Rommel, the Germans' brilliant field commander, was badly wounded after a Hawker Typhoon strafed his car. He never returned to the field.

Das Reich division was supposed to arrive at Normandy at D+3. It did not go into action until D+13, and some elements did not begin fighting until D+24. By then, the Allies had blasted gaping holes in the overstretched German lines, and instead of counterattacking, German generals were forced to try to just hold on.

Das Reich troops **slaughtered** 642 people in Oradour-sur-Glane.

# Shadow Knights

German armor was **savaged** by Allied fighter-bombers.

It was too late. Germany's only real chance, as Rommel had known, had been to defeat the Allies on the beaches. But by June 30, when the last Das Reich units finally began fighting, that chance was gone. The Allies had 800,000 troops on French soil. Weeks of hard fighting lay ahead, but by August the Allies had broken out of the Normandy bridgehead and General Patton's Third Army began racing east.

Now the Allies hit Hitler hard from the south. Five weeks after D-Day, in one of the least-known major combat operations of the war, Operation Dragoon, 94,000 American and French troops swarmed ashore on some of the swankiest beaches of the French Riviera and began moving north. Allied planners had assumed they would not make it to Grenoble until D+90. But as the Allies headed north on the old Route Napolitaine, they discovered that the route had been completely cleared by resisters, many of them part of Francis Cammaert's Jockey circuit. In the town of Gap, resistance fighters forced 2,000 German soldiers to surrender, piled their guns outside the movie theater, herded them in and locked the door, with two teenagers standing guard outside.

One American officer recognized what the *maquis* had done, and insisted that it be recognized. On D+6, August 21, a German major was waiting with a white flag as the first American vehicle arrived on the outskirts of Grenoble. The American commander refused to accept the German's surrender unless it was made jointly to him and to the *maquisard* commander at his side, around whose shoulder the Yank had draped his arm.

SOE's performance, as Gubbins exulted, had been a "howling success." Baker Street's underground army had performed far beyond anyone's expectations. General Maitland Wilson, commander of Dragoon, estimated that the resistance "reduced the fighting efficiency of the Wehrmacht in southern France to forty per cent." In

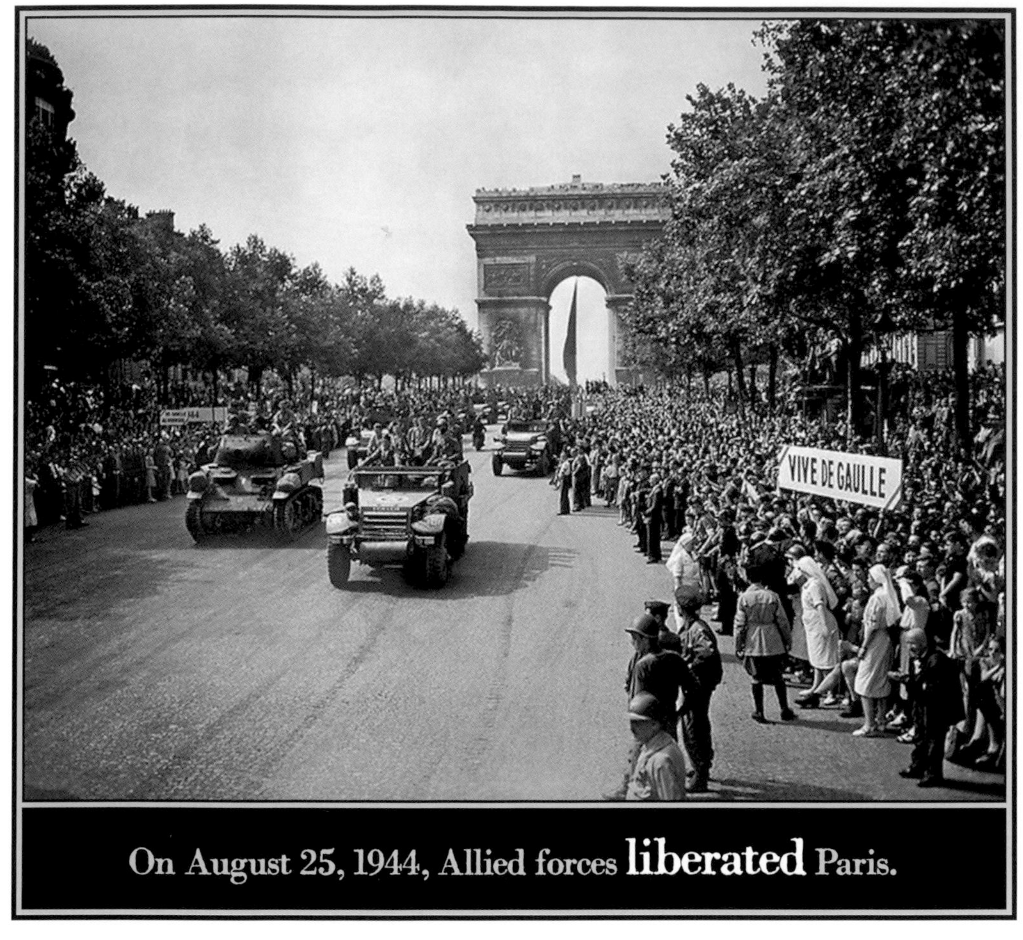
VIVE DE GAULLE

On August 25, 1944, Allied forces **liberated** Paris.

a letter he sent to Gubbins after Germany surrendered, Supreme Allied Commander Dwight D. Eisenhower wrote, "I consider that the disruption of enemy rail communications, the harassing of German roadworks and the continual and increasing strain placed on the German War Economy and internal services throughout occupied Europe by the organized forces of resistance, played a very considerable part in our complete and final victory."

The liberation of France was an epic, and any one of thousands of episodes could be singled out to represent SOE's part in it. But perhaps the tale of the two bicyclists best sums it up.

Tony Brooks, the 22-year-old head of SOE's Pimento circuit, had learned that the Germans planned to ship Das Reich's tanks on train cars hidden in railroad sidings in villages near Montauban. He dispatched two subagents. Night after night, past curfew, the two agents rode their bikes up to the cars and siphoned off the axle oil from the train cars. Then they replaced it with ground carborundum, an abrasive grease manufactured by SOE's dirty-tricks labs. When the Germans tried to ship their tanks north, the trains froze up after a few miles. It took the Wehrmacht a week to find other railway cars, and they were more than a hundred miles away. This act of sabotage was a big part of the reason that it took Das Reich two weeks longer than it should have to arrive in Normandy.

The two bicycle-riding agents were sisters. One was 16 years old. Her little sister was 14.

```
Morning
September 13, 1944
Dachau concentration camp
Near Munich
Germany
```

One day, the French prisoners saw Noor walking in the courtyard, dressed only in a sackcloth. She looked at their window and smiled at them. That night, she wrote on the bowl, "Don't look at my clothes. They have taken away my own. Forgive me!"

Sometime later, Noor sent a final message to them. They found the words "I am leaving" scratched on the bowl in a shaky, trembling hand. They did not know where she had gone.

On September 11, Noor was removed from Pforzheim Prison and driven to Karlsruhe, where she was brought to the office of the head of the Gestapo. At 2 a.m. that night three other SOE agents—Yolande Beekman, Eliane Plewman and Madeleine Damerment—were brought into the room.

The four women were told that they were being transferred to Dachau. They were driven to the train station and put first on a train to Stuttgart, then one to Munich. On the train to Munich they were given window seats. The women relaxed, talked, had lunch, enjoyed the scenery and smoked English cigarettes. Their Gestapo guards, Christian Ott and Max Wassmer, painted a

**Noor and her fellow agents were transferred to Dachau.**

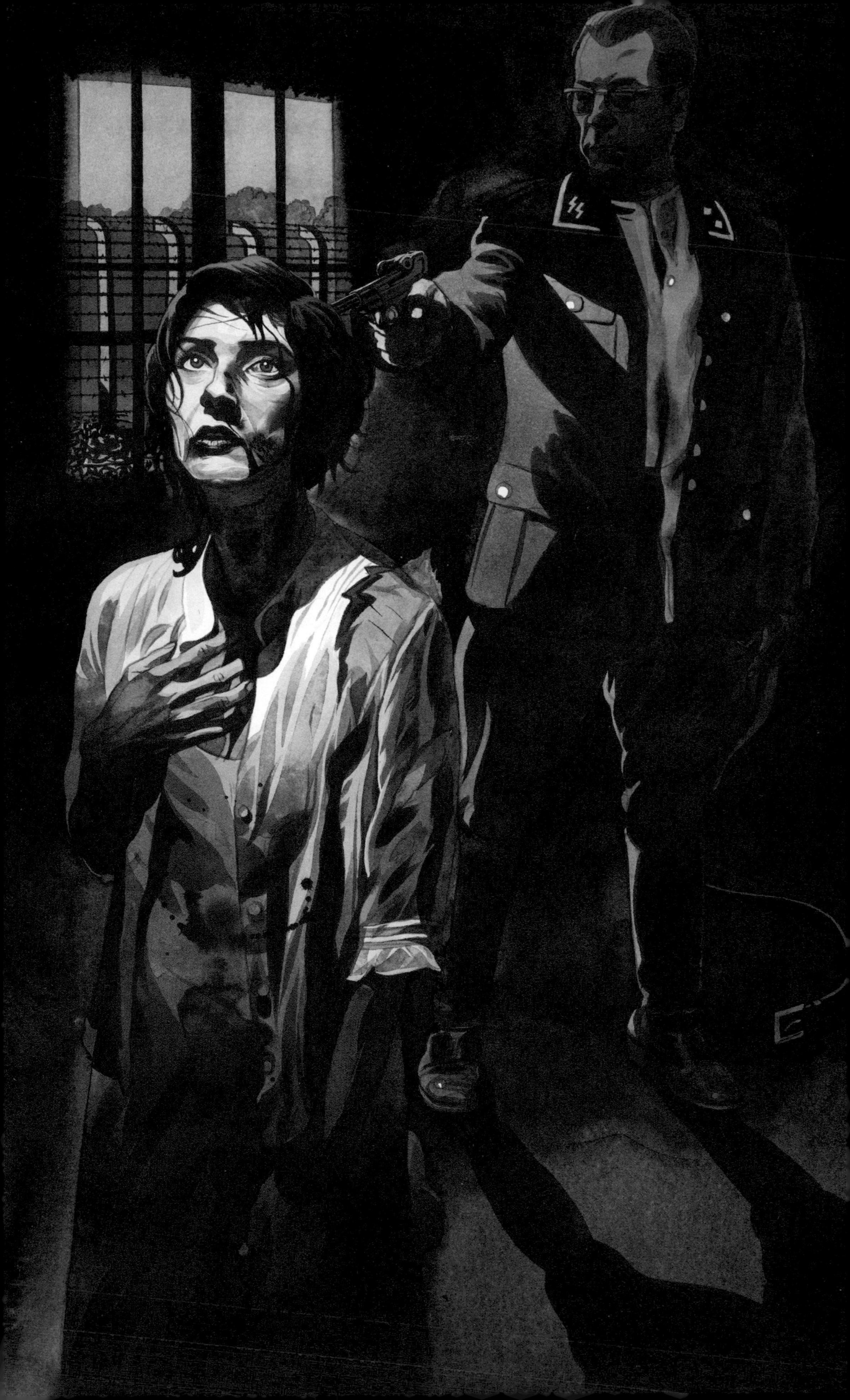

pleasant picture of Dachau, describing it as an agricultural camp in the country.

At Munich, the women and their guards changed trains again, and rode into the Bavarian countryside. They arrived around midnight at the notorious concentration camp, which was named after the nearby medieval town, and the women were placed in separate cells.

What happened next will never be known. The official version, based on testimony given by Wassmer and Ott, is that between 8 and 10 the next morning Noor and the other three agents were taken from their cells, marched to the crematorium, forced to kneel down in pairs and then, holding hands, were shot in the back of the neck.

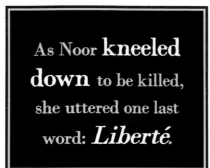

As Noor **kneeled down** to be killed, she uttered one last word: *Liberté.*

But this version is probably not true. Both Ott and Wassmer changed their stories. And during a later interrogation, Ott said that when he asked Wassmer what really happened to Noor, Wassmer replied, "Do you want to know what *really* happened?"—implying that it was something dreadful.

After the war, Noor's biographer Jean Overton Fuller received letters from two men who claimed that Noor was tortured and abused all night by German guards, who stripped her naked and brutally kicked her. Noor's dark skin led her racist captors to treat the "Creole" even more viciously. The second letter claimed that Noor's tormentor was an officer named Ruppert, who kicked her until she was "a bloody mess," then taunted her by telling her he was going to kill her, forced her to kneel down and shot her through the head.

Vera Atkins, the formidable head of F Section intelligence who after the war undertook an exhaustive mission to find out what had happened to her missing agents, privately believed that Noor had been not only tortured but raped before she was killed.

The truth is lost. All that can be said for certain is that on September 13, 1944, Noor Inayat Khan and fellow SOE agents Yolande Beekman, Eliane Plewman and Madeleine Damerment were murdered in Dachau and their bodies immediately thrown into the crematorium. Noor was 30 years old.

Perhaps it is as well that the details of her last moments are unclear. For Noor's death is as impossible to contemplate as that of another gentle, soft-voiced princess who could not tell a lie, Cordelia in *King Lear.* At the end of the play, when Lear enters carrying his daughter Cordelia's dead body in his arms, he asks heaven uncomprehendingly, "Why should a dog, a horse, a rat, have life, and thou no breath at all?" Noor's death summons the same anguished question, which boils down to one unanswerable word: Why?

The Nazis intended Noor, like the millions of other human beings they murdered, to vanish into night and fog. And yet in her final moments on earth, as throughout her short life, the young woman whose name means "Light of Womanhood" left a ray of light. As she kneeled down to be shot, according to one of the men who said he witnessed her ordeal, she spoke one last word: *Liberté.* Freedom.

The last time Noor saw Jean Overton Fuller, a few days before she went to France, she told her friend about a story she had written, one that she considered her most important work.

# Shadow Knights

The story was set in Switzerland, where two children noticed that in the evenings the mountain peaks turned to gold. The children decided to climb the mountains, get some of the gold and give it to the poor people in the village. On their way up, they met a herdsman who told them a secret they must keep if they were to reach their goal. Afterward the children were accosted by robbers, who demanded the secret and tortured the children to get it. But the children kept the secret, and to reward their bravery a fairy appeared who showed them the way.

When they finally reached the top of the golden mountain, the children discovered they had become gold themselves.

In a state of exaltation, they collected as much of the gold as they could and began to climb down. But as soon as they left the summit, the golden objects they were carrying turned into stones and dirt. They realized that the gold existed only on the summit and could not be brought down. At first they thought their trip had been for nothing. But then they realized that they could still teach the poor people in the village how to climb the mountain. That, however, would be much harder.

Noor-un-nisa Inayat Khan was killed by the Nazis at Dachau. But sometimes a life can be a path, and some paths are cut out of granite. Noor showed a way to climb up.

# Aftermath

Overlord was the ultimate vindication for Colin Gubbins and SOE. But as Allied politicians turned their attention to the postwar world, Gubbins found himself dousing many of the flames SOE had lit. As the Allied armies closed in on Berlin, Churchill quickly lost interest in the resistance forces and became increasingly concerned about the threat of Communism. The romantic rebels that had fired his imagination now seemed a threat to the established order.

Even as the brash OSS—forerunner to the CIA—geared up for the postwar world, its older brother was being shut down. As early as May 1944, Churchill had told Selborne that he did not envisage any future for SOE, saying, "The part your naughty deeds in war play in peace cannot at all be considered at the present time." By 1945, it was becoming clear to Gubbins and the rest of SOE's staff that the organization would not outlast the war. In May 1945, Selborne argued that SOE should be retained, on the dubious premise that "Himmler is preparing a German maquis... to achieve a third world war." But Whitehall had made up its mind, and on January 16, 1946, just five months after the Japanese surrendered, SOE was disbanded. It died as quickly as it had been born.

Colin Gubbins's association with the freebooting SOE blighted his career. He received many honors, but the military he loved offered him no further employment. He remarried, went into business and spent his last years on the Isle of Harris, pursuing the maxim that to live a happy life one should "know everything about something, know something about everything and play a musical instrument." He died in 1976, forgotten by all but his former agents, a handful of military historians—and those resistance fighters around the world who knew the name of the man who headed the organization that helped them break their chains.

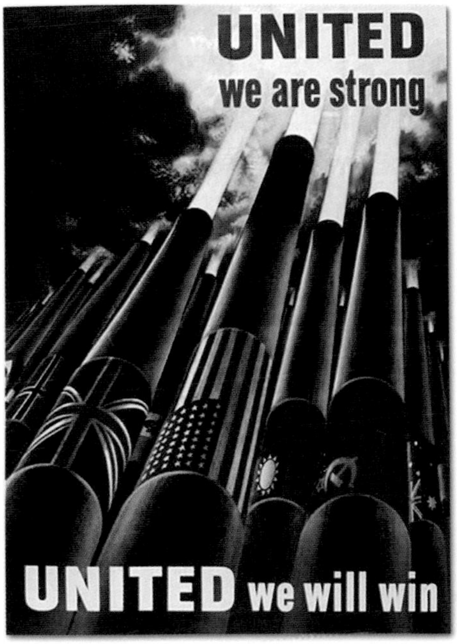
UNITED
we are strong
UNITED we will win

It is all too easy to mythologize our Last Good War.

SOE's legacy remains shrouded. Because it was the paradoxical precursor both of insurgent movements like Fidel Castro's guerrillas and covert state agencies like the CIA, it is not easy to sum up its impact on the postwar world. Some argue that its dirty war tactics helped legitimize terrorism. But the painful truth is that the greatest terrorism in World War II was practiced not by underground warriors but by conventional forces. Both sides in WWII practiced state-sponsored terrorism on an unprecedented scale. The sum total of the SOE's bloodshed pales in comparison to the Allied "strategic bombing" that killed millions of German and Japanese civilians. World War II was total war before SOE ever set off its first explosive. For both sides, the ends justified the means. We forgive those means because we believe the Axis had to be defeated.

Nor can SOE be blamed for the ascendancy of meddling covert state agencies like the CIA. The American superpower that emerged from World War II would have created a secret military/intelligence arm if SOE had never existed. Unlike the CIA, SOE was a gun that was built to be fired only once.

But if what SOE did was justifiable in the context of a necessary war, that does not mean it was innocent, or that its actions do not raise ethical questions. All instruments of war are dirty, and SOE was no exception. It violated the rules of war. Although it tried to minimize reprisals, SOE inevitably took actions that led to the death of uninvolved civilians. And it also bore a unique responsibility, one not shared by regular fighting forces: it was responsible for the fate of those people who would not have joined resistance movements without it.

The appalling nobility of SOE is that it encouraged total war, but of a different sort than that planned by statesmen and generals. It brought the war into the lives of men and women who the day before had not dreamed they would decide to risk everything for a cause. If SOE had not existed, some of those ordinary people would never have joined resistance movements, and many would not have suffered imprisonment, torture or death. That is a heavy moral debt.

But SOE discharged that debt in two ways. It helped win the war. And it brought people suffering under Axis tyranny a gift.

SOE gave those people the ability to fight back. It gave them back their human dignity. It gave them a chance to make something larger of their lives.

The gift was not one given by the courageous to the weak. It was a gift between equals. SOE agents were not better or braver than the people they lived with, and the best of them always emphasized that in their accounts of the secret war. They knew that the housewife who risked her family was just as courageous, or more, than they were. Nor did they quickly judge those who did not join the resistance. They knew war too well to play at being God.

> SOE gave occupied people a **dangerous** gift: the chance to **fight back.**

There is a humility, an altruism, that shines through the words and careers of agents like Harry Ree and Benjamin Cowburn and Francis Cammaerts. To help others fight back was an honor for them. As Cowburn wrote, "Beside the official, loud-mouthed, arrogant world of collaboration and the sad, sullen world of official everyday life, was beginning to form the hidden, glowing world of faith and resistance. It was the privilege of a special agent to discover and recruit these fine people."

In a poem he wrote as the world descended into darkness, W. H. Auden called upon himself to show "an affirming flame." The men and women who made up Cowburn's "hidden, glowing world," and the agents who helped them, heard their own calls, lit their own flames. Many of them were consumed by them.

It is all too easy to romanticize SOE. Its uniqueness—its connection to our last mythical Good War, the dramatic frisson of being a "secret agent," the easy triumphalism that hovers over a long-ago struggle against a regime so evil as to seem almost like Tolkien's Mordor—combine to make it all seem like a thrilling escapade out of a boys' adventure novel.

But that is a superficial response. World War II may have been necessary, but it was still war, that special hell that humans bring upon themselves. In a speech he gave in 1970, Harry Ree said that he had not spoken in public about his experiences for 25 years because when he did in 1945, his audiences wanted only thrills and excitement. More than anything, Ree did not want to glamorize war. "I am afraid I was not prepared to offer up information about real, suffering, innocent and dead human beings, if it was going to be inevitably and innocently misused by my audiences; as if I were offering a kind of pep pill or stimulant."

David Howarth, who helped run the legendary small-boat service between Scotland and Norway for SOE, made the same point at the end of his memoir *The Shetland Bus*. "[T]o ascribe glory to the violent death of any young man loving life," Howarth concluded, "is only to add further folly to the failure of human wisdom which is the cause of war."

So let these tales of SOE's shadow knights add no further glory to war. Let them honor something larger: the mysterious power that sometimes allows human beings to reach beyond themselves.

## 4 p.m.
## May 9, 2009
## Fazal Manzil
## Suresnes, Paris

Today, many people traveling from London to Paris head to St. Pancras Station, where they board the sleek Eurostar train. They relax in comfortable seats, enjoying drinks from the dining car, while the high-speed train whisks them smoothly across southern England, under the Channel and through the fields of northern France, finally emerging in the heart of Paris at the Gare du Nord. The entire trip takes only a little over three hours.

It is hard to imagine that just a few decades ago making this trip was like traveling to a neighborhood in hell.

On a sunny spring afternoon in Suresnes, a group of children are walking past the Fazal Manzil. The House of Blessing still stands, not far from the bridge that crosses the Seine near the leafy Bois de Boulogne. On a stone wall near the house's green doorway, a plaque reads, "Noor Inayat Khan lived here. 1914–1944. Madeleine in the Resistance. Shot at Dachau. Radio operator in the Buckmaster circuit. Cross de Guerre 1939–1945. George Cross."

In *The Silent Company,* the resistance leader called Rémy wrote, "On a sunlit lawn, as I write these words, my children are laughing and playing. It is to my friends who are dead, my friends who were tortured, my friends who were deported, my friends who would not speak, that I owe the fact that my children's laughter was not stifled in their throats. A fearful thought, yet an entirely true one, has come to me. Their laughter is made up of the silence that my friends kept."

The children pass under the plaque and disappear in the distance, their high, small voices fading down the street.

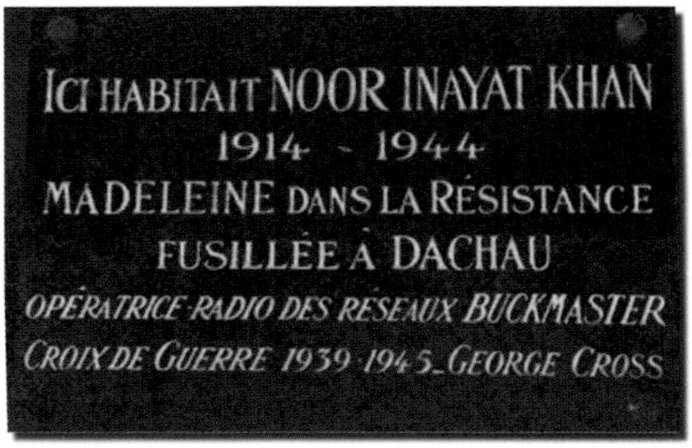

ICI HABITAIT NOOR INAYAT KHAN
1914 - 1944
MADELEINE DANS LA RÉSISTANCE
FUSILLÉE À DACHAU
OPÉRATRICE-RADIO DES RÉSEAUX BUCKMASTER
CROIX DE GUERRE 1939-1945_GEORGE CROSS


**The plaque honoring Noor on the wall of the Fazal Manzil.**

# Bibliography

## Noor Inayat Khan

*Spy Princess: The Life of Noor Inayat Khan* by Shrabani Basu (Charleston, SC: History Press, 2006)

*The Women Who Lived for Danger* by Marcus Binney (New York: Harper Perennial, 2004)

*Noor-un-nisa Inayat Khan (Madeleine)* by Jean Overton Fuller (Middlesex, UK: East-West Publications, 1988)

*The Sufi Message of Hazrat Inayat Khan: Sufi Teachings* (vol. 8) by Hazrat Inayat Khan (London: Barrie & Rockliffe, 1963)

*Twenty Jataka Tales* retold by Noor Inayat Khan (Philadelphia, PA: David McKay, 1939)

Noor Inayat Khan's personnel file, Public Record Office, National Archives, Kew, England

## The heavy-water raid

*Assault in Norway* by Thomas Gallagher (Guilford, CT: Lyons Press, 2002)

*Skis Against the Atom* by Knut Haukelid (Minot, ND: North American Heritage Press, 1989)

*The Real Heroes of Telemark* by Ray Mears (Philadelphia, PA: Coronet Books, 2004)

*The Making of the Atomic Bomb* by Richard Rhodes (New York: Simon & Schuster, 1986)

## Harry Ree

*Secret War Heroes* by Marcus Binney (London: Hodder & Stoughton, 2006)

*They Came from the Sky* by E. H. Cookridge (New York: Thomas Y. Crowell Co., 1967)

*The Fourth Dimension of Warfare* (vol. 1), edited by Michael Elliott-Bateman (Santa Barbara, CA: Praeger, 1970)

*Undercover: The Men and Women of the SOE* by Patrick Howarth (New Haven, CT: Phoenix Press, 2000)

Harry Ree's personnel file, Public Record Office, National Archives, Kew, England

## General

*Forgotten Voices of the Secret War: An Inside History of Special Operations During the Second World War* by Roderick Bailey (London: Ebury Press, 2008)

*Secret Agent's Handbook,* introduction by Roderick Bailey (London: Max Press, 2008)

*Set Europe Ablaze* by E. H. Cookridge (New York: Thomas Y. Crowell Co., 1967)

*Beaulieu: The Finishing School for Secret Agents* by Cyril Cunningham (Barnsley, UK: Pen & Sword Books, 2005)

*Sabotage and Subversion: The SOE and OSS at War* by Ian Dear (New York: Cassell Military Paperbacks, 1996)

*SOE in France* by M. R. D. Foot (London: Whitehall History Publishing, 2004)

*SOE: The Special Operations Executive 1940–46* by M. R. D. Foot (London: BBC Books, 1984)

*The Secret History of SOE: Special Operations Executive 1940–1945* by William Mackenzie (London: St. Ermin's Press, 2000)

*Special Operations Executive: A New Instrument of War,* edited by Mark Seaman (London: Routledge, 2006)

*Britain and European Resistance, 1940–1945* by David Stafford (New York: Macmillan, 1980)

*Churchill & Secret Service* by David Stafford (New York: Overlook, 1997)

*Secret Agent: The True Story of the Covert War Against Hitler* by David Stafford (New York: Overlook, 2001)

*Baker Street Irregular* by Bickham Sweet-Escott (London: Methuen, 1965)

*Gubbins and SOE* by Peter Wilkinson and Joan Bright Astley (London: Leo Cooper, 1993)

## Books by or about SOE personnel

*They Fought Alone: The Story of British Agents in France* by Maurice Buckmaster (Watford, UK: Odhams Press, 1958)

*No Cloak, No Dagger: Allied Spycraft in Occupied France* by Benjamin Cowburn (Barnsley, UK: Pen & Sword Books, 2009)

*Double Agent?* by Jean Overton Fuller (London: Pan Books, 1961; originally published as *Double Webs*)

*No. 13, Bob* by Jean Overton Fuller (London: Little, Brown, 1954; originally published as *The Starr Affair*)

*A Life in Secrets: Vera Atkins and the Missing Agents of WWII* by Sarah Helm (New York: Anchor, 2007)

*The Shetland Bus* by David Howarth (Nashville: Thomas Nelson, 1953)

*We Die Alone* by David Howarth (Guilford, CT: Lyons Press, 1999)

*Flames in the Field: The Story of Four SOE Agents in Occupied France* by Rita Kramer (New York: Penguin, 1995)

*Knights of the Floating Silk* by George Langelaan (Mechanicsburg, PA: Quality Paperback Book Club, 1959)

*Between Silk and Cyanide: A Codemaker's War 1941–1945* by Leo Marks (New York: Free Press, 1998)

*The White Rabbit* by Bruce Marshall (New York: Permabooks, 1954)

*Christine: SOE Agent & Churchill's Favourite Spy* by Madeleine Masson (London: Virago Press, 2005)

*Waiting in the Night: A Story of the Maquis, Told by One of Its Leaders* by George Millar (New York: Doubleday, 1946; originally published as *Maquis*)

*Ill Met By Moonlight* by W. Stanley Moss (New York: Macmillan, 1950)

*Report on Experience* by John Mulgan (London: Oxford University Press, 1947)

*Death Be Not Proud* by Elizabeth Nicholas (London: White Lion, 1958)

*Rake's Progress* by Denis Rake (London: Leslie Frewin, 1968)

*Unlikely Soldiers: How Two Canadians Fought the Secret War Against Nazi Occupation* by Jonathan F. Vance (Toronto: HarperCollins, 2008)

*We Landed by Moonlight: The Secret RAF Landings in France 1940–1944* by Hugh Verity (Manchester, UK: Crecy, 2000)

*An Army of Amateurs* by Philippe de Vomécourt (New York: Doubleday, 1961; originally published as *Who Lived to See the Day*)

## Other

*Partisans and Guerrillas* (World War II, vol. 12) by Ronald H. Bailey (New York: Time-Life, 1978)

*France Under the Germans: Collaboration and Compromise* by Philippe Burrin (New York: New Press, 1996)

*Red Acropolis, Black Terror: The Greek Civil War and the Origins of Soviet-American Rivalry, 1943–1949* by Andre Gerolymatos (New York: Basic Books, 2004)

*London Calling North Pole* by H. J. Giskes (New York: Bantam, 1982)

*Das Reich: The March of the 2nd SS Panzer Division Through France, June 1944* by Max Hastings (New York: Jove Books, 1986)

*The Jedburghs* by Will Irwin (New York: PublicAffairs, 2005)

*In Search of the Maquis: Rural Resistance in Southern France 1942–1944* by H. R. Kedward (New York: Oxford University Press, 1995)

*The Partisans of Europe in the Second World War* by Kenneth Macksey (London: Hart-Davis MacGibbon, 1975)

*The Shadow War: Resistance in Europe 1939–1945* by Henri Michel (New York: Harper & Row, 1972)

*The Silent Company: Memoirs of a Secret Agent of Free France* (vol. 1) by Gilbert Renault-Roulier ("Remy"), translated by Lancelot C. Sheppard (New York: Whittlesey House, 1948)

## Films:

*Now It Can Be Told* (Imperial War Museum: The Official Collection, 1946, 2007; originally titled *School for Danger*)

*The Sorrow and the Pity,* directed by Marcel Ophüls (1969)

# Picture Credits

Page 10: Illustration by Jeffrey Smith

Page 13: The Hardangervidda, photo © Yann Arthus-Bertrand/CORBIS

Page 14: Illustration by Jeffrey Smith

Page 16: Jens Poulsson, Norges Hjemmefrontmuseum, Oslo

Page 16: Knut Haugland, Norges Hjemmefrontmuseum, Oslo

Page 16: Claus Helberg, Norges Hjemmefrontmuseum, Oslo

Page 16: Arne Kjelstrup, Norges Hjemmefrontmuseum, Oslo

Page 18: Illustration by Jeffrey Smith

Page 20: Winston Churchill, photo © Bettman/CORBIS

Page 23: Paris sidewalk café after the German invasion, photo by AP/Wide World Photos

Page 23: La Place Blanche festooned with signs, photo © Bettmann/CORBIS

Page 24: Map by Norma Tennis

Page 25: Adolf Hitler, courtesy of the Imperial War Archives

Page 26: Illustration by Jeffrey Smith

Page 28: The Fazal Manzil, Noor Inayat Khan family

Page 30: Illustration by Jeffrey Smith

Page 33: Vidkun Quisling, Norwegian War Archives

Page 34: Illustration by Jeffrey Smith

Page 36: Illustration by Jeffrey Smith

Page 38: Charles Portal and Winston Churchill, photo by Fotosearch/Getty Images

Page 40: Illustration by Jeffrey Smith

Page 45: Noor in WAAF uniform, courtesy of the Imperial War Archives

Page 46: Illustration by Jeffrey Smith

Page 49: Arisaig House, photo © Jim Bain

Page 50: SOE training, photos courtesy of the Imperial War Archives

Page 53: Glider crash, courtesy of the National Archives, Kew

Page 54: Joachim Ronneberg, Norges Hjemmefrontmuseum, Oslo

Page 54: Knut Haukelid, Norges Hjemmefrontmuseum, Oslo

Page 54: Birger Stromsheim, Norges Hjemmefrontmuseum, Oslo

Page 54: Fredrik Kayser, Norges Hjemmefrontmuseum, Oslo

Page 54: Kasper Idland, Norges Hjemmefrontmuseum, Oslo

Page 54: Hans Storhaug, Norges Hjemmefrontmuseum, Oslo

Page 56: Gus March-Phillips, courtesy of The National Archives, Kew

Page 58: German propaganda map, courtesy of Deutsches Bundesarchiv (German Federal Archive)

Page 60: Soldiers at El Alamein, courtesy of the Imperial War Museum

Page 62: Illustration by Jeffrey Smith

Page 63: Helge Ingstad, photo © 1932 Glydendal Norsk Forlag

Page 67: Double transposition code, Pierre Loraine

Page 68: Map by Norma Tennis

Page 70: Illustration by Jeffrey Smith

Page 72: Vemork raid re-creation, Innovation Norway

Page 73: Vemork raid re-creation, Innovation Norway

Page 74: Noor's SOE file photograph, photo by Martin Langfield, courtesy of the National Archives, Kew

Page 77: C-type supply container, courtesy of www.millsgrenades.co.uk

Page 80: Illustration by Jeffrey Smith

Page 82: Norsk Hydro plant, courtesy of the National Archives, Kew

Page 84: Canisters before the raid, Norsk Industriarbeidermuseum

Page 84: Canisters after the raid, Norsk Industriarbeidermuseum

Page 85: Gorge and Vemork bridge, Stuart Burns

Page 87: Illustration by Jeffrey Smith

Page 88: Lysander, illustration © Clavework Graphics

Page 89: Armed *maquisard,* courtesy of the National Archives, Kew

Page 90: Illustration by Jeffrey Smith

Page 93: Nikolaus von Falkenhorst, Heinrich Hoffman

Page 94: Nazi propaganda poster, courtesy of Dr. Robert D. Brooks

Page 96: Henri Déricourt, courtesy of the National Archives, Kew

Page 96: Jean Overton Fuller, John Cooper

Page 97: Elizabeth Nicholas, Special Forces Club

Page 98: Gilbert Norman, courtesy of the National Archives, Kew

Page 98: Andrée Borrel, Special Forces Club

Page 100: French Resistance poster, R. Louvat and G. Kanova, 1944

Page 104: Besançon, Ville de Besançon, 1943

Page 105: Besançon, Ville de Besançon, 1943

Page 106: Lapp leading reindeer, photo by Mark Kauffman/LIFE/Getty Images

Page 108: Illustration by Jeffrey Smith

Page 111: Peugeot plant, Peugeot Fans Club

Page 112: "Ski-hunter" recruitment poster, courtesy of Deutsches Bundesarchiv (German Federal Archive)

Page 116: Illustration by Jeffrey Smith

Page 118: King Haakon leaflet, the PsyWar Society

Page 120: Illustration by Jeffrey Smith

Page 124: Illustration by Jeffrey Smith

Page 127: Joseph Terboven and troops, Associated Press

Page 128: Prisoners at Grini, photo by SCANPIX

Page 130: *Maquis* with Sten gun, Keystone Press Agency

Page 132: Illustration by Jeffrey Smith

Page 137: Rat sketch, courtesy of the National Archives, Kew

Page 137: French resistance fighter, courtesy of the National Archives and Records Administration

Page 138: Colin Gubbins, photo by Paul Popper/Popperfoto/Getty Images

Page 143: The ferry "Hydro," Anders Beer Wilse, 1925

Page 144: Illustration by Jeffrey Smith

Page 148: Das Reich, photo by Friedrich Zschäckel, courtesy of Deutsches Bundesarchiv (German Federal Archive)

Page 149: Omaha Beach, photo by Chief Photographer's Mate (CPHOM) Robert F. Sargent, U.S. Coast Guard

Page 150: Christine Granville, Jolanta Countess Mycielska

Pages 152-153: Illustration by Jeffrey Smith

Page 155: German soldier and vehicle, U.S. Army photograph

Page 156: Paris liberation, photo by Jack Downey, courtesy of the Library of Congress Prints and Photographs Division

Page 157: Dachau concentration camp, Denis Toomey, www.dogfacesoldiers.org

Page 158: Illustration by Jeffrey Smith

# About the Author

GARY KAMIYA was a cofounder and longtime executive editor of the groundbreaking website *Salon*. His writing has appeared in *Artforum, The New York Times Book Review, Sports Illustrated,* and many other publications. He lives in San Francisco.

# About the Illustrator

JEFFREY SMITH is an internationally known artist whose work frequently appears in *Rolling Stone, Sports Illustrated, GQ, Newsweek,* and many other publications. He has been honored with gold and silver medals from the New York Society of Illustrators.

PULP HISTORY
DEVIL DOG
THE AMAZING TRUE STORY OF THE MAN WHO SAVED AMERICA
By DAVID TALBOT
Illustrated by SPAIN RODRIGUEZ

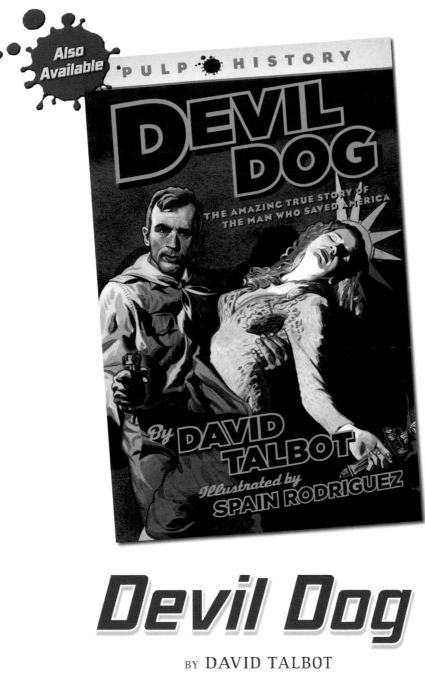

# Devil Dog

BY DAVID TALBOT
ILLUSTRATED BY SPAIN RODRIGUEZ

*The amazing true story of the man who saved America.*

**THE AMAZING, ILLUSTRATED TALE** of the Marine who fought around the globe and blew the lid off a plot against FDR.

Major General Smedley Darlington Butler joined the Marine Corps at age sixteen, and two years later took a Chinese bullet to the chest. Butler then fought in Haiti, Nicaragua, and France—and then realized that "war is a racket." Back home, he cleaned up crime in Philadelphia, faced down Herbert Hoover to help destitute veterans, and foiled a plot against FDR masterminded by J.P. Morgan and the DuPonts.

Available wherever books are sold or at www.simonandschuster.com.